HISTORY OF THE ESTABLISHMENT
OF
BRITISH RULE IN INDIA

HISTORY OF THE ESTABLISHMENT

OF

BRITISH RULE IN INDIA

REV. SIR GEORGE W. COX, BART., M. A.

GYAN

Published by

Gyan Publishing House
5, Ansari Road
Daryaganj, New Delhi-110002
Phone: 011-47034999, 9811692060
E-mail: books@gyanbooks.com

Distribution Network
gyanbooks.com
India, USA, Canada, UK, Australia, France

ISBN: 978-81-212-8872-9 (PB)
First Published, 1881

2nd Impression 2023

Printed at: Gyan Press, Delhi.

HISTORY OF THE ESTABLISHMENT OF BRITISH RULE IN INDIA
AUTHOR: GEORGE W. COX

HISTORY OF THE ESTABLISHMENT

OF

BRITISH RULE IN INDIA.

INDIA.
70
80
90
30
20
10
Cabul
Srinagar
Cashmere
Lahore
Quetta
Himalaya Mountains
Bhutan
Rajputana
Sinde
Udaipur
Agra
Allahabad
Benares
Patna
Chota
Nagpore
Central Provinces
Nagpore
Cuttack
BAY OF
BENGAL
DECCAN
BOMBAY
Bustar
Hyderabad
Mysore
MADRAS
Pondicherry
Porto Novo
Laccadive Is
Cochin
C. Comorin
CEYLON
Kandy
Pt de Galle
Maldive Is
Coromandel Coast

English History Reading Books

HISTORY OF THE ESTABLISHMENT

OF

BRITISH RULE IN INDIA

BY THE

REV. SIR GEORGE W. COX, BART., M.A.

LONDON

LONGMANS, GREEN, AND CO.

1881

TO

MY SONS

EDMUND C. COX

ASSISTANT POLITICAL AGENT, KOLHAPUR, BOMBAY PRESIDENCY

AND

GEORGE W. STIRLING COX

ASSISTANT SUPERINTENDENT OF POLICE, BENGAL

I DEDICATE THIS SKETCH

OF THE HISTORY OF BRITISH RULE

IN A COUNTRY

WHICH IT IS THEIR DUTY TO KNOW WELL

PREFACE.

In this volume I have sketched the history of India before the earliest voyages of the Portuguese, the English, the Dutch, and the French, only so far as it seemed necessary to do so in order to make the narrative of European settlement and conquest intelligible.

The history of Asiatic countries is in many aspects uninviting. That of India before the rise and after the decay of the so-called Mogul empire is singularly intricate, and for all but professed historical students perplexing. From the time of its early Aryan lords the land has been divided amongst a multitude of dynasties, some more or less permanent, some lasting for little more than the moment; and these dynasties are established or supplanted by statesmen whose favourite weapons are for the most part intrigue, conspiracy, falsehood, and treachery.

There is, however, a real connexion running through the whole, and bringing before us, if not a national life, yet a life of the people, which may be traced through the long series of the ages, and which has been, and will in the future still more largely be, influenced by European civilisation, modes of thought, usage, and law.

From this point of view the whole history becomes full of vivid life, and as interesting as it is important; and it is in this light that I have striven to present it in these chapters, which may, I hope, incite many to a more systematic study of a subject calling for the most patient care and attention of Englishmen. The first and the last duty of the historian is to speak the truth. This duty with reference to the course of British rule in India involves the bestowal of much praise and of much blame; and if we are honest, the latter must be as outspoken as the former. But even in those cases in which the strictures are necessarily most severe, there is great encouragement for the future in the fact that the measures which have wrought most mischief have been condemned by such men as the Duke of Wellington, Lord William Bentinck, Mr. Elphinstone, Lord Canning, Lord Mayo, Lord Lawrence, and Lord Northbrook.

On such matters even the youngest reader must have some opinion; and in this volume he may, I hope, find a narrative which will help him towards forming a more matured judgment hereafter.

The spelling of names, geographical and personal, occurring in the history of India has been scarcely yet reduced to a system; but many have become household English words, and these are given in their familiar forms. We have the same plea for retaining names like Delhi, Benares, Cawnpore, Meerut, as for writing Thebes, Athens, Naples, Corinth.

The map of India given with this history contains only those names which are mentioned in it, and not quite all of these; but the text will in each case explain the position of the few places which from want of space could not be included in the map.

PORTUGUESE, DUTCH, AND FRENCH SETTLEMENTS IN THE EAST INDIES.

	A.D.
The Portuguese establish a factory at Calicut	1500
" " declare Goa the capital of the Portuguese dominions in India	1510
" " settle in Java	1511
" " gain possession of Bombay	1530
" " settle at Diu, at the entrance to the gulf of Cambay	1535
" " settle at Amboyna	1564
" " cede Bombay to the British Crown	1662
" " expelled from Salsette and Bassein	1739
The Dutch settle in Java	1595
" " seize Amboyna	1607
" " settle at Chinsura	1657
The French purchase Pondicherry	1672
" " settle at Chandernagore	1676
" " take Madras	1746
" " " the fort of Jinji	1750
" " build the column at Dupleix Fatihabad	
" " obtain the Northern Circars	1751
" " take Vizagapatam	1757
" " surrender the fort of Jinji	1760

CONTENTS.

CHAPTER I.

THE HINDUS OR ARYAN INVADERS OF INDIA.

CHAPTER II.

GEOGRAPHY OF INDIA—ABORIGINAL TRIBES—RELIGIONS AND CASTE AMONG THE HINDUS.

CHAPTER III.

MAHOMETAN CONQUESTS IN INDIA—INROADS OF GENGHIZ AND TIMOUR—LOCAL DYNASTIES—EARLY VOYAGES AND SETTLEMENTS OF THE PORTUGUESE.

CHAPTER IV.

FIRST VOYAGES OF THE DUTCH AND THE ENGLISH TO JAVA AND INDIA.

CHAPTER V.

REIGNS OF THE FIRST THREE MOGUL EMPERORS OF INDIA.

CHAPTER VI.

THE REIGN OF JEHANGÍR—PROGRESS OF THE ENGLISH AND THE DUTCH.

CHAPTER VII.

THE REIGNS OF SHAH JEHAN AND OF AURENGZEBE AS ALAMGÍR, 1627–1707.

CHAPTER VIII.

RIVALRY OF THE FRENCH AND ENGLISH IN INDIA.

CHAPTER IX.

REIGNS OF THE SUCCESSORS OF AURENGZEBE.

CHAPTER X.

DUPLEIX AND CLIVE.

CHAPTER XI.

CLIVE AND SURAJ-U-DAULA—BATTLE OF PLASSY.

CHAPTER XII.

RELATIONS OF THE ENGLISH WITH THE MOGUL EMPIRE.

CHAPTER XIII.

THE ADMINISTRATION OF WARREN HASTINGS.

CHAPTER XIV.

LORD CORNWALLIS AND THE LAND SETTLEMENT OF BENGAL.

CHAPTER XV.

FALL OF THE MYSORE SULTAN—MAHRATTA WARS—BATTLE OF ASSAYE—SIEGE OF BHURTPORE.

CHAPTER XVI.

ADMINISTRATIONS OF LORD MINTO AND LORD HASTINGS—OPERATIONS IN NEPAL AND AGAINST THE PINDHARRIES.

CHAPTER XVII.

THE DETHRONEMENT OF THE PESHWA—INTERNAL ADMINISTRATION OF LORD HASTINGS.

CHAPTER XVIII.

BURMESE WARS—SECOND SIEGE, AND CAPTURE OF BHURTPORE.

CHAPTER XIX.

ADMINISTRATION OF LORD WILLIAM BENTINCK, 1827-1835.

CHAPTER XX.

THE FIRST AFGHAN WAR.

CHAPTER XXI.

THE SIKH WARS.

CHAPTER XXII.

THE POLICY OF ANNEXATION.

CHAPTER XXIII.

THE GREAT MUTINY, 1857–8.

THE ESTABLISHMENT

OF

BRITISH RULE IN INDIA.

CHAPTER I.

The Hindus, or Aryan Invaders of India.

1. It has been often said that when the English found their way to India they were brought into contact with a kindred people, and that, as they gradually worked their way northwards and westwards, they were drawing nearer and nearer to the common home which both they and the people whom they were conquering had left many thousands of years ago. In substance this is true: but we must see carefully what is meant by it. There was a time when the forefathers of Englishmen, Hindus, and Persians, of Greeks and Romans, of Frenchmen and Germans, of Danes and Norwegians lived together, either as a single people or as a group of clans or tribes, on the high table-lands of Central Asia. To these tribes we give the name of Aryans, not because we can say for certain that they so called themselves, but because, after they had been scattered, the word was used by their descendants as a title of honour which distinguished them from all who belonged to any other race or stock. Thus in the oldest Hindu books, which were put together many hundreds of years before the Christian era, India is spoken of as the abode of the Aryas, and the Aryas are contrasted with the Dasyu, the conquered inhabitants of the country. So the Persians called their land Iran, while the rest of the world was to them An-Iran, or, as we should say, not-Iran. It is not unlikely that the word originally denoted ploughmen, the tilling of the soil being the most honourable work for the man of free or noble birth.

2. How long the forefathers of the Aryan nations of Europe and Asia dwelt together we do not know; but we may safely say that, when the time for separation came, some turned their steps to the south-east, and others towards the south-west and the west. To the east and the north the huge mountains which are formed into a vast bow, with the ranges of the Hindu Khush in the centre, rose up as an effectual barrier. Beyond those stupendous walls, which stretch for hundreds of miles to the north-east under the name of the Altai mountains, and to the east as the Himalayas, the abode of everlasting winter and snow, lay the home of other tribes which are classed together under the common name of Turanians, but which really formed a multitude of nations, all of them more or less like each other, but quite unlike the Aryans. In after ages these tribes, known as Mongols, Tartars, Huns,

Turks, and by other names, have burst like floods of devouring fire into the Aryan world: and the forefathers of the Aryan nations, in the home which seems to have been their birthplace, may have known that if they ventured to advance eastwards they would have to contend with human enemies not less savage than the mountains which hemmed them in.

3. There was, indeed, nothing to attract them towards these bleak and dismal regions; and so, when the old home became too small, one portion of the Aryan race moved towards the south and south-east, and having crossed the great river Indus, grew into the people known as the Hindus, whose abode was Hindustan. Another portion found their way into the regions lying to the south of the Caspian Sea, and set up a new Iran as Persians. A third, either by the same path or working round by the north of the Caspian, reached Europe, and grew into the Hellenic or Greek and Latin tribes in the south, and into the Celtic, Teutonic, and Scandinavian tribes in the north.

4. But we must not suppose that the ancestors of all these tribes left their common home at the same time. They went, we cannot doubt, as successive waves, which gained greater volume as they moved along; and ages probably passed between the migrations of clans or tribes the most closely related to each other. Thus the Celtic tribes went before those which we call Teutonic or Dutch. Their word for running water was *avon*, a name familiar to us still. These were followed by a Teutonic people, whose word for the stream or brook

was *beck*, and then again by another Teutonic people, who called it *water*. But sometimes the second comers, from ignorance of its meaning, kept the first name, adding their own to it: the third comers did the same, and thus we have in one instance the name Wansbeckwater, which tells its tale of at least three conquests or immigrations.

5. If we are asked how we know all this, we are forced to confess that we have no written records which tell us any part of this history, and that no records of it ever were or ever could have been written. The evidence for it is found in such words as Wansbeckwater; and the answer to the question is that the ancient history of mankind is embedded in their language. So long as we keep strictly within the limits of this evidence we are walking on sure ground; and it tells us vastly more than we might expect to learn about a time for which we have no record or writings of any sort. A comparison of the dialects spoken by Greek, Roman, Persian, Teutonic, and Scandinavian tribes has taught us that the structure of all is in the first framework the same, and has enabled us to see in great measure what the language of their common forefathers was. It was not the same as the language spoken afterwards by any of the Aryan nations after the separation; but the grammar of it was the foundation on which all the later dialects grew up, and the words which are common to all, or to most of them, are words which were spoken by the Aryans before they were scattered from their early home.

6. It is from these words that we learn the

history of their growth. They show us that these, our distant forefathers, were not savages; that they built themselves houses; that they spun wool for cloth and flax for linen; that they were subject to laws carefully drawn out; that they could plough, sow, and reap; that they had a large farming stock of horses, sheep, and cattle; that they made use of dogs as we do; that they lived in families, in which the sacredness of marriage was strictly maintained, while the different degrees of kindred were marked out more minutely than they are amongst ourselves; and that they spoke of God by the name which their descendants have used after them in the most distant parts of the earth.

7. Such as these were the Aryan people, who found their way into India from the north-west, a people which had grown up in habits of the most orderly life, deeply impressed and almost overwhelmed by the mystery of creation, and living already more in the future than in the present. That their families grew into clans, the clans into tribes; that they had villages, towns, and cities; that they had armour and weapons of offence and defence; that they were ruled by kings, who had priests and warriors for their counsellors, we learn clearly from their language. But when we find that the word which for the Greek and the Roman meant a plough (Gr. *arŏtron*; Lat. *arātrum*), meant for the Hindu, as it does for us, a rudder, we learn not merely that the Aryans who used it in this sense had reached the sea, but that they described the action of the rudder in the water by a metaphor

taken from that of the plough on land. We may go into the matter, if we please, still more minutely. The Teutonic or German tribes kept together for a long time, and the words common to them show what progress they had made in what we call civilisation before they parted company. Thus Germans and Englishmen have the same word for shoe; but the Germans have another word (*strumpf*) for stocking; and therefore though they had shoes, Germans and Englishmen had no stockings while they remained together.

8. In this way we know a great deal of the history of the Hindus even before they reached India, as we know that of Englishmen before they forced their way into the country now called England. But it is the history of the people as a whole, and nothing more. Of the lives and acts of individual men and women, whether kings or queens, warriors, priests or traders, we must frankly confess that we know nothing, and that, so far as we can see, it is impossible that we should ever know anything. All nations, or at least all who have risen above the stage of savage life, have expressed their thoughts or their recollections in what we call epic poems, long before they have felt the desire for possessing any records of past events which can be in any sense called historical. In these poems the heroes and heroines love much and suffer much; but the story of their fortunes is told in almost all the epics of the Aryan nations with so striking a likeness, both in the framework and in the details, as to leave little room for doubting that in each case it is the same

story changed to suit the needs of different countries and climates.

9. The great epic poems of the Hindus are the Mahabhārata and the Ramayana; and although these, like the Homeric poems of the Greeks, reflect the habits and conditions of society under which the poet lived, they give us nothing which can fairly be called history. Nor can we look on their pictures of royal magnificence as on scenes which ever passed on earth before their waking eyes. The palaces of the wealthiest kings have never had doors of gold and walls of silver, or been lined with colossal statues of the same precious metals. The imagination of the poet was kindled, not by the sight of any earthly abode, but by the cloud-capped towers and gorgeous palaces seen in the gleaming heavens, as the sun amidst a blaze of living fire plunges into the western sea.

10. We cannot, therefore, say when the Hindu left his primæval home in Central Asia, or how long the work of conquest may have lasted in the country which he invaded. The so-called chronology of the Hindus stretches over myriads and even millions of years; and this fact has been taken as proof of their incapacity for preserving any historical records by those who assert that in this respect they were altogether surpassed by the Egyptians. The truth is that whether in India or in Egypt there is no chronology at all; and it seems only fair to remember that there never was any intention of passing it off as such. In the belief of the Hindu, the history of the world is bounded within the limits of four vast periods, from the beginning of which nearly four millions of years have passed away. It has been supposed that the Hindus claim this antiquity for themselves, and claim it to the exclusion of other nations. No notion could be more groundless. The Hindu has never made any special boast of the antiquity of his race; and in his chronology of the world he has sought only to express his ideas of the origin and duration of our globe and of the universe to which it belongs. They imagined themselves as living in the last of four *Yugs* or ages into which its existence was divided, and the character of this *yug* stood out in dismal contrast with those of the earlier periods. In short, we have here only another form of the golden, the silvern, the brazen and iron ages, in the last of which the Greek poets supposed that the present race of toilworn men were living.

CHAPTER II.

Geography of India—Aboriginal Tribes—Religion and Caste among the Hindus.

1. The land which the Hindu chose for his new home was the vast peninsula which may be described as bounded by the river Indus, the Himalayas, and the Ocean. We may form some notion of its size when we learn that its extreme length from north to south is about 1,900, and its extreme width 1,500

English miles. About half-way down this peninsula the Vindhya mountains, running from west to east between the twenty-second and twenty-fourth parallels of north latitude, separate the valley of the Nerbudda from the table lands of the region commonly known as Central India. The whole country to the north of this range of hills is Hindustan, or the abode of the Hindu. The region to the south of the Nerbudda valley and the Satpúra hills is called the Deccan.

2. Taken roughly, Hindustan may be regarded as consisting of two huge river basins, the one being that of the Indus, the other that of the Ganges. Both these mighty streams issue from the snow-clad chains of the Himalayas. Flowing first to the north west, the Indus sweeps round the mountains which hedge in the beautiful Land of Srinagar or Cashmere; and then turning to the south after receiving the waters of the Cabul river near Attock, it is swollen by the streams of the Jhelum, the Chenab, the Ravee, and the Sutlej, which with the Indus determined the name of the Punjab, the land of the five rivers, the rich prize first seized by the Aryan invaders, as they found their way into the country from Central Asia. Still pursuing the same course with a slight bend to the west, the Indus finds its way through a delta into the Arabian Sea. The other great river of Hindustan, the Ganges (the ganging or running stream) has its sacred source at Gungootri, about 200 miles to the north of Delhi. Flowing to the south-east, it receives at Allahabad the dark waters of the Yamuna or Jumna, and finally,

like the Brahmapootra, which, flowing from the north-east, has likewise hurried down from the Himalayas, forces its way into the bay of Bengal through a delta which has for its base a line drawn from Calcutta to Chittagong.

3. The lower half of the Indian peninsula, lying to the south of this vast basin of the Ganges, may be described as a region of which the central portions are cut off from the sea by ranges of hills, which leave a strip of open land along the whole length of the coast. Starting from the river Tapti to the south of the Satpúra hills, the Western Ghauts, rising to their greatest height in the peaks of Mahableshwar, look down on the cities of Bombay and Goa. Running on to the south under the name of the Nilgherries, these hills sink into the great gap or valley of Coimbatore, which extends from sea to sea to the north of the hills of Travancore. Separated from the western range by this gap or valley, which is watered by the Cauvery, the eastern Ghauts form with a few breaks a similar rampart, the open country between them and the sea being known in its southern portion as the Carnatic, with the cities of Pondicherry and Madras on the coast.

4. To these vast and varied regions the Hindu was to give his name, and over large portions of it Hindu dynasties were to bear sway. But as each man in his journey through life has his special dangers and temptations springing out of his own dispositions and appetites, so is it with tribes and nations. When he crossed the Indus, the Hindu entered a land already inhabited, nor did he gain

possession of it without severe and perhaps repeated struggles. These earlier inhabitants have been classed among Turanians; but this classification tells us little more than that they were not Aryans. They are also thought by some to be the aborigines or first natives of the country; and they may have been so. But in no case has it been possible to prove that races of which every vestige has disappeared may not have preceded them. It is wiser to content ourselves with saying that in India they are older than the Hindu; that throughout India these non-Aryan tribes belong seemingly to one type; and that this type has been found in almost all parts of the world. Their chief physical features, their habits, and modes of life are everywhere virtually the same. Their weapons are formed and used in the same way, and the boomerang of the Australian may be seen in the wilds of Southern India. Black in colour, they have the woolly hair, the thick lips, and the broad noses and cheek-bones of the negro, although they clearly do not belong to the negro stock. Not a few of these still haunt the wilderness and the jungle, which for all but themselves are laden with death. Here they live without clothing and with scarcely a roof to cover them. Others dwell in villages and make some feeble attempts at cultivating the soil.

5. The number of these savage tribes, of which many, like the Bheels and Khonds, are or would be cannibals, is estimated still at about twelve millions; and we can scarcely suppose that they have increased since the times of the first Aryan conquests. It is far more likely that they were then vastly more numerous, and much more fierce, than they are now; and in this case the impression which they made on their conquerors is accounted for. For these they were beings like the Trolls and Ogres of Scandinavian legend, and their coarse woolly hair obtained for them the name of Varvara, the *woolly*, the *barbarian* of the Greek and the Roman. The Hindu always spoke of them as Dasyu or enemies, and rejoiced in the victories which made him Dasapati, their *despot* or lord. He put his ban upon them as Rakshasas, spiteful and malignant imps, who have no human feelings about them, but who, like the giants of European stories, are as stupid as they are malicious.

6. This loathing of the native races carried with it a serious danger for the new-comers, whose natural tendency it was to form themselves into exclusive societies, thus weakening, if not destroying, their capabilities for national union. But how far the religious division of the people into castes had been carried before they crossed the Indus, we cannot say. The fact that this system has nothing to do with a man's civil dignity or position seems to show that it was not wholly the result of conquest, although conquest probably made it more rigid and unbending.

7. The original number of the castes is commonly said to have been four. It would be more exact if we gave it as three. The natural divisions of a free or dominant race are those of priests, warriors, and traders or tillers of the soil; and thus among the Hindus we find from an early age the three great

castes of Brahmas, Kshatryas, and Vaisyas. It is true that the most ancient collection of Hindu laws, known as the Code of Menu, speaks of the fourth or Sudra caste as the slaves of the other three; but it speaks of them in a way which shows that they were not in strictness of speech a caste at all. They were not entitled to the sacred thread which marked the members of the three higher castes as *dwi-ja* or twice born. Into this fourth class the non-Aryan or indigenous tribes of the country might be absorbed to any extent; but the object of caste was to make it impossible for them to emerge from their servile state to a higher condition. All marriages between them and members of the three great castes were absolutely forbidden. They were, in fact, outside the social pale. But within it a hard fight was kept up to maintain the same distinctions. When the system of caste, or as the Hindus call it, of *varna* or colour, was in its full strength, a member of one caste might not marry a member of another. If such marriages took place, the children were called Varnasankara (a word corrupted into Burrensunker), or strictly a mongrel breed; and such confusions of caste were ascribed to the laxity or misgovernment of wicked and irreligious kings. But this is enough to show that the system has undergone great changes; and the fact chiefly to be noted is that in its later form it has no authority in the Rig Veda, the most ancient religious book of the Hindus.

8. Only one of the hymns in this book mentions the four castes at all; and this passage, which is probably of later date, speaks of them as proceeding from the different parts of the body of Brahma, the Brahman from his mouth, the Kshatrya (here called Rajanya) from his arms, the Vaisya from his thigh, the Sudra from his feet. All therefore are Brahma-born, and hence it has been well said that 'there is no authority whatever in the hymns of the Veda for the complicated system of castes; no authority for the offensive privileges claimed by the Brahmans; no authority for the degraded position of the Sudras.' The claims which exalted the Brahmans as gods over all classes were of later growth; and the oppressiveness of the system set up by them provoked a strong reaction which we shall have to notice presently. This reaction, we may fairly say, left the Brahman as the only pure caste in existence. The Kshatryas and Vaisyas practically disappeared, and the mixed castes which remained have been split up into sections, which amount, it is said, to nearly forty, all maintaining the same rigid exclusiveness. The result to the people is an intolerable oppression; but it has had the further effect of leaving them virtually at the mercy of every invader. In a society so constituted national union becomes impossible. The Brahman and the Varnasankar will never combine permanently for any purpose. They were banded together for a time during the great mutiny of 1857; but they would have been severed by victory as certainly as they were sundered by defeat.

CHAPTER III.

Mahometan Conquests in India—Inroads of Genghiz and Timour—Local Dynasties—Early Voyages and Settlements of the Portuguese.

1. For a long series of generations the Aryan conquerors of India remained undisturbed in their possessions. The general course of their later history would seem to show that Hindu kingdoms, independent of each other, sprung up in different parts of the country, and that the fact of their descent from a common stock would no more prevent the outbreak of quarrels and wars among them than it has preserved an unbroken friendship between the several branches of the Teutonic race. Many of these kingdoms were wealthy and powerful, although their cities, built chiefly of clay or wood, were neither magnificent nor durable. But if we compare their condition with that of the German tribes of the same age, we shall see that the Hindu was in the van of the nations, and had so outstripped all others in the race as to make the very idea of rivalry absurd.

2. From the European nations they were separated by a vast distance; but the Aryan sovereigns of Persia were nearer at hand, and the first attempt at invasion is said to have been made by Darius in the sixth century before the Christian era. About two centuries later Alexander the Great set out on the wonderful expedition which was professedly

a requital of the invasion of Europe by Xerxes, the son of Darius. This marvellous leader of men crossed the Indus, defeated Porus near Attock (p. 9), and, reaching the banks of the Sutlej, looked forward to seeing in a few days the waters of the Ganges. But the patience of his men was worn out; and twelve mighty altars remained to mark the spot where they refused to march further on his errand of conquest. The so-called Greek kingdom of Bactria existed for a time after his death; but the Hindus preserved, it is said, no record of his expedition or of its results. This, like their chronology (p. 8), has been taken as a proof of the weakness of their historical faculty; but we have to remember that astonishing as Alexander's enterprise may seem to us, it was to the Hindus a matter of very trifling importance, and unknown probably to those who lived beyond the Sutlej.

3. Two years after his death a man named Chandra-Gupta, who had served in the army of Porus, usurped the throne of Pataliputra, called by the Greeks Palibothra, a city which stood on or near the site of the modern Patna, and was the capital of the kingdom of Magadha. This sovereign, the founder of a dynasty known as the Mauryan, was the Sandrocottus of the Greeks; and the date of his reign, thus definitely fixed, constitutes at least one certain point in the chronology of early Indian history. Having successfully withstood Alexander's general, Seleucus, now king of Babylon, Chandra-Gupta received as his ambassador the philosopher Megasthenes, whose long residence at Pataliputra

enabled him to draw a valuable picture of the Hindu people of that age (B.C. 325–300).

4. The historians of Alexander the Great make no mention of the great religious change which was then being brought about in India. If we follow the common account, two centuries and a half had passed away since Gautama, a prince of the Kshatrya caste, set himself to the task of delivering the people from the thraldom of Brahman tyranny. Renouncing his position, and stripping himself of his wealth, Gautama withdrew into the wilderness, and there attained the sanctity which made him known as Sakya-Muni, the *monk*, and the wisdom which exalted him to the title of Buddha, the *wise*. Gautama raised his voice not against the institution of caste, but against the oppressiveness of the Brahmans as a priestly order. He could allow no interference between each individual man and his Maker. 'My law,' he said, 'is a law of grace for all.' And again: 'My doctrine is like the sky. There is room for all without exception—men, women, boys, girls, poor, and rich.' It was scarcely necessary for him to say that: 'As the four rivers which fall into the Ganges lose their names as they mingle their waters with the holy river, so all who believe in Buddha cease to be Brahmans, Kshatryas, Vaisyas, and Sudras.' His doctrine that every man is bound to subdue his passions until he is ready to give up everything, even his own self, and that this task of self-renunciation could be achieved by himself alone, was a weapon which could scarcely fail to strike a deadly blow at the system of caste and the ascendency which it secured to the Brahmans.

5. For nearly three centuries this teaching worked its way silently. But at length Asoka, the grandson of Chandra-Gupta, became for Buddhism what Constantine was for Christianity. He made it the religion of the state, and Brahmanism seemed to have lost its power for ever. The snake, however, was only scotched, not killed. In the fourth century of our era the Chinese traveller Fa-hian speaks of it as again raising its head in the country; and in the days of Hiouen-thsang, another Chinese traveller, about two centuries later, many of the Buddhist sacred places were in ruins, and the old system had virtually displaced the more merciful teaching of Sakya-Muni. But although the latter, perhaps, gave more free play to the national instincts of the Hindu mind, it was by no means likely to make the desire for self-conquest a master-passion, and its ascetic side repelled more than it attracted. Thenceforth Hindu dynasties displaced those which had professed the faith of Buddha, and the predominance of modern Hinduism with its grotesque and cumbersome pantheon and its coarse mythology was effectually secured.

6. But a teacher was now in the world who proclaimed himself as the wielder of a sword which God had placed in his hands for the conversion of the nations. To all men the last of the prophets offered the choice of the Koran or death, or of tribute more terrible than death, for the giver forfeited all civil rights and the protection of the

law. The year 622 of our era witnessed the Hejira, or flight of Mahomet from Mecca to Medina. Within thirty years the followers of the prophet were masters of Syria, Persia, and of Egypt. A few years later, A.D. 664, they had reached Cabul, and the Afghans made their submission to Islam; and when the Saracens under Taric were overthrowing the Gothic kingdom of Spain, A.D. 700, the Governor of Bassora despatched an expedition which achieved the conquest of Sinde. But if Rajpoot tradition may be trusted, the fortunes of the Mahometan invaders were less happy in the East than in the West, and within a century they were defeated and driven out from India.

7. This unsuccessful enterprise was, however, only one of a series of efforts which were in the end to establish Mahometan ascendency in India. This ascendency, it must not be forgotten, was that of a religion rather than of a people. When we speak of Arab or Saracenic conquests, we mean conquests which may have been achieved by genuine Arabs, but which may have been the work also of men who had no Arab blood in them. The disciples of the prophet himself raised his standard in triumph at Jerusalem, Cairo, and Damascus; but when whole nations had been brought to the acknowledgment of Islam, the choice between the Koran or the sword was enforced in many lands by men who might be in no way akin to the conquerors of Egypt, Syria, or Persia.

8. Thus, when Sebektegín became sovereign of Ghazni, A.D. 976, the people were under a chief who

claimed descent from Yezdegerd, the last of the native Persian kings, who had escaped as a miserable fugitive from the field of Nehavend, A.D. 637. Sebektegín, A.D. 976, made himself lord of Candahar, and defeated the combined armies of Jeypal, the Hindu master of the Punjab and Cashmere, and the kings of Delhi, Kalinga, Ajmír, and Kanouj. The smallness of the force which scattered their unwieldy hosts foreshadowed the victories to be gained, many centuries later, by Clive, Coote, and Wellesley. In this instance the aggression came from Jeypal, who could not rest with a Mahometan power growing up so near him as at Ghazni; and the consequence was not merely his own overthrow, but a series of invasions (some say thirteen) in which Mahmoud, the son and successor of Sebektegín, showed his zeal for Islam by destroying the idols and plundering the temples of the Hindus (A.D. 997–1030). This is the Mahmoud of the story in which the owls wish long life to the king who fills the country with ruined villages. The tale comes from one who saw that Mahmoud, whose ambition it was to be known for ever as the idol-breaker, was in truth more intent on robbery and plunder.

9. But although the campaigns of Mahmoud had no permanent results, they prepared the way for the conquests of later kings. A century and a half later, A.D. 1180, his successor, Khosru, fell into the hands of Shaháb-u-dín, brother of the sultan of Ghór, and the Ghaznevide dynasty of Sebektegín came to an end. Shaháb-u-dín continued to fight the battles of the Ghórian sovereigns, not always

with success. Ten years after the conquest of Lahore he was defeated at Narrain, A.D. 1194, near the Sarasvati river, by the Hindu kings of Delhi and Ajmír. But the fatal want of cohesion, which marks the character of the Hindus, deprived of all its fruits a victory which might easily have been made decisive; and in the following year, 1195, on the same battle-field, Shaháb-u-dín recompensed himself amply for his past reverse. The king of Delhi was slain in the fight, and his capital fell into the hands of Kootub-u-dín, whom Shaháb-u-dín, who is known also as Mahomed Ghóri, left as his deputy. Kootub was a Turkish slave, and is therefore said to have been the first of the slave kings of Delhi.

10. It was in the reign of Kootub's son-in-law and successor, Shemsh-u-dín Altamsh (1210–1235), that the vast highlands between China, Siberia, and the Caspian Sea poured forth once more a deluge of merciless marauders for the desolation of the world. The roving tribes of these cheerless wastes have, for the most part, but a slender union; but, if they can be brought together by a leader of commanding genius, they may for the time be irresistible. These savage hordes are commonly known to Europeans as Mongols, much in the same way, perhaps, as all Europeans are known to Asiatics as Feringhis or Franks; and the long line of Indian emperors, which began with Baber and ended with the miserable old man who was transported for life after the Indian mutiny, is spoken of as the dynasty of the Great Mogul, with as much, or as little, reason as

the Danes, on their first coming into this country, could be called English.

11. This time the wild tribes of the desert were welded into a single body by the imperious will and rough justice of Temugin, who called himself Genghiz Khan, or King of Kings. The paltry wall which was supposed to guard the empire of China from invasion was soon passed, and the power of Temugin was acknowledged from the walls of Pekin to the banks of the Volga. India itself was but little affected by the appalling deluge. The troops of Temugin wasted the country as far as Lahore, and then withdrew to Ghazni (A.D. 1202–1227).

12. About 180 years later, Timour, or, as he is also called, Tamerlane, crossed the Indus with a host of Tartars and other hordes, not less terrible than those of Genghiz, whom he claimed as his ancestor. Timour advanced on Delhi by way of Panipat, carrying with him a multitude of captives, who, on seeing the king of Delhi come forth with a reconnoitring force, expressed a natural hope of his success and of their own deliverance. The king was driven back, and Timour ordered all the prisoners to be killed. He also imposed a heavy contribution on the city. Many refused to pay, and the place was handed over to the will of his men, who amused themselves with a general massacre of the inhabitants (1398). But the inroad of Timour left no more permanent effects than that of Genghiz; and after his departure India remained, as it had been before, parcelled out amongst a number of Mahometan and Hindu dynasties. Of these kingdoms some were set up by

rebellious viceroys or deputies; some were created by sovereigns who bestowed a portion of their dominions on some favourite minister. Some lasted but for a short time and achieved nothing; others attained to considerable splendour and power. The desolate ruins of Gour, long since abandoned to wild beasts and jungle, attest the wealth and prosperity of the Mahometan kings who ruled over Bengal and Behar, from the middle of the fourteenth century, for nearly 200 years.

13. Still more wealthy and powerful were the sovereigns belonging to the Bahmani Mahometan dynasty of the Deccan. Here, also, a viceroy or deputy had thrown off his allegiance to his master who ruled at Delhi. In 1347 Zuffur Khan, a Mahometan, was crowned under the title of Alla-u-dín Gungoo Bahmani. The title was a strange one for a follower of the prophet of Mecca; but Zuffur Khan had received great kindness from his former master, a Brahman named Gungoo; and he showed his gratitude not merely by adopting his name, but by making him his treasurer,—the first recorded instance of a public office bestowed by a Mahometan king on a Hindu. The power of the dynasty thus established was greatly shaken when Mahmud Gawan, a man fairly entitled to be spoken of as both righteous and wise, became the victim of a base conspiracy towards the end of the reign of Mahommed Shah the Second (A.D. 1481). This conscientious minister had brought the finances of the state into thorough order, had promoted the education of the people, and had raised the army to a high degree of efficiency; but his uprightness and loyalty only made his enemies the more eager for his downfall, and a letter coming professedly from Gawan and offering to betray the kingdom to the raja of Orissa drew from Mahommed Shah an order for his instant execution. The letter was forged; and Gawan, on being led away to die, told the king that the death of an old man (he was nearly eighty years of age) was a thing of no moment, but that to him it would be the loss of his character and the ruin of his empire. His warning was realised. Within half a century the great Bahmani dynasty had come to an end.

14. Thus far the several regions of India had been governed by their own kings or chiefs; and if conquests had been made by foreign invaders, these again were kings, chiefs, or leaders of armies in their own countries, and had crossed its limits for professed purposes of plunder or with the avowed intention of enlarging their dominion. But there were now at work, almost, it might be said, at the other end of the world, influences of a very different kind, which were to produce in India political changes more stupendous than any which had been brought about by those who had entered it with the drawn sword in their hands. The new comers now presented the guise of peaceful traders; and, although they might not be over scrupulous in pushing or defending their commerce, their motive for coming was, undoubtedly, not the winning of territory, but the acquisition of wealth and, with it, of knowledge. It might perhaps be not unfair to say that in some of them the desire of knowledge was stronger than even the love of money.

15. The history of trade, and the history of the state to which the traders belong, run often in very different channels; and the trader is generally far in advance of the financier and the statesman. Long before Britain was known to the Romans, the tin of the Cornish mines and the amber from the shores of the Baltic were carried overland to Marseilles and the head of the Adriatic sea. Merchants, it has been well said, travelled before they sailed; and the goods of northern India found their way to Europe by way of Cabul, Candahar, Samarkand, Astrakhan, and the shores of the Caspian and the Euxine Seas. Another road ran through Persia to Damascus and Alexandria. For this southern trade emporiums were found in Alexandria, Smyrna, and other Mediterranean ports; and a virtual monopoly of the carrying trade from these ports was in the hands of the merchants of Genoa and Venice, whose ships depended on the overland transit of goods to the harbours from which they conveyed them to Europe.

16. But where men cannot use the land, they will resort to the sea; and the sea had long furnished a highway for the commerce of central and southern India. During the months of November, December, January, and February safe and rapid voyages might be made to the Persian Gulf, to Aden, or even to the Egyptian coasts, from which the south-west monsoon would bring ships back with equal ease and quickness. The same needs led the Portuguese to look with longing eyes on the ocean which stretched away to the south, under the conviction that, if they could turn the southern corner of Africa (if it had such a corner), they might sail to the countries which produced the goods now furnished to Europe only by the merchant-ships of Genoa and Venice.

17. The same desire prompted the great enterprise of Columbus. The result of it was the discovery of a new continent, not of a short road to the land of the Indus and the Ganges; and the Portuguese kings naturally turned their attention again to the sea way round Africa. The aid of the sovereigns of England and other European countries was sought in vain; and the Portuguese kings had to content themselves with the blessing of the pope and with such resources as lay at their command. The expedition of Diego Cam, sent out by John II., reached the twenty-second parallel of southern latitude, and one of his men succeeded in making his way from that point to India; but before his return Bartholomew Diaz had rounded the promontory now known as Cape Agulhas, and was made aware of this fact on seeing that the land trended away to the north-east on his left hand while to his right all was open sea. (A.D. 1486.)

18. For Diaz the southern cape of Africa was a Cape of Storms. To Vasco de Gama, who was more favoured by the weather, it seemed a Cape of Good Hope, and so he therefore named it. On Christmas day, 1497, he sighted the country which, from this circumstance, he called Natal. At Melinda, somewhat to the north of Zanzibar, he found the harbour filled with vessels from India, and, securing the services of a pilot from Guzerat, found himself in May 1498 at Calicut, in sight of the beautiful peaks of the Nilgherries. Here De Gama was allowed to open trade; but his departure from the port was not effected without some difficulty.

19. Soon after his return to Portugal a second expedition was despatched under Pedro Cabral which reached Calicut in September 1500. Cabral obtained leave to establish a factory; but the Mahometans stormed it. In retaliation Cabral seized some ships belonging to Mahometan traders, and having transferred their cargoes to his own vessels, set them on fire. He then bombarded the town, and thus between the Portuguese and the Zamorin, or chief, of Calicut there was virtually a state of war. The latter attacked Juan de Nueva, who reached India soon after Cabral's departure; but his seamen were unable to withstand the gunnery of the Portuguese, and his own overtures to de Nueva were received with suspicion. The experience of both the captains convinced the king of Portugal that any subsequent expeditions to India must be of a military not less than of a mercantile character.

20. The truth is that in those days, and indeed almost down to our own, trade was understood to be a thing from which no nation or band of merchants could reap sufficient benefit unless they excluded all others from it. It is easy for us to condemn the early traders, whether from Portugal or from England; but we have to remember that, in the first instance, they were met on the part of the Mahometans of southern India with the same spirit of exclusiveness which afterwards marked their own dealings with them. We have seen that, thus far, the produce of India found its way into the countries of Europe almost wholly by the ships of Genoa and Venice, and of this trade the Mahometans of the Red Sea and the Persian Gulf had practically a complete monopoly. The idea that freedom of trade instead of impoverishing one or more sets of merchants would be the means of enriching all, had never dawned on their minds, or indeed on the minds even of the most sagacious European statesmen and thinkers. Hence for the trader his ledger was scarcely more necessary than his sword, which he might at any moment be called to draw in defence of his life as well as of his property.

21. Still the temper of the Portuguese was not one which was likely to pour oil on the troubled waters. The expedition of twenty ships despatched in 1502 under Vasco de Gama was sent not merely to trade, but with the avowed purpose of excluding from it the Mahometans of the Indian Ocean. His operations began with a deed of horrible and wanton cruelty. A ship full of pilgrims going to Mecca fell into his hands near Cannanore. Gama reserved the children for slavery. The crew and passengers, numbering about 300, were battened down in the hold and the ship was set on fire. Gama's next task was the chastisement of the Zamorin of Calicut. As he sailed into the bay he captured the crews of the small craft about him, and sent a message to the Zamorin that these should all be hung unless his demands were instantly complied with. Not receiving an answer, or not receiving it as soon as he wished, he carried out his threat, and sent the hands and feet of his victims to the Zamorin.

22. Four or five years later, Almeida, arriving from Portugal with the title of Viceroy of India, found himself confronted by a formidable combination of enemies whose fears had been thoroughly roused by Portuguese interference with their commerce. In the naval action which followed Almeida underwent a severe defeat; and the position of the Portuguese might have been seriously endangered had it not been for the arrival of two fleets under Tristan d'Acunha and Alfonso Albuquerque. These commanders had attacked the Mahometan strongholds in the Red Sea and Persian Gulf, and taken Ormuz and Muscat. In 1510 Goa, for the second time, fell into the hands of the Portuguese, and was declared by the Viceroy to be the capital of their dominions in India. Albuquerque had achieved a great success. The Mahometan trade between the Levant and Western India was effectually intercepted, and Lisbon took the place of Genoa and Venice as an emporium for the produce of the east.

23. The subsequent history of the Portuguese in southern India was not such as to make the opposition of the natives a matter of wonder, or to reflect much credit on themselves. An alliance with the king of Guzerat secured to them the possession of Diu at the entrance to the Gulf of Cambay. Here they were blockaded in 1537 by a large fleet sent from Egypt, and underwent the utmost miseries of a siege, until it was raised by the arrival of another fleet under Juan de Castro. This officer had burnt and sacked a multitude of towns and villages along the coast, and indiscriminately massacred or sold into slavery the men, the women, and the children.

24. The next fifty years witnessed a long and uncertain struggle between the Portuguese and the Deccan kings, of which the latter at last grew weary; but towards the end of the sixteenth century the Portuguese found themselves in face of dangers far more serious than any which were to be apprehended from Indian Rajas. Two Dutch ships were intercepted on their return to Europe in 1597; but the States of Holland were not prepared to have the highway of the seas closed against them, and early in the sixteenth century the Portuguese were confronted by the English as well as by the Dutch. In the end their maritime supremacy was destroyed, and they had never made any attempt to establish themselves on land except in positions which might be guarded from the sea. Some of their acts already noticed furnish a gloomy picture of cruelty and vindictiveness; but its dark colouring is terribly heightened by the execrable tyranny of the Holy Office set up at Goa. Something more than the chivalry of Albuquerque was needed to redeem the infamy brought on the Portuguese in India by the processes and acts of the Inquisition.

CHAPTER IV.

First Voyages of the Dutch and of the English to Java and India.

1. The first victory of English over Portuguese ships in Indian waters was won in 1612. The nation which was to outstrip all other European peoples in the race for Eastern dominion was late in the field, and slow and uncertain in its early movements. During the ages of land transit for Indian produce, even the name of India was known probably to but few in England. Alfred the Great, it is true, is said to have sent an embassy to that country on behalf of the Christians of Meliapuram; but the significance of the fact, if it be a fact, is purely religious. The illustrious English king had sent gifts to Rome and to Jerusalem; and in the same way, in fulfilment of a vow made while London was in the hands of the Danes, he sent gifts, we are told, to the Indian churches of St. Thomas and St. Bartholomew by the hands of Æthelstan, who is called an alderman, and Sighelm, who nearly thirty years later was appointed bishop of Sherborne. To William of Malmesbury, living in the twelfth century, the sight of gems said to have been brought back by these messengers or ambassadors, furnished sufficient evidence for the truth of a story which rests, it must be confessed, on a very frail foundation.

2. The first thoughts of the English on Eastern trade turned rather towards China than to India.

The memorial presented to Henry VIII. by a merchant named Robert Thorne, set forth the advantages of a direct trade with the former country, by means of a north-west passsage. In 1553 three ships under Sir Hugh Willoughby set out on this enterprise, but they were separated in the White Sea. Two were frozen in, and the crews died. One only returned to England. Subsequent attempts ended in like disasters, until at last the voyage of Henry Hudson in 1597 convinced all that the idea of a northwest passage to India must be abandoned. The notion next taken up was that of reaching India by way of the Straits of Magellan or Cape Horn, and Sir Francis Drake, taking this route with five small vessels, crossed the Pacific in 1577, and on his return doubled the Cape of Good Hope, without having reached the country to which he had been sent.

3. Drake's enterprise called forth remonstrances from the Portuguese, who nervously dreaded any interference with their fancied monopoly; but Queen Elizabeth contented herself with declaring that the sea, like the air, was common to all men. The formation of a Levant Company, chartered in 1581, came too late; for the Mediterranean trade had been broken up by the Portuguese monopoly, and it was resolved to act on the Queen's declaration that her subjects had a right to sail where they pleased. But an expedition sent out in 1582 to reach India direct got no farther than Brazil, and one only of four ships came back to England. No other efforts were made till after the defeat of the Spanish Armada; but three years after that event three ships were des-

patched from London under Lancaster, 1591, experienced no better fortune than those of Willoughby. One of the ships was sent back from the Cape of Good Hope, which the English had thus reached at last; another, it was supposed, foundered at sea; the third made its way to the Straits of Malacca, and returned by Ceylon. On the Brazilian coast, the carpenter cut the ship's cable, while the crew were on shore, and the vessel drifted out to sea. Lancaster, it seems, was the only one who ever saw England again. The Dutch were more lucky. Houtmann, the commander of an expedition sent out in 1595, was imprisoned by the Portuguese at Bantam, a factory in Java, but made his escape, and returned to Holland in 1598. Another expedition, sent out immediately, brought back rich cargoes in fifteen months, and the trade of Holland with the East was established, all their companies being combined into one under a single charter.

4. The same course was taken in England. The Governor and Company of the Merchants of London trading to the East Indies received their charter from the Queen in 1600, and in the following year Lancaster was again sent to India, which he was fated never to reach. He established a factory at Bantam, and having swelled his valuable cargo with the still more valuable plunder of a large Portuguese ship, returned to England. The next fleet, under Middleton, sailed in March 1604, and reached Bantam at the end of the year. The friendly greetings of the Dutch were followed by signs which showed that they were resolved on having a monopoly of the spice trade;

but the English, by confining their operations to places where the Dutch had no excuse for interference, avoided a collision and returned home in 1606. In his next expedition Middleton was more fortunate. In a small vessel of only 150 tons burden he found his way safely to Bantam, where he took in a cargo of pepper; but some cloves purchased from a Java junk for 3,000*l.* realised in England nearly 37,000*l.* The two other ships under his command sailed three weeks after his departure; and of these the 'Hector' under Captain Hawkins sailed to Surat, and was thus the first English ship that reached India. Hawkins remained on shore and sent his ship to Bantam.

5. The profits of the London Company of Merchants far exceeded already their most sanguine expectations. They therefore lost no time in obtaining from James I. a charter which confirmed them in all their privileges, and despatched another expedition of three ships under Sir Henry Middleton A.D. 1607. On reaching Surat, Middleton found that the Portuguese were prepared to resist him, if need be, by force, and that the terror which they inspired rendered the notion of trading there impracticable. Following the advice given to him, Middleton sailed for Gogo on the peninsula of Guzerat, carrying with him Hawkins, the captain of the 'Hector,' who had just returned from Agra.

6. This journey of Hawkins marks a new stage in the history of English settlement in India. After sending away the 'Hector' to Bantam, he found that he had no chance of establishing a factory with any safety at Surat, unless he could first obtain the per-

mission of the Emperor. Carrying with him the letter addressed by King James I. to the Great Mogul, he resolved to present it in person. At Agra he had an audience of the sovereign who was now lord paramount of Hindustan. Jehangír received him with friendly courtesy, and assigned him a large stipend. But the interference of the Portuguese missionaries frustrated all his hopes. The imperial firman or decree was not given ; his income was not paid ; and his life was at the mercy of men who had shown how little they scrupled to remove by any means the obstacles which might stand in their way. He had no choice therefore but to make his way to Surat, where the timely arrival of Middleton brought his anxieties to an end.

CHAPTER V.

Reign of the first three Mogul Emperors of India.

1. Jehangír was the fourth so-called Mogul sovereign of India. His great grandfather Baber claimed to be sixth in direct descent from Timour or Tamerlane, who in like manner claimed descent from Genghiz Khan. He was therefore, in the technical phraseology of lawyers, a Mongol ; but ten or twelve generations may do much towards modifying hereditary characteristics, and even towards bringing about a complete change of natural disposition. How much blood alien to that of the Moguls had been blended with that of his Mogul ancestors between the days of

Genghiz and his own it is impossible to say; but it is certain, that although his mother was said to be a Mongol woman, Baber always professed the greatest horror of the tribe. For all practical purposes Baber, we are told, was a Turk, and his memoirs were written in Turkish, while his army also was Turkish. Whether between Mongols and Turks there was the same amount of difference as we see or seem to see between Teutons and Celts, it might be hard to determine; but certain it is that Baber and some of his successors exhibited a power of growth in all that tends to civilise a people, for which we look in vain in Tamerlane or Genghiz. It matters little, therefore in comparison, whether he were Tartar, Turk or Mongol. He was not Aryan: yet he was a man who exhibited in himself some of the best qualities of Aryans, and who was to have as his grandson and second successor the most illustrious and the most righteous of Eastern monarchs, of any age or country.

2. It might be said, not without some reason, that the establishment of a new dynasty would be a pure benefit to the people of India, if its sovereigns were just and energetic men. Five hundred years had passed since the first Mahometan inroads; and if it be urged that the Mahometan invasions preceding the one which made Kootub-u-dín master of Delhi were mere inroads which led to nothing more than the setting up of some military posts in the country, still Mahometan kings had ruled successively in the land during the three centuries which intervened between the battle of Narraiń (p. 21) and the victory of Baber at Panipat in 1526.

During this long period the condition of the country, if it had changed at all, was changed for the worse rather than the better. The faith of the Hindu had been fiercely assailed; but the people would not be attracted to the doctrine of the Unity of God when it was preached at the point of the sword. Whole districts had been desolated by ruthless massacres; myriads had been sold into slavery; Hindu temples had been sacked and the idols and their shrines shivered and crushed; but the people still clung to their ancient worship in spite of the vengeance threatened in royal edicts. In the sight of their Mahometan conquerors they stood beyond the pale of the law, and had no right even to the air which they breathed. The trade of the country had declined, and with foreign countries, except on the western coast, there was none. The old Hindu literature had died out, and that of the Mahometans was an exotic brought by poets and others who came from countries as distant even as Mahometan Spain. If old roads were sometimes cleared from jungle overgrowth, no new ones were made; and even the buildings by which the kings might have been expected to exhibit their wealth and power could make no claim either to magnificence or to beauty. The Mahometans had established themselves in the land as a dominant order; but on the body of the people they had made no permanent or deep impression. Hindu dynasties were swept away; and except as collectors of revenue, Hindus could hope for no public employment, and were wholly debarred from all influence as statesmen.

3. But for all practical purposes the country remained independent of its conquerors. The Aryan invaders of India had brought away with them from their ancient home the system of self-governing village communities. In these societies trades and occupations are hereditary; and the village council arranges the distribution of land, settles disputes, and fixes with the officers of the state the amount of revenue to be levied on the village. With the individual inhabitants of the village the state has no concern, and no purpose can be answered by interfering with them. Against such a system as this the extremest tyranny will in all likelihood spend its force in vain. The people may be hunted from their homes; but if ever they return they go back quietly to the old course of things, and, although politically outcasts, retain some substantial freedom.

4. The father of Baber, the fifth in descent from Timour, had been transferred from the sovereignty of Cabul to that of Ferghana, a beautiful country on the upper course of the Jaxartes; and here Baber was born. His mother claimed descent from Chagatai Khan, one of three sons among whom the empire of Genghiz was divided; but, as we have seen, this fact in no way lessened the contempt and hatred with which Baber always spoke of Mongols. His life was passed in alternations of conquest and defeat which sent him from one country only to win and to lose a throne in another. Again and again he became master of Samarcand, and again and again he left it as a lonely fugitive. At last he turned his eyes towards the richer and more inviting countries of India. The

tyranny of Ibrahim Lodi at Delhi was making all his subjects his enemies. In Behar and elsewhere his governors revolted and proclaimed their independence; but the Viceroy of the Punjab, instead of following their example, invited Baber to seize a throne which, as he asserted, belonged to him by right of the conquests of his ancestor Timour.

5. In no way loth to put forth his claim, Baber advanced on Delhi. The army of Ibrahim faced him on the field of Panipat, and underwent a crushing defeat. Ibrahim was slain, and Baber became the first of the so-called Mogul sovereigns of Delhi, 1526. But his main work was still before him. In the north-west there was no opposition; to the south and the east he had to deal with the revolted chiefs who had risen up against the tyranny of Ibrahim. His army was dispirited, but Baber roused their failing energies. His son Humayun soon reduced the greater part of Bengal and Behar; the power of the Rajpúts was broken on the field of Sikri; and the defeat of Mahmoud Lodi near Benares secured for him the Delhi territory to the south of the Ganges. Baber was now barely fifty years of age; but the hardships of his life and perhaps his love of wine had impaired his constitution, and he died at Agra in 1530, having given orders that his body should be laid in the beautiful tomb which is still the holiday resort of the people of Cabul. On his last journey he had ridden from Calpí to Agra, 160 miles, in two days; and in the same journey had twice swum across the Ganges.

6. His son Humayun had the changeful fortunes,

but lacked the genius of his father. Against Bahadúr Shah, the king of Guzerat, who denied that he owed any allegiance to the House of Timour, he achieved some success. Bahadúr's guns were served by the Portuguese, who had aided him in defeating the Rajpút chief of Chittore; but the skill and science of the strangers were of no use to him now. Leaving Guzerat in the charge of his brother Mirza Askari, Humayun turned to put down the revolt of Shere Khan in Bengal; but in Shere Khan he had to encounter an enemy whose military capacities far exceeded his own. He allowed himself to be decoyed into ground where the rising of the Ganges kept him a prisoner; and when his movements were free, he attacked Shere Khan in his entrenched camp before he had finished the bridge of boats which might have secured his retreat (1539). His army was virtually destroyed, and Humayun escaped with a scanty force to Agra. He had expected that Shere Khan would advance to attack him; but the revolted chief remained quiet in Bengal, and Humayun took the field against him with the same ill-luck as before. He had just conveyed his army by a bridge of boats over the Ganges when Shere Khan fell upon him and drove the greater part of his host into the river.

7. Once more Humayun escaped as a fugitive to Agra, whence he hurried to Lahore, where he supposed that his brother Kamran would hold his ground. But Kamran ceded the Punjab to Shere Khan, and withdrew to Cabul, leaving Humayun to find his way, as best he could, to Sinde. Here his hopes of succour were again disappointed; and he

was compelled to cross the desert to Jodhpore, a city lying to the north of the Aravulli hills. Here, too, the rajah repulsed him, and the emperor, with his helpless followers, was driven into the howling wilderness. The few wells in the desert were in the hands of pitiless marauders, who refused to give him water; and the cavalry of Jodhpore, without attacking him, pressed him further into the treeless waste, where clearly they meant that he should die. At length they relented. The son of the Raja approached with a flag of truce, reproached Humayun with the wantonness of his invasion, gave him water and some food, and let him go. At length, with only seven followers, he brought his wife to Amerkote, where their son Akbar was born, 1542.

8. Humayun now made another attempt to recover Sinde, but failing in it made his way to Candahar, having given up all hope of recovering his power in India. Here the reports which reached him of his brother Kamran's unpopularity at Cabul led him to think that he might get possession of that city. His army was so swelled on its march that Kamran made no resistance, and Humayun entered the town in triumph, 1551. In no long time he was joined by his wife with her son Akbar, now a child of four years. Taking the boy in his arms, he said, 'Joseph was cast by his brothers into a well, but he was raised, as thou shalt be, to great glory.'

9. At Cabul Humayun received from his friends at Delhi and Agra letters begging him to strike a blow for the recovery of his lost empire. After much hesitation he consented. A decisive victory at

Sirhind led to the capture of those two great cities, and Humayun was again seated on his father's throne. But he had regained as yet only a fragment of his old dominion, and in what remained to be done he was to have no share. The staircases to Eastern houses are often narrow steps on the outside with a parapet perhaps not more than a foot in height. Humayun was descending such a flight of steps when, hearing the muezzin's call to prayer, he sat down to repeat his creed. As he rose, the staff which he used to support himself slipped on the smooth marble, and the emperor fell over the parapet into the court below. He was mortally injured, and in a few days Akbar was emperor of Hindustan, 1556.

10. To that much-loved son Humayun left, on the whole, a good example. No act of wanton aggression, of injustice, or of bigoted intolerance, no massacres or torturings are laid to his charge; and if he had not the natural powers of his father, he had his cheerful and genial temper, his kindliness, and his courtesy. In his memory Akbar built afterwards the simple and stately marble mausoleum, from which the last titular sovereign of his house was dragged forth as a prisoner during the mutiny of 1857.

11. That the boy to whom the sceptre of Baber had descended would make himself in reality as well as in name emperor of Hindustan, none probably ventured either to think or to hope. He had shown his bravery in the battle of Sirhind, but he had fought under the guidance of his general and tutor, Behram Khan. His own cavalry numbered not more than 30,000; his enemies could bring 100,000 horsemen into the field. With sound judgment he appointed Behram Khan his chief minister. From the first the campaigns which he projected or in which he took part were successful. In Behram he had an experienced and able military leader; and if his tutor was apt to be imperious and exacting, Akbar was wise enough to submit. He had his reward in another victory, won on the field of Panipat, where his army encountered that of Mahommed Shah Súr Adily under his Hindu minister, Hemú, 1556. Hemú was brought as a captive into his presence, and Behram bade him slay the infidel. Akbar burst into tears, and lightly touched the prisoner with his sword. But Behram was not the man to content himself with a mere form or symbol of conquest, and he smote off the captive's head. So died the first Hindu who had risen to high office under a Mahometan chief, and who had shown himself singularly worthy of the trust reposed in him.

12. Had Akbar obeyed the bidding of Behram, the very act of slaying in cold blood might have marred his character through his whole life. As it was, the boy grew up with a sense of duty which seemed to embrace all mankind in its far-reaching beneficence. His justice and his tact were to be conspicuously shown with reference to Behram himself, who was guilty of some acts of gross heartlessness. Akbar sent him a message, telling him that thus far his mind had been taken up with his education, but that as he must now govern his people by his own judgment, he advised his well-wisher to withdraw from all worldly concerns, and spend the rest of his days in prayer at Mecca. Behram started on his pilgrimage, but abandoned it for rebellion, in which he was unsuccessful. His entreaty for forgiveness obtained from Akbar not merely that boon, but his restoration to all his former honours. A few months later Behram was murdered by a man whose father he had slain in battle. His pupil always spoke gratefully of his teaching and his great services.

13. Akbar's position was still most critical; and his dynasty might well be considered as resting on weaker foundations than those of any which had preceded it. His generals gained victories, and having gained them, behaved as if they were not his officers, but independent chiefs. Instead of summoning them into his presence, Akbar went to them in person, and his courteous reproof generally secured their loyal submission. He had already marked out a definite policy for himself, and this was a policy designed to fuse Hindus and Mahometans into a single nation. Far from imitating the example of Mahmoud the idol-breaker, he married a daughter of the Rajpút chief of Sumbhul, whom he enrolled among the nobles of his court. To the Hindu or Aryan rajas this attitude was at first unintelligible, and may have even awakened in their minds suspicions of treachery; but it soon won the attachment of most of them.

14. With open and determined rebels Akbar could deal promptly and even severely; and for the repression of such revolts he moved with astonishing rapidity. His bravery in the field was equal to that of Bayard or of Tancred, and he had further the advantage of immense bodily strength, and a constitution which, unlike Baber, he never weakened by excess of indulgence in wine. In Rajpútana only, it would seem, was Hindu opposition followed by a woful catastrophe. The garrison of Chittore, the stronghold of Hindu independence, rendered desperate by the loss of their leader, slew their women and children, and burnt them along with his body, and refusing all quarter when the fort was stormed, were cut down to a man (1568). It was a hard necessity; but it removed what might have been an insurmountable hindrance to the political union of the Hindu with the Mahometan princes and people.

15. Dealing thus with his enemies Akbar soon became master of Bengal and Behar, of Orissa and Cuttack. But his career of success was broken by some reverses. His friend and companion, Raja Bírbul Singh, fell with 8,000 men under the swords of the Usufzye Afghans, who had drawn them within their mountain defiles; but this disaster was compensated by the annexation of Cashmere.

16. A long list of conquests excites in some minds a natural feeling of repulsion against the conqueror, and is apt to leave the impression that his only business must be that of deluging the earth with blood. But in the case of Akbar we have to remember that every one of his campaigns was forced upon him, and that in every instance his victory implied relief from oppression not unfrequently almost intolerable in its weight. Wherever Akbar was master, the evil of a dominant order, which deprived the subject population of all benefit of law, was at once done away; and when towards the close of his reign his empire embraced Afghanistan, Cashmere, and the Punjab, Oude and Bengal, Cuttack and Orissa, Malwah, Sinde, and Guzerat, throughout this whole region no man could say that his religion or his race placed him in a better or a worse position in reference to his fellow-subjects. Conquered chiefs had no cause to fear tortures or death at his hands. Instead of being trampled under the feet of elephants, or blinded and thrust for life into a dungeon, they were invariably raised to high honours, and often confirmed in all their possessions.

17. In times past Hindus taken prisoners in war had been slain by thousands, and their women and children sold as slaves. By Akbar's edict this was absolutely forbidden, and their transportation beyond the sea rendered impossible. Another edict permitted the re-marriage of widows, and laid a ban upon the rite of suttee in all cases in which the widow had not deliberately resolved on it herself. The rajah of Jodhpore, he heard, was going to force his daughter-in-law to ascend his son's funeral pile. Akbar mounted his horse, and rode off to prevent the murder. He was still scarcely more than a youth when he abolished the jezia, or capitation tax, that most hateful of all imposts, in return for which Mahometanism allows to conquered populations not the right but the sufferance to live. Together with this horrible badge of subjection, he swept away all taxes on pilgrims. They fell, he granted, on a vain superstition; yet as all modes of worship were designed for one great Being, it was wrong, he urged, to

throw an obstacle in the way of the devout, and to cut them off from their mode of intercourse with their Maker.

18. Carrying out these righteous reforms, he declared that rational persuasion (all thought of force being abandoned) should be the only weapon employed in inducing men to change their opinions or their faith. Persecution, he urged, after all defeats its own ends; it obliges men to conceal their opinion, but produces no change in them. In truth, throughout his whole system there is not a trace of bigotry or exclusiveness. The Hindu temples were not only not thrown down, they were carefully protected, and their priests and their wealth were sedulously guarded. Far from enforcing the alternative of the Koran or death, he formed for himself and encouraged for others unions by marriage with Hindu families which remained Hindu. Rajpút princes, Hindus of the Hindus, were amongst his generals and his statesmen; his great finance minister, whose settlement of the land has been maintained, in some parts of the country at least, from that day to this, was Todar Mul, a Hindu. More than all, the Hindus had the free administration of their own laws, which were recognised in the courts of the Mahometan judges.

19. This is indeed a wonderful picture, a picture the truth of which seems almost to pass the bounds of belief, when we call to mind the condition of the whole world in the age of Akbar and in the ages which had gone before it. It has been well said that both in his theory and in his practice Akbar stood absolutely alone, and that Catholic and Protestant Christendom might both have gone and sat at his feet. An Eastern despot was insisting on universal toleration at a time when the Holy Office of the Inquisition was torturing and slaying its thousands, when Calvin was entrapping Servetus to his doom, and when men and women in England and Scotland were being hurried to the gallows and the stake for the absurd and impossible crime of witchcraft.

20. The lesson may well be taken to heart, as having for us a political as well as a religious force. In Akbar we have an instance, we are told, of a Mahometan ruler who could be just to all his subjects and tolerant to all mankind. If it were so, the idea that Mahometanism and equal justice for believers and unbelievers cannot go together must be given up. But the answer is short. Akbar was not a Mahometan. That from his boyhood onwards he was working towards conclusions which deny absolutely the infallible truth and authority of any faith propounded by any man, there can be no question; but it was no heat of youthful zeal, it was no rashness which betrays lack of experience, that moved Akbar to make the confessions which revealed his virtual apostasy from Islam. His reforms preceded these expressions; and Akbar had passed the threshold of middle life, he had indeed held the sceptre of Baber for a quarter of a century, before he declared that we should not adopt a creed or practise a ritual on the authority of any man, as all men were liable to vice and error. There was no God but God, he said, in his confession of faith, and Akbar was his Caliph;

in other words, his vicar for the administration of justice.

21. That he was not only not an orthodox Mussulman, but that he intended deliberately to discourage Mahometanism, so far as this could be done by exposing its absurdities and iniquities without passing the bounds of thorough toleration, has been admitted by almost all historians. Mahometans, like all the rest of his subjects, were left free to eat pork, to drink wine, to play at dice, if it pleased them to do so; the making of pilgrimages, fasting, and worship of any kind were left wholly to their option. More significant, perhaps, as an intentional slight on the Mahometan system, was the substitution of the solar year for the Arabian lunar months, the discouragement of the Arabic language, and the abandonment of the usual daily salutation for one which, although it could offend neither Mahometan, Christian, nor Hindu, was not the one in vogue among orthodox Mussulmans.

22. That such a man should be accused of systematically persecuting the followers of the prophet of Mecca, is not wonderful. The only remark to be made is that the charge is not true. It is the fact that when a courtier asked him what orthodox princes in other lands would think or say of him, the emperor ordered him to leave the room. It is the fact that he told another who had stigmatised his advisers as 'hellish,' that such language deserved a blow. But the blow, though deserved, was not inflicted, and it would perhaps be not easy to find any one who would venture to speak of this as persecution. His own creed was indeed simple enough. It was that God should be reverenced, worshipped, and loved by all, and that all were bound to serve Him by living righteously, by subduing their passions, and doing the good which would add to the happiness of their fellow creatures and bring the peace of a quiet conscience to themselves.

23. This, we must remember, was the avowed conviction of a man brought up in a faith which looked upon and treated all who did not belong to Islam as unfit to live, and which suffered them to live only on condition of their paying tribute and giving up all that preserves to a man his self-respect and renders his life bearable. It may well be said that a mightier genius and a nobler heart can scarcely be conceived than that of a man who, being a Mahometan and a despot, could reach such convictions and act upon them; but the lesson which the history teaches is that he could not reach them without abandoning Islam, without denying the special mission of Mahomet, without forbidding absolutely the enforcement of his law in all its essential features. His tolerance only proves after all that Mahometanism cannot be tolerant; his impartial and unswerving justice only shows that Islam can reform itself only by ceasing to be Islam. The moment that the Mahometan begins to move on the track which Akbar marked out for himself, he ceases to be faithful to the religion which he professes; and before he can reach the conclusion that justice is a thing to which all men have an equal and an indefeasible right, he must have ceased to be a Mahometan at all. The lesson is one of the utmost importance, for it teaches us how the professors of Islam should be dealt with when they proceed to carry their theories into practice at the expense of those who are not Mahometans.

24. After all, beautiful though it be, the system of Akbar, if so it may be called, began and ended with himself. No other result could well be looked for. Akbar's temper of mind and modes of thought, his premises and conclusions, were to all intents and purposes, unintelligible both to Mahometans and to Hindus. His reforms came from himself, and may be said to have been forced on the people without reference to their will in the matter. But the history of the world shows that those reforms only are permanent which a nation slowly and with much effort wins for itself. The downward growth is almost always a fruitless one. Akbar worked alone, and he did his work by running counter to the system in which he had been trained. His successors reverted to the old orthodox paths, and by so doing they pulled down the empire which Baber had founded and Akbar had striven to organize in all its parts. They were thus preparing the way again for foreign ascendency; they were in fact doing the work of the English almost before any Englishman had set foot on the soil of India. But it is well, nay, it is absolutely necessary, to know what were the conditions of the country at the time of their landing, and what they had been in times past, if we would form a judgment on the policy and principles which Englishmen have professed to follow and the motives which have determined their action in relation to the people once righteously ruled by the brave and magnificent Akbar.

CHAPTER VI.

The Reign of Jehangír.—Progress of the English and the Dutch.

1. The death of Akbar was probably hastened by the conduct of his sons. A love of wine was a strong feature in the character of the family. Baber, it can scarcely be doubted, shortened his life by his drinking bouts. His son Humayun might with advantage have been somewhat more temperate. It is still more to the credit of Akbar that he should have set himself to conquer this tendency in his early manhood, and that he should have seen the wisdom of urging on others the duty of moderation rather than total abstinence. But in his children it became a violent malady. His favourite son Daniel died of its effects. The same cause made his son Selim a gloomy and cruel tyrant, and Akbar could scarcely have failed to see that there would be no one to carry on his great and beneficent work.

2. But when Selim, on his father's death in 1605, ascended the throne under the title of Jehangír, or conqueror of the world, the expectations which his temper and habits might have led others to form were for the moment agreeably disappointed. He ordered many useful reforms, some of which showed a political dis-

cernment keener perhaps than that of his father; but the spirit which had prompted his father's acts was gone. He adopted the orthodox formulæ of Islam, and issued edicts about wine which he had no intention of obeying himself. But he was capable of deeds of unspeakable cruelty, and one such deed on a stupendous scale roused horror at Lahore at the outset of his reign.

3. At Agra the emperor admitted to his presence Captain Hawkins of the 'Hector,' and beheld before him one of the people who in after days were to rule his vast dominions. Jehangír saw the duty of a politic ruler to the strangers who asked his aid. He not only gave leave for the establishment of English factories at Surat, Cambay, Gogo, and Ahmedabad, but he expressed a wish to welcome an ambassador from the English court. King James I. accordingly, in 1615, accredited to the sovereign of Hindustan Sir Thomas Roe, who had already at Constantinople acquired a large experience of Eastern life. But all that Roe had thus far beheld had not enabled him to form any adequate idea of the magnificence of the Mogul court at Delhi or at Agra. He had never seen, he tells us in his journal, such inestimable wealth; and if he could have witnessed it in the days of Akbar, he would have seen in the sovereign one whose personal life, he was told, was as simple as his regal pomp was splendid.

4. During the years immediately preceding Roe's embassy, English trade had gone on with a strange and irregular growth. After the return of Captain Hawkins from Agra (p. 35), Sir Henry Middleton betook himself to the straits of Bab el Mandeb, where he intercepted ships laden with Indian produce, in exchange for which he compelled the masters to receive part of his own cargoes. Such acts were little better than piracy; but the progress of trade and of the British factories in India was so slow as to make it evident that the difficulties to be encountered could be overcome only by enterprises on a larger scale. A fleet of four ships fully armed, sent from England in 1612, engaged and defeated a Portuguese squadron in the harbour of Surat (p. 31). The victory added greatly to the reputation of the English, who had thus far been looked upon as mere traders, wholly unable to cope with the Portuguese, and obtained for them from the emperor Jehangír a treaty which granted them permission to trade on condition of paying import dues amounting to no more than 3½ per cent.

5. This treaty may be regarded as establishing the English in India. Roe on his arrival not only obtained from the emperor the dismissal of his governor at Surat, but sent to the Portuguese viceroy at Goa a plain warning of the consequences if he should persist in courses which 'can only bring forth war, revenge and bloodshed.' 'The English,' he added, 'intend nothing but free trade open by the law of nations to all men. It is not the purpose of the English to root out or hinder your trade, or to impeach the receipt of your revenues, and it is strange you should dare to infringe upon the free commerce between their masters and subjects.' In case of his refusal or silence, letters of reprisal, the viceroy was

warned, would be granted to make war upon him in all parts of the Indies. No answer was given, and war was declared accordingly against 'the Portugals in the East Indies.'

6. Before his sojourn in India had come to an end Roe drew up twenty-one articles regulating the English trade, most of which were confirmed by the emperor. But the animosity of the Dutch against the English was not a whit less virulent than that of the Portuguese. A treaty had been made between the two nations in 1619, but it remained a dead letter; and a second treaty was in course of negotiation when news reached England of a crime of singular foulness and cruelty on the part of the Dutch at Amboyna. Under the pretence that they were conspirators in a plot for seizing the castle, the English residents at the place, ten in all, were arrested, put to the most fiendish tortures, and then beheaded on evidence obtained by agonies beyond human powers of endurance (A.D. 1623). Before the execution, the condemned men, we are told, 'went one to another, begging forgiveness for their false accusation, being wrung from them by the pains of torture; and they all freely forgave one another, for none had been so falsely accused but he himself had accused another as falsely.' The indignation excited in England by these horrible murders was intense; and King James I. professed to share, perhaps he really shared, the feelings of his subjects. But the United Provinces were then struggling to shake off Spanish domination in the Netherlands, and as during this struggle a rupture between the court of St. James's

and the Hague was to be avoided if possible, the Amboyna massacre was suffered to pass unavenged.

7. The English continued slowly to make way. A small factory established at Armegore to the north of Madras was the first place fortified by them in India; but the position proved to be less desirable than that of Masulipatam. In 1632 they obtained some privileges of trading in the Persian Gulf; in 1634 a factory was set up at Piply near the mouth of the Hugli or Hooghly. But the idea of freedom of trade was still a theory, not a reality; and the existence of one company suggested naturally the formation of another. Charles the First charged the first company with violation of their privileges. Their servants, he said, were underpaid, and a vast amount of illicit traffic went on with their connivance. He was therefore ready to listen to those who contended that the existing company had established no permanent forts, and done nothing towards extending the greatness and wealth of the kingdom. The real truth was that the king wanted money, and that the promoters of the new company were ready to supply it. A charter was therefore granted to Sir Thomas Courten and his fellow-merchants; but the old company had, after all, the start of the new, and the latter could scarcely be regarded as a success. In 1650 a resolution of the House of Commons decided that one company only should carry on the trade. Some years later a charter, which has never been forthcoming, was, it is said, issued by Cromwell, which combined the old company and the merchant adventurers into a single joint-stock society. Surat was declared a presidency for

the western side of India, and Fort St. George, or Madras, for the eastern. In 1661 Charles II. granted a new charter which authorised the company to make war upon any power not Christian, as well as to suppress the trade of all unauthorised persons, and to administer British law within their jurisdiction.

8. In the same year Bombay was ceded to the English crown on the marriage of the king with the Infanta of Portugal; in 1688 it was handed over to the East India Company with full powers of local government. The presidency of Surat was transferred to Bombay; and the arrival of a fleet of ten ships, well armed, and bringing about 1,000 Europeans, was supposed to mark the beginning of a more enterprising and successful policy. But the seizure of some vessels conveying pilgrims to Mecca proved that the English could not yet venture to match themselves with the Mogul emperor. Jehangír, indignant at the presumption which dared to lay hands on his sacred ships, ordered their expulsion from India. Their factories were attacked, Surat was taken, and the goods in the factory seized and sold. Bengal was abandoned, and the company remained possessed of only Madras and Bombay. It was clear that the English had reckoned without their host. The governor of Bombay humbly besought peace from Jehangír, and recovered the former privileges of trading on payment of a sum of 15,000*l.* and a promise of good behaviour for the future.

9. There were still many real and some supposed difficulties to contend with. The French were settled at Chandernagore on the Hooghly, the Dutch and Danes at the neighbouring station of Chinsura, the French at Pondicherry, and their trade was regarded as an interference with that of the English merchants. The intrusion of private English traders was held to be an annoyance still more serious, and complaints were made that the English markets were thus glutted with Indian produce. Manufacturers in England, declaring themselves to be undersold, clamoured for higher import duties, and the general body of traders to India agreed to the formation of one United East India Company which, in 1702, received a charter from Queen Anne. All that remained now to be done was that the two companies should arrange their financial affairs together. Six years were granted for making this adjustment, and the task was brought to an end under the award of Lord Godolphin.

10. The English now seemed on the high road to success. In Bombay they had an impregnable stronghold. On the Eastern coast they had an important fortified post in Madras. A new factory had been set up at Chutanuttee on the left bank of the Hooghly; and the rebellion of the last of the old Afghan chiefs of Bengal compelled the Mogul viceroy to issue an order that the English must defend themselves. The result was the erection of Fort William for the protection of the settlement now called Calcutta. But the most important fact of all, although for the present it might seem to portend difficulties and reverses, was the decline of the empire of the great Mogul.

CHAPTER VII.

The Reigns of Shah Jehán and Aurengzebe, 1627–1707.

1. Jehangír had embittered the last days of his father; the conduct of his son Khurrám was to darken his own. Under the title of Shah Jehán, or king of the world, Khurrám was declared heir and successor to the emperor. But he had an enemy in the beautiful and imperious Noor Jehán, wife of Jehangír, whose object it was to secure the throne for her own son Shahriar. Being ordered to recover Kandahar from the Persians, Khurrám regarded the command simply as a pretext for getting him out of the way, and instead of obeying he advanced upon Agra. For a time he held his ground; but at length, defeated by an army under the command of his brother Purvíz and the general Mohobut Khan, he submitted himself to his father, who made the surrender of Dara and Aurengzebe, the sons of Khurrám, a condition of his forgiveness.

2. Mohobut Khan had thus far abetted Noor Jehán in her schemes against Khurrám; but now she set herself to bring about his disgrace, for which on other grounds there may have been ample reason. Mohobut saw through her intentions, seized the bridge of boats by which the emperor was about to cross the Jhelum, and took him prisoner while he slept. Noor Jehán made a vain but gallant attempt to rescue him. Mohobut now marched with his prisoner to Cabul, where his wife succeeded at last

in setting him free. But the climate was too severe for the emperor, and he died on his way to Lahore in the sixtieth year of his age and the twenty-second of his reign, 1627. An effort to secure the succession for Shahriar failed, and Shah Jehán was crowned in January, 1628. Noor Jehán, withdrawing into private life with a pension of 250,000*l.* a year, gave herself up, it is said, to works of charity, and clothed herself in white garments for the rest of her days.

3. For twenty-eight years Shah Jehán ruled as the master of an empire which stretched from Bengal to Persia; and although it cannot be said that the wheels of government always ran smoothly for him, his sound judgment and prudence surmounted frequently the gravest difficulties, and his civil administration probably surpassed that of Akbar. He found his treasury fairly filled; he left it overflowing with wealth. Nor is his title to our respect weakened by the fact that, while he is free from charges of oppressive exaction, he raised some of the most magnificent and beautiful buildings on which the eye of man has ever rested. The peacock throne, so-called from the outspread tail in which the feathers with their natural colours consisted of the costliest diamonds, sapphires, rubies, and other gems, may be dismissed with something like contempt as a costly toy or bauble; but a very different feeling is excited by the majestic forms and beautiful work of his mosques and palaces. The splendour of his new city at Delhi, the exquisite gracefulness and touching simplicity of the Taj Mahal (so-called as being the sepulchre of his wife, Mumtaz Mahal), keep alive

the memory of the great sovereign who, with Akbar's faith, might have been greater even than Akbar.

4. The clouds which threatened future storms were already in the heavens. From the heaven which rests over despotic monarchies even of the best type they never can be long absent. There is a perpetual temptation for viceroys and deputies to act in their own interest while they profess to promote that of their master; and if a chance of rapid and easy aggrandisement presents itself, the temptation becomes irresistible. The Mogul viceroy of the Deccan was an Afghan adventurer, Khan Jehan Lodi, who had long aimed at securing his own independence. The emperor, suspecting his designs, could look only to the vassal kings of the Deccan, whose alliance with the viceroy might render him irresistible, and he resolved to go in person into the Deccan, 1629.

5. The result was that he detached from Khan Jehan Lodi his Mahratta ally, Shahji Bhosla, the father of the renowned Sivaji. Later on, the name of Mahratta was to become a sound of terror from one end of India to another; but at this time none knew the mighty force which lay hid in the wilds of the hills which line the western coast of the great peninsula (p. 10). Speaking a dialect closely allied to that of the earliest Aryan invaders of India, they clung to the Hindu creed which they probably supposed that those invaders had cherished; and even now some among them were thinking of the day when the children of Bhowaní and Indra should smite down and drive out of the land the disciples of the prophet

of Mecca. But for the present Shahji Bhosla declared himself the faithful servant of the emperor, and on entering his service with a large body of retainers, he received a patent of nobility and was confirmed in the possession of his estates. Within three years circumstances had arisen which cooled his loyalty; but again he saw the prudence of submission, and was again pardoned.

6. Some years had passed away when the name of Sivaji, the younger son of Shahji Bhosla, began to be more formidable than that of his father had ever been. His childhood and boyhood had been spent in the wild valleys of the Western Ghauts, whence he had issued, with such supporters as he could find among the sons of the smaller landowners, on plundering raids into the lowlands. He would not learn either to read or to write; but he was profoundly impressed by the revelations which his mother averred that she had received from the goddess Bhowaní,—revelations which foreshadowed his future greatness as the destroyer of the Mahometan creed and the restorer of the Hindu faith. His mind was set on the great work; but he saw the need of moving warily. The acquisition of the hill fort of Poona might have aroused suspicion, had he not undertaken to hold on lease the district in which the fort was situated. A hoard of gold found within its walls enabled him to put them into thorough repair and to fortify the summit of another hill to which he gave the name Rajgurh. His faith in himself kindled a like faith in others, and Sivaji ventured to intercept imperial treasures. Shah

Jehán retaliated by arresting his father and placing him in a dungeon in which he was all but walled up, with the threat that the few remaining bricks should be fixed in their places if he failed in securing the submission of his son. Sivaji, thus sorely pushed, threw himself on the emperor's grace, and was not only forgiven but received into favour, while his father was brought out of his dungeon and after a time set free. When both were thus safe, Sivaji took to his old courses, seizing on the hill forts and making himself an impregnable stronghold, which he called Pertabgurh, on a hill some miles to the south of Poona.

7. To the troubles raised up for the Emperor by revolted viceroys or Hindu zealots were added anxieties arising from the likelihood of struggles between his sons after his death. As viceroy of the Deccan, Aurengzebe had shown equal ability and unscrupulousness, and he had thrown in his lot with the dominant fanatics of Islam. His brother Shuja had inherited in its full force the failing of the family and was a confirmed drunkard. As a professor of the Shiah faith, which looked on the caliphs after Ali as intruders and impostors, he was also violently disliked by the orthodox Mussulmans of the Sonnite sect. Another brother, Murad, shared his vice, but lacked his powers of mind. There remained yet one other, Dara, a man more able than the rest, conscientious and just, but afflicted with the opinions and prone to adopt the belief and imitate the practice of Akbar. It was clear that the next in succession must be Dara or Aurengzebe; but Dara was heavily weighted in the

race. Mahometans had borne with Akbar because he had been their sovereign for years before he avowed himself a heretic; they were not likely to submit to one who had made the same confession before he ascended the throne.

8. But the royal titles were assumed not by Dara or Aurengzebe, but by the drunkards, Shuja and Murad, and Aurengzebe befooled the latter by promising that he would see the sceptre placed in his hand and then depart on a pilgrimage to Mecca. Dara took the field against them, but was utterly defeated. Hastening to Agra, Aurengzebe strove first to conciliate his father, and failing in this, he deposed him, 1658, and kept him a prisoner within the walls of his palace. So ended virtually the reign of Shah Jehán, though he lived on for rather more than eight years longer. Aurengzebe found in the treasury 24,000,000*l.*, besides a large quantity of jewels and bullion; nor were these the savings of a tyrant who had thought of nothing but his own enrichment. Every department in the state was admirably organised, and all payments had been full and punctual; and oppressive taxation was not the besetting sin of the early Mogul sovereigns.

9. Aurengzebe was about forty years of age when he dethroned his father; and he was now to reign, as Alamgír, for half a century, like Akbar whose wonderful life was closed in his sixty-third year. Between the two reigns there are points of likeness as marked as the points of difference. In both we see the same unwearied energy of body and mind, the same rapidity of movement, the same readiness in discerning the

causes of danger and to a certain extent the same sagacity and skill in dealing with them. For any of those qualities which have won for Akbar a place among the best as well as the most illustrious of mankind, we shall look in vain. The career of Sivaji wakened in him feelings of well-grounded anxiety; but although he may have gained his immediate object for the moment, he made a fatal mistake when he suffered him to increase and consolidate his power in order the more effectually to weaken his vassal kingdoms of Bejapur and Golconda.

10. Sivaji was thus left to carry out his designs unhindered, and the wily Mahratta chief laid a deadly trap for the general of the raja of Bejapur and his army. By pretended professions of submission he enticed him within the defiles of the mountains, and prevailed on him to visit him with a small escort at Pertabgurh. Here Sivaji, having received the special blessing of his mother on his righteous deed, welcomed his guest and thrust him through with a dagger. The army, left in the defile, was mown down like grass by men who started up from ambush round about, and the camp with all its contents, its horses and elephants, fell into the hands of the conqueror. To a certain extent the king of Bejapur retrieved this disaster; but at the close of the struggle in 1662, Sivaji was in possession of 300 miles of coast territory 100 miles in width, and an army of nearly 60,000 men.

11. Aurengzebe had put down all opposition to himself on the part of his brothers three years earlier. There could be no renewal of it, for all were dead. Dara was accused of apostasy from his religion, and murdered in prison. The same fate befel Murad, and the sons of Dara were poisoned. Shuja alone had escaped, but he was supposed to have died in Arracan.

12. To Sivaji the passing years seemed only to bring fresh accessions of power. He had plundered Surat and levied exactions on the Dutch and English factories. He had laid the seaports under contribution as far south of Goa as Barcelore, and plundered the inland districts as far as Dowlutabad. The emperor now sent against him a force under Raja Jey Singh, a Hindu; and against Hindus Sivaji, we are told, shrank from fighting. He therefore submitted himself to the emperor, and accepted his invitation to Delhi, where he looked for a reception according with his ideas of his own importance, 1666. But he found himself slighted, if not insulted; and, as there were reasons for fearing harsher usage, Sivaji made his escape, and, after an absence of nine months, reached Rajgurh. In no way cast down, he applied himself steadily to the regulation of his civil government and of his army; and this work was carried out, we are told, in its minutest details, with wonderful ability.

13. But his best ally after all was Aurengzebe himself. The reforms or changes of Akbar, which had for their object the fusing of Hindus and Mahometans into a single body, were all swept away. Insurrections, if any took place, were punished with the savage cruelty of old times; the capitation tax was reimposed on all infidels; and the affections of

the Hindu population were most effectually alienated. In the genuine spirit of Mahometan bigotry, half the customs duties were remitted to Mahometans; the full duties were exacted summarily from the Hindus, who were further excluded from all public offices. Marriages between Mahometans and Rajpúts or other Hindus were strictly forbidden. Poets and authors of every kind, musicians, singers and dancers were driven from the court, and were prohibited by edict from plying their craft elsewhere.

14. Aurengzebe was, in fact, establishing his title to being regarded as a Mahometan saint, if not as a benefactor to mankind. Of a truth, he had his reward; and it took the form of a weakening and disruption of his empire. The Rajpúts, instead of being loyal servants as they had been to Akbar, became his bitter enemies. Their hatred manifested itself in rebellion which was put down with the natural ferocity of Islam. Their country was laid utterly waste, their men were slain, and their families sold into slavery. The Rajpút catastrophe may have strengthened, it could not have weakened, the aims and policy of Sivaji, who now declared himself independent, and was, for the second time, enthroned. Sanscrit titles for his officers displaced the Persian names thus far in use, and the Mahrattas were exhibited to the world as a nation. He lived about six years longer. He had scarcely realised the dreams or revelations vouchsafed to his mother; but he had left his followers in no doubt as to the means which must be employed if they wished to destroy the Mogul power. They had their mountains from

which they could issue with the force of the hurricane, and to which they might return, leaving their baffled enemies in despair of finding them.

15. Sivaji was unscrupulous and wise; his son Sumbaji (1680-1689) was unscrupulous and indiscreet. His barbarous executions called forth the protests of his Peshwa, or chief minister, and the imprisonment of the Brahman Kuloosha roused a bitter feeling against him in the public at large. Aurengzebe thought that he now saw his opportunity for putting down the dynasties of Bejapur and Golconda; but when he had succeeded in this task, he found himself no nearer than he was before to the affections of the people, who looked back with regret to the rule of their former masters. Rebellions followed one after another in quick succession, and the attempts to collect the capitation tax added fuel to the flame. But he received some compensation in the capture of Sumbaji, who, on refusing to become a Mahometan, was put to death with savage tortures.

16. For the time the Mahratta power seemed broken. But the loss of a chief could have no permanent effect on an organization like that of the Mahrattas, who could disappear in their fastnesses when the odds against them were too heavy, and swoop down again on the low country when the enemy was withdrawn. In these inroads they found that they had a weapon which even the power of the house of Timour would not, in the issue, be able to withstand. After sixteen years of strife Aurengzebe found them as resolute in their antagonism as ever;

and a series of reverses, all tending to their aggrandisement and his own weakness, darkened the closing months of his life. At ninety years of age this gloomy despot may be said to have died in harness, 1707. His energy had never faltered, his resolution had never been shaken. He had sometimes misjudged the means needed to reach his ends; but he had never hesitated to make use of any which seemed to him likely to secure them. In sweeping away the kingdoms of Golconda and Bejapur he had demolished the bulwarks which might have defied the assaults of Mahratta chiefs. By reimposing the capitation tax he had made three-fourths of his subjects his enemies. But he did his duty as a disciple of Mahomet, and the blame of his failure must rest on Islam.

CHAPTER VIII.

Rivalry of the French and English in India.

1. While the empire of the great Mogul was thus hastening to decay, the strangers from Europe were gaining strength, and were deciding among themselves by negotiation, intrigue, or open war, the question of supremacy in India. It was settled first against the Portuguese, who were expelled from Salsette and Bassein by the Peshwa of the Mahratta sovereign in 1739. A long controversy remained between the English and the French, and even to the most sagacious of politicians the issue might well have seemed for a long time doubtful. Its history brings before us a terrible state of confusion and violence, of oppression and cruelty, of utter uncertainty of law, and of a general helplessness of the people, which would have overtaxed the powers even of an Akbar, but which was directly aggravated by the folly or the tyranny of his successors.

2. The foreigners were rising to power nominally under the protection or as the allies of the Nizams or viceroys of the sovereign of Delhi, or of Nuwabs, who were deputies of the Nizams; but Nuwabs and Nizams alike were sometimes at the mercy of the vassal kings of the Mogul Empire, or of savage invaders like the Mahrattas of Sivaji. In Madras the lack of great rivers practically confined the English to the coast: in Bengal they ascended the Ganges and established a factory at Patna, distant four hundred miles from Calcutta, and another at Cossim Bazaar, near the great city which takes its name from the Nuwab Murshed Kuli Khan.

3. This man had risen from insignificance to be governor of Bengal, Behar, and Orissa. He was neither the best nor the worst of Mahometan rulers. In other words, he acquired their usual reputation for oppressiveness and bigotry, and showed their usual fondness for badges marking the inferiority of infidels. The wealthiest Hindus were forbidden to make use of palankeens, and Hindu defaulters in rent were hung up by the feet, bastinadoed, and left exposed to the burning sun. Murshed had no son; and his son-in-law, Shuja Khan, looked forward to being his successor. For him Murshed had no liking, and he used all his influence at Delhi to secure the

post for Shuja's son, his own grandson Sarfaraz Khan. But in the contest of bribery Shuja was victorious. His own rule was lighter than that of Murshed, and the release of the Zemindars and Rajas—in other words, of the landowners and chiefs—whom Murshed had imprisoned, made him popular.

4. But at Patna, his deputy or Nuwab, Alavardi Khan, won a darker reputation. The Hindu Rajas under his government may have been, and probably were, disorderly oppressors; but the way in which he beguiled them by false promises, and then put them to death, covered him with infamy. By a long standing agreement, thirty men were sent yearly to a certain spot to receive the tribute of the Raja of Monghyr, who was in like manner pledged to bring only the same number of followers. In 1735, Alavardi sent his thirty, and with them another force which was to lie in ambush. The Raja came with his men and paid his tribute. All were murdered. Two Englishmen, Mr. Holwell and Captain Holcombe, passing by with a convoy containing treasure from Patna to Calcutta, saw a boat going by with baskets which they supposed to contain fish. In the baskets were found thirty heads. One man had escaped the massacre and carried the tidings to the Raja's wife. She set the palace on fire and died with her son in the flames. That night the city was sacked and burnt by the troops of Alavardi Khan. The two Englishmen saw the smoke and blaze from the river where they lay at anchor. Such was a specimen of administration in Behar by a deputy of the viceroy of the Great Mogul.

5. At length on the death of Shuja in 1739 the hopes of Sarfaraz Khan were realised. The richest Hindu banker in the empire lived at Murshedabad. His grandson was married, and Sarfaraz Khan insisted on seeing the bride without a veil. The aid of Alavardi Khan was invoked to avenge the deadly insult. He was at the gates of the city before Sarfaraz was aware of his danger. The officers and men were bribed, and loaded their muskets with powder only. Sarfaraz Khan was killed and Alavardi Khan took his place. He exhibited the imperial letters which appointed him Nuwab, 1740. The letters may have been forged, but it mattered little whether they were forged or not. Rival claimants were sometimes visited by imperial messengers, who brought to each the insignia of office; the messengers being men bribed to play the part on either side.

6. Alavardi Khan, in this his more exalted state, lay on no bed of roses. Year by year the Mahratta hordes spread like locusts over the land, devouring all that came in their way. They left the European strangers unmolested; but the alarm of the English induced them to throw up round their settlement at Calcutta the trench and rampart still known as the Mahratta ditch, and Alavardi Khan was at last compelled to surrender to them the province of Orissa, with a sum of 130,000*l*., or thirteen lakhs of rupees, as the chouth or tribute of Bengal, 1751.

7. In 1732, the Nuwab Saádut Oolla had died at Arcot, a town about seventy miles to the west of Madras. His nephew, Dost Ali Khan, took his

place, without reference either to his own master the Nizam, or the Nizam's master, the emperor or Great Mogul. He also withheld the tribute which the Nuwabs had hitherto paid to their superiors. The Nizam was deeply offended; but his own anxieties, arising out of Mahratta invasions and Delhi intrigues, made it for the time impossible for him to interfere. From the former cause Dost Ali was soon to be a sufferer. The Mahratta bands again overran the Carnatic, and Dost Ali fell in battle. His son, Sufder Ali, agreed to pay 1,000,000*l*. to the Mahratta chief on condition of being recognised as Nuwab of the Carnatic in his father's room. But Dost Ali had also two daughters, who were married the one to Mortiz Ali, the other to Chunder Sahib. It was the object of Sufder Ali to get rid of his brothers-in-law, who might seek to deprive him of his dignity; and he made a secret agreement with the Mahratta chief, allowing him to seize Trichinopoly, where Chunder Sahib had taken refuge, on condition of their carrying him away. The Mahratta leader fulfilled his compact; but before Chunder Sahib had retreated to Trichinopoly, he had sent his wife and children to Pondicherry, and placed them under the protection of the French governor, Dupleix.

8. Sufder Ali now thought that he had gained his ends; but he continued to walk in the ways of his father. He made himself Nuwab, and in accordance with this theory he paid no tribute. He had also allowed the Mahrattas to gain an important military post in Trichinopoly. The patience of the Nizam was overtaxed, and he demanded from Sufder

Ali all arrears of unpaid tribute. Unable to pay, he fled to the strong fort of Vellore, which was commanded by Mortiz Ali; but if he could thus escape the importunities of the Nizam, it was impossible to evade the demand of the Mahrattas. The million which he had promised to them must be paid, and must be raised by exactions on the towns throughout the province. Mortiz refused to pay his share. Sufder Ali insisted that he must, and in the festival of the Moharram, when the Shiahs weep and mourn for the death of the sons of Ali, he was murdered.

9. Mortiz was now proclaimed Nuwab, and entered Arcot in state; but the soldiers were unpaid, and demanded payment of arrears in instalments. Mortiz refused, and they declared that they must be paid in full at once. The Nuwab saw the storm coming, quailed before it, and fled back to Vellore. Sufder's young son was set up in his place; but the Nizam now resolved to visit the Carnatic himself, and appointed Anwar-u-dín Nuwab, giving out that he was only to hold the post during the minority of Sufder's son (1743). A few months later the boy was murdered. The outcry was great against Anwar-u-dín as the murderer; but there was no one else who could succeed except Chunder Sahib and Mortiz Ali. The latter was more hated than ever; the former was in a Mahratta prison. Anwar-u-dín was confirmed in his appointment by the Nizam, and soon found himself playing a part in the struggle between the hat-wearing strangers from Europe.

10. In 1744 war was declared between England and France in the quarrel of the Austrian succession.

In the following year an English fleet appeared off the Coromandel coast with the avowed purpose of destroying the French settlements. In great alarm, Dupleix, the governor of Pondicherry, besought the aid of Anwar-u-dín, and the latter, satisfied with the presents of Dupleix, forbade the English to commit any act of war in any part of his dominions, assuring them at the same time that the same injunction should be laid upon the French. In 1746, a fleet was again to be seen on the same coast; but this time it was French, and it threatened the English settlement of Madras. The English reminded Anwar-u-dín of his promise; but they sent no present, and Anwar-u-dín held his peace. The walls of Fort St. George were in no condition to stand against a bombardment by a European fleet, and the French commander, Labourdonnais, received the town into a capitulation which made all the stores within it the prize of the victor, left the English inhabitants prisoners of war on parole, the town itself remaining in the hands of the French until it should be ransomed. The ransom Labourdonnais pledged himself should be a moderate one.

11. These terms caused more than vexation to Dupleix. He asserted that all French conquests in the East must be disposed of by the governor of Pondicherry alone, and he ordered that Madras should be rased to the ground, and that the English should be brought as prisoners to Pondicherry. Dupleix had long seen that a handful of Europeans were more than a match for a multitude of Asiatics, and the capitulation of Madras seemed to lay open before

him a long vista of magnificent conquests. If the English could be borne down and driven away, Frenchmen would be in possession of the field. By a strange irony of fortune, the very step which he took for the aggrandisement of France set free the man who was to lay the foundations of British empire in India. The monstrous order of Dupleix was justly regarded as absolving the inhabitants from their parole. To Robert Clive, the future victor of Arcot and of Plassy, it came as a deliverance, not merely from captivity, but from a drudgery which he hated.

12. The son of a country gentleman in Shropshire, Clive had perplexed his friends and his instructors by his dislike of books, and the singular daring and impetuosity of his disposition. At the age of eighteen he was sent to India as a writer to the Company, then purely a trading association; and with the utmost horror he faced the prospect of a life to be spent in the inspection of stores and the balancing of ledgers. The pay scarcely sufficed for subsistence, and the license for private trading was of little use except to the richer among the clerks. Clive now escaped from Madras in the dress of a Mussulman, and taking refuge at Fort St. David, begged for a commission as an ensign in the Company's service. Having received it, 1747, he showed at once the great military genius with which he was endowed. But his hopes were dashed when the tidings of peace between England and France sent him a few months later back to his writing desk; and he might have sunk into lifelong insignificance if the ambition of Dupleix had not provoked a struggle between the

English and the French in India, which could end only in the downfall of either the one or the other.

13. Dupleix was well aware that although the Hindus and Mussulmans of India might be worth little against Europeans as soldiers so long as they were under native leaders, they would furnish materials for splendid armies in the hands of Europeans. He also saw that for the purposes of conquest no more convenient machinery could possibly be devised than that which was supplied by the imperfect organization of the Mogul empire. It was easy to make an alliance with a genuine viceroy or with a pretender, and in either case to use him simply as an instrument. A nuwab might be treated as an independent prince, for he often was so in fact, or as a vassal of the emperor, for he always was so in theory. It was with such ideas that Dupleix had first sought the help of Anwar-u-dín; but their friendly relations were brought to an end by the capture of Madras. Dupleix in vain promised to give up the town to him. Anwar-u-dín saw that he was speaking falsely only in order to keep him from helping the English. He resolved, therefore, to seize the place for himself, and approached it with an army of 10,000 men and a large force of artillery. To his profound amazement he saw his troops utterly routed by 400 Frenchmen with two guns, and to his bitter humiliation he discovered the reason for the deference which the foreigners paid to the representatives of the lord of Delhi.

CHAPTER IX.

Reigns of the Successors of Aurengzebe.

1. The peace of Aix-la-Chapelle interrupted in India a contest in which the French had thus far the advantage. They had taken Madras, and the English in spite of all their efforts had failed to take Pondicherry. This year, 1748, witnessed the death of the Nizam, who had reached the wonderful age of 104 years, and that of his master, Mohammed Shah, the last of the Mogul kings on whose behalf any pretensions even to ordinary respect could possibly be urged.

2. There is little indeed to attract us in the tale which relates the fortunes of Baber's dynasty after the death of Aurengzebe. Under the pillow of Alamgír a paper was found in which he expressed a wish that the imperial title should be borne by Moazzim, who should share the empire with his brother Azim, the kingdoms of Golconda and Bejapur being reserved for Cambaksh. Azim was nearer at hand and had himself proclaimed sovereign of all India; but he was slain in the battle fought with the army of Moazzim, who had been crowned at Cabul with the title of Bahádur Shah, having reached the mature age of sixty, 1707.

3. Azim was dead, but Cambaksh refused to acknowledge the sovereignty of Moazzim, and their armies joined battle near Hyderabad. Cambaksh was mortally wounded, and Bahádur Shah was now able to turn his thoughts to pressing questions in other quarters. With the Mahrattas he had little difficulty. The infant grandson of Sivaji had grown up in the court of Aurengzebe, who gave him the familiar name of Saho. On his last march Azim had set him free, thinking that at least some of the Mahratta chiefs would take up his cause, and that the controversy thus aroused would deprive them of the power of active interference elsewhere. He had judged rightly; but it was Bahádur Shah who reaped the benefit of his wisdom. The breaking-up of the Rajpút confederacy was a task not less pressing. He had partly carried it through (chiefly by conceding to some of the chiefs a real independence while retaining a nominal sovereignty), when he was called away by the news of a rising of the Sikhs.

4. Few chapters in the history of religion are more strange than that which relates the origin and fortunes of this singular people. We are apt to think of them as a nation, and if regard be had only to present circumstances, we are right in thinking so. But they were originally a sect, and a sect founded for the purpose of cherishing a form of piety absolutely alien to their present character. Nanek, the founder, a Hindu, claiming to be of the Kshatrya caste (p. 13), underwent at an age far earlier than Gautama Buddha (p. 17) the change which makes a man wholly indifferent to all earthly interests. Like Gautama, he married and took part in the active business of life; but his longing was for a vision of truth and careful study of the Vedas, and the Koran convinced him that the worship of

Hindus and Mahometans was alike and equally acceptable in the sight of God, and indeed that all forms were a matter of complete indifference. There must, therefore, be for all and amongst all a thorough toleration, and all must be always united in the service of the one God, who requires that all men shall live for the good of their fellows.

5. The disciples of such a teacher would scarcely fail, we might suppose, to live in undisturbed tranquillity; but the teaching of Buddha, not unlike it in some respects, could not keep a permanent hold on Hindus, and that of Nanek roused the vehement opposition of Mussulmans. Toleration, impartial, absolute, and universal, is a lesson which, as Akbar saw, Islam could never learn without ceasing to be Islam; and Akbar had not been long dead before the spiritual chief of the Sikhs fell a victim to Moslem bigotry. A century had passed away since Nanek began to preach peace and goodwill for all; but with this deed of cruelty the scene was changed as with the waving of a magic wand.

6. They had thus far been passive quietists: they now became warriors as stern and self-sacrificing as Cromwell's Ironsides. They took up arms under Har Govind, the son of their martyred chief, and were driven as rebels from Lahore to the northern mountains. Quarrels broke out amongst themselves, but these only intensified their hatred of Islam, until Guru Govind, the grandson of Har Govind, formed them into a religious and military commonwealth. All caste distinctions were wholly done away with and forbidden to its members, who were to be marked by a peculiar dress and by peculiar manners. They were to slaughter no cattle; but otherwise they were left to their own choice and tastes in meat and drink. They were to reverence the Hindu gods and respect the Brahmans; but the old worship was laid aside, and new modes of salutation were provided, with new ceremonies on the chief events of life. The tradition ran that he formed a Khalsa, or brotherhood of faith, of five disciples, a Brahman, a Kshatrya (p. 13), and three Sudras, giving them the name of Singhs, or lion-warriors, and telling them that whenever five were gathered in his name, his presence would be always with them. As soldiers of this holy-fellowship, they were divided into twelve communities known as Misl, a word having the same meaning with the Spartan Homoioi, peers or equals. The leader of each Misl was called a Sirdar; and the Sirdars were both warriors and judges, presiding over and disciplining a society in which every man was a soldier. Distinct from these in some respects are the fanatics known as Akalis, who ascribe their confederacy to Guru Govind, and who exhibit certain points of likeness to the military orders of the crusades. In the issue, the Sikhs acquired a distinct national character; but for the most part they have long since left their fanaticism behind them, and they are credited with a great love for pleasure of every kind.

7. But this change has taken place since the days of Guru Govind, who vainly strove with his followers to make head against enemies merciless in

their creed and in their acts. Fire and sword, plunder, torture, and massacre, pursued them all their days; but the result was to make them savagely stern and vindictive. Under a religious ascetic, named Bandu, they overran the east of the Punjab, and it must be confessed that they used a scourge of scorpions, 1709–1716. If they were driven back, it was only to advance again with greater fury, and their raids against Lahore and Delhi itself brought the emperor into the field in person. Bandu was compelled to take refuge in a fort; but in a desperate sally he made his escape. Beaten down, the Sikhs were not dismayed, and their power was again becoming formidable, when Bahádur Shah died, 1712.

8. We come now to the time when a crafty minister sets up a *roi-fainéant*, a do-nothing king, because he wishes to be master himself. Jehándár Shah was thus placed by Zulfikar Khan on the throne of Baber; and the first step of the miserable tyrant was to slay all his near kinsfolk. One, however, Farokhsir, escaped; and by the aid of two brothers, Hosein Ali and Abdullah, the former governor of Behar, and the latter of Allahabad, returned to win a victory which made him master of Jehándár Shah and his treacherous counsellor. Both were put to death, and Farokhsir was emperor, 1713.

9. The two brothers who had won him his throne, and who, as belonging to the family of the prophet of Mecca, were known as Syuds, expected to find in him a tool such as Zulfikar had thought to secure

in Jehándár. Like Zulfikar they were disappointed; and a wretched state of suspicion and intrigue on both sides was the consequence. But the Sikhs were again in motion under Bandu; and their ravages were such as might well rouse the deepest wrath and indignation. At last Bandu was taken with many of his followers, and, as we may suppose, the reprisals were savage. Clothed in a robe of cloth of gold, with a scarlet turban on his head, Bandu was shown to the crowd in an iron cage; and then, torn to pieces with hot pincers, he died, thanking God that he had been raised up by Him to be a scourge for the injustice and oppression of the age (1716).

10. In the end, 1720, Farokhsir was put to death by the orders of the Syuds, who set up in succession two princes, each of whom died, within a few weeks, of consumption. Their third choice was more lucky, and Roushem Akhter was crowned as the emperor Mohammed Shah (1720–1748). But the murder of Farokhsir and the early death of his two successors roused against the Syuds a general feeling of suspicion, which it was not easy to lull. The fabric of the empire was seriously shaken. A revolted Afghan chief defeated the royal troops in the Punjab, and a struggle between Hindus and Mahometans was causing the death of thousands in Cashmere.

11. But a sign still more ominous of future evil was furnished by the attitude of Chin Kilich Khan, known also as Asof Jah, or Nizam-ul-Múlk, from whom springs the line of the Nizams or viceroys of the Deccan. The government of the single province of Malwá seemed to him but a poor return for his services to the Syuds; but the disturbed state of that province gave him an excuse for raising troops, and the Syuds in alarm offered him the choice of four governments. Asof Jah saw at once the path which he ought to follow. Marching to the Nerbudda, he gained possession of the fort of Asírgurh, and in two great battles defeated the imperial commanders sent against him. The terror of the Syuds was increased by a severe shock of earthquake, and they acted with hesitation when promptitude was sorely needed. The knowledge of their fears led the emperor to think that he might now deliver himself from his masters. By the aid of Mohammed Amin and of Sadat Khan, the viceroy of Oude and the ancestor of its later kings, he brought about the assassination of Hoseyn. His brother, Abdallah, set up an infant prince as king, and continued to act in his name. But the fortune of war went against him. He was taken prisoner, and Mohammed Shah entered Delhi in triumph. Mohammed Amin became vizir, but died almost immediately.

12. Generally, such a death would be set down to poison. It was now accounted for by the story that a saint, whose arrest the new vizir had ordered, had smitten him with sickness, and that the saint, when taxed with the fact, admitted it, but said that his shaft, once shot, could not be recalled. The vacant office was reserved for Asof Jah, who returned to Delhi with the determination of bringing about large reforms. The changes which he wished to introduce had no attractions for an emperor whose one

desire was that of enjoyment, and who found not a little pleasure in burlesquing the old-fashioned dress and grave manners of his minister. Disgusted with the state of things in the capital, Asof Jah resigned his office and returned to his vice-royalty. This act was a virtual declaration of independence, and the emperor sent orders to the governor of Hyderabad to drive out Asof Jah and to take his place. This order only brought about war between Asof Jah and the governor, who fell in battle; but as the emperor had not avowed the order, the Nizam sent him the governor's head with his own congratulations at the happy failure of his rebellion. Henceforth he remained at Hyderabad, sending gifts from time to time to his nominal master, but acting otherwise as an independent sovereign.

13. The Nizam was now compelled to consider his relations with the Mahrattas. His purpose had been to further the case of Samba, if the ascendency of Saho had not been secured by the genius of Balaji Visvanath. This man was a Brahman who had been the hereditary accountant of a village in the Concan, but at length he obtained the office of Peshwa, which answered to that of Nuwab in the imperial system. Thus far the exactions of the Mahrattas had been mere robberies; a treaty made with Mohammed Shah gave them at least an appearance of legality. But even now Balaji shrunk from any definition of the rights of collection thus conferred.

14. For this he had two motives. The subdivisions and partitions of revenue in the same province gave to each chief an interest in its increase, while they prevented him from acquiring resources which might make him independent; and, further, the greater the complication of the system, the more power would be thrown into the hands of the Brahman caste to which the Peshwa belonged, and so into his own. Balaji was succeeded by his abler son, Baji Rao. There were some who counselled him to bring the internal government of the Mahratta possessions into better order before undertaking any more extended enterprises. Baji Rao saw that with the masses of Mahratta horsemen running wild over the country such an attempt would be very ill-advised, and he proposed the invasion of the imperial domain itself. 'If we strike the withered trunk,' he said, 'the branches will fall of themselves.' His master shared his enthusiasm. When Baji Rao asked his permission to carry the standard beyond the Nerbudda, the Raja's reply was that he should plant it on Himalaya. Thus was established what may fairly be called the Brahman dynasty of the Peshwas; and with it rose to power the great Mahratta families of Holcar and Sindia. The former was a shepherd; the latter a menial servant of Baji Rao, whose recognition converted them from random adventurers into officers acting in his name and with his authority.

15. The Peshwa now had the Nizam almost in his grasp; but he saw that his enmity might involve serious danger in the future. The Nizam, on his side, could not feel sure that the emperor might not transfer the vice-royalty to the Peshwa. The two potentates agreed, therefore, to join forces for the

pulling down the dominion of their common lord; and they worked together, until the Nizam saw reason for suspecting that the Peshwa was reaping solid advantages at the Nizam's expense, and that nothing could prevent this result except his own reconciliation with the emperor. This step determined the action of Baji Rao, who suddenly appeared with his hosts before the gates of Delhi itself, 1737. His purpose was to strike terror, not to destroy; and he retreated before Asof Jah could face him in the field. No pitched battle was fought; but the Nizam was so pressed and harassed by the enemy that he agreed to a convention which ceded to the Peshwa the whole country from the Nerbudda to the Chambal, and guaranteed the payment of half a million of pounds sterling. Before this convention could be confirmed, a catastrophe occurred which laid Delhi in ashes and filled the world with horror.

16. The dynasty of the Sufavy or Sufi kings of Persia was crumbling away like that of Baber in India. But their yoke had been a galling one for the tribes inhabiting the high table lands of Afghanistan, and at length Mir Weis, the chief of the Ghilzai tribe, resolved on invading Persia and avenging himself on the immediate authors of the wrongs complained of. After his death, the details of the scheme were drawn out by his son Mahmud, who marched from Candahar with 25,000 men, and laid siege to Ispahan. The gallantry with which the people bore up for more than six months against the horrors of famine and thirst shows that the old Persian spirit had not altogether died out. But their endurance was of no avail; and at last the king issued from its gate, and placed his crown on the head of the invader, A.D. 1722. His success, it is said, tempted Mahmud into strange acts of cruelty; but the number of his victims is in all likelihood vastly exaggerated. Within two years he died, or was murdered, in a state of raving madness.

17. His nephew and successor, Ashref, was attacked by Russians and Turks together. The latter he defeated; from the former he was delivered by the death of the Czar, Peter the Great, after they reached the southern shores of the Caspian. But a more formidable enemy was nearer to him than either Turk or Russian. The son of the last Sufi king had made his escape and was living as a fugitive with the tribe of Kajar, when he was joined by Nadir Kuli, who brought about another of those strange revivals which have marked the history of Persia. With an energy even more wonderful than that of the founder of the Sassanid dynasty, Nadir roused the people to fiery action, reconquered Meshed, recovered Khorasan, and scattered the armies of the Ghilzais to the winds. But while he was advancing on his career of victory, the king whom he had restored to titular sovereignty took on himself to act as if he were an independent ruler. This Nadir could not brook. He deposed Tahmasp and put his infant son in his place. But when his task was over, when he had wrested from Russian and Turk every inch of Persian soil, he assumed the royal title, 1736, stipulating that the Persians should abandon their Shiite heresy, and conform to

the orthodox Sonnite doctrine. In this Nadir was committing a blunder. The convictions of the Persians were not touched by his demand; but their suspicions were roused and their affections estranged.

18. Although he was, perhaps, unaware of this fact, he saw that a power established by force must be maintained by new enterprises and victories, and he set out with a vast army to besiege Candahar. The city fell, and his conquest of the Ghilzai country brought him close to the frontiers of the Mogul empire. Across this border some Afghan fugitives had made their way. Nadir demanded their seizure or expulsion. Receiving no answer he advanced towards Delhi, 1739, and a battle near Karnál ended in the signal defeat of the Indian army. With a few attendants, the representative of Baber and Akbar entered the Persian camp, and was courteously received by the conqueror. The two kings entered the capital together, and took up their abode in the palace.

19. By the orders of Nadir, some Persian troops were distributed over the town, with a strict charge to keep good order and to protect the people. But the terror and disgust of the inhabitants had reached a height which is but little removed from madness; and a report of Nadir's death spread abroad on the following day kindled the slumbering fires. The multitude fell on the Persian guards. The nobles, it is said, gave up to slaughter the soldiers who were protecting their houses and property, and when Nadir came out in the hope of appeasing the tumult he saw around him the dead bodies of his soldiers, and was assailed with volleys of stones as well as with arrows and musket-balls. At last one of his officers fell at his side, and Nadir gave the order for a general massacre. For six hours 20,000 men were employed in the work of slaughter, and it is probably far below the mark if we set down the number of the slain at less than 30,000. The blood streamed along the streets, the flames of burning houses shot up into the sky, and every form of brutal cruelty was exhibited in all its ghastly nakedness. The work of vengeance, however, did not cause Nadir to forget that he had come chiefly on an errand of plunder. The imperial jewels were swept into the coffers which were to bear them away; the peacock throne was borne from the magnificent hall which it had filled with the glory of its radiant jewels. The nobles were compelled to yield up the whole or the greater part of their vast wealth, and even the poorest were robbed of their scanty resources. Cruel scourgings extorted confessions of buried hoards. Many died under the torture, and many slew themselves to escape from the scene of their agony.

20. When the work was done and nothing more was to be gained by staying, Nadir made ready to return home. But he went back a changed man. For some time the business of war concealed the extent of the change; but when Turks, Lezgi, and other enemies had all been subdued, the horrible fact was made manifest. The discovery that in spite of his wishes and injunctions his subjects were still Shiahs made him look on every Persian as his personal enemy. Exasperated by his suspicions, he put out the eyes of his son, and then reviled those who had failed to save him. His daily murders were accompanied by daily robberies, and his words breathed nothing but hatred and loathing for his subjects.

21. Such a career could not last long. The tyrant was heard to appeal to Afghans to cut down his Persian guards, and seize on his chief nobles. That night he was slain (1747). The annals of the world contain few more appalling narratives than the story of his life; but its awfulness must not make us forget the provocation which let loose the tiger nature in Nadir Kuli. The horror which the thought of the man and his deeds must awaken in us cannot wholly lack a feeling of pity.

22. The city and empire which he had left behind him seemed smitten with palsy, or sunk in a stupor which left no room for thought. The people had been decimated, the treasury was empty, the army broken up, and the regions not wasted by Mahrattas were now left desolate by the Persian hosts. The Mogul dynasty might have been brought to an end at once if the very completeness of the catastrophe had not struck terror into the hearts of the Mahrattas themselves. 'Our domestic quarrels are now nothing,' wrote Baji Rao; 'there is but one enemy in Hindustan. Hindus and Mussulmans, the whole power of the Deccan, must assemble.' The words point to an awakening of something like the European feeling of patriotism; but we have seen why the continued growth of such a feeling is in the circumstances of Eastern society altogether impossible. The old dissensions were soon renewed, and Baji Rao was in his turn made to feel that greed of land and wealth is not a condition fruitful of happiness. His anxieties seem to have hastened his death, and his office descended to his son Balaji Rao, a man not less sagacious and vigorous than his father. Eight years later Mohammed Shah also passed away.

CHAPTER X.

Dupleix and Clive.

1. The battle for English or French supremacy was now to be fought out in Southern India. On the one side was Dupleix, a man of great political genius, lacking perhaps in physical courage, but quick to see opportunities for action, speedy in availing himself of them, and aided by military leaders not less able and more conscientious than himself. On the other there was a council which saw but dimly the significance of the struggle, and had a still more vague idea of the right mode of carrying it through; slow in forming resolutions, and uncertain in their execution. But these disadvantages were more than compensated by the energy and judgment of Clive.

2. The peace of Aix-la-Chapelle and the restoration of Madras to the English would, it might have been thought, carry with them heavy discouragement for Dupleix. But he was not cast down. Englishmen and Frenchmen could no longer face each other in battle as such, but they were free to take part in the politics of the native kingdoms. The death of Chin Kilich Khan (Asof Jah, and Nizam-ul-Múlk), had removed the protector of the Nuwab Anwar-u-dín. Chunder Sahib, who laid claim to his office as the son-in-law of Dost Ali, was in a Mahratta prison; but his wife and children were guests of Dupleix. From the wife of the captive Madame Dupleix, familiarly known in Indian history as Jan Begum, learnt that lack of money was the only hindrance to his liberation; her husband saw that in the name of Chunder Sahib as Nuwab of the Carnatic he might make himself the real master of Southern India. Seven lakhs (70,000*l.*) were sent to Chunder Sahib, and a French force was despatched to aid him in bringing matters to an issue with Anwar-u-dín in 1748. But a more splendid prospect still was opened to him by the death of the Nizam. His son, Nasir Jung, in the absence of his elder brother, seized his treasury, and his largesses to the army secured his recognition as viceroy of the Deccan. But the succession to an office, which in theory was not hereditary, was claimed by Mozuffer Jung, a favourite grandson of the old Nizam, who exhibited a will, probably forged, naming him the heir; and delegates, real or pretended, from the Great Mogul brought to both the rivals the insignia of their dignity. Freed from his prison, Chunder Sahib now proposed an alliance with Mozuffer Jung, the plan being that their united forces should recover first the Carnatic and then the Deccan. Mozuffer Jung heartily accepted the proposal, which was approved not less cordially by Dupleix. At Ambúr a battle was fought in which Anwar-u-dín fell, and his son Mohammed Ali, the last of his house, fled to Trichinopoly. The capture or death of the latter would settle the controversy in the Carnatic, and the whole powers of the two claimants, backed by that of the French, might be applied to the establishment of Mozuffer Jung as viceroy of the Deccan, where, under cover of his name, Dupleix would be virtually the king. With feverish anxiety he proposed and urged the reduction of Trichinopoly; and his allies professed to set about the task. But they wanted money, and shrank from confessing the fact. The 70,000*l.* of Dupleix may have been all paid as Chunder's ransom to the greedy Mahrattas; and their only course was to halt at Tanjore and demand the arrears of tribute alleged to be due from the raja to the Nuwab. But before this business could be ended, Nasir Jung entered the Carnatic with a force which to the two claimants seemed irresistible. Mozuffer Jung surrendered himself; Chunder Sahib fled to Pondicherry; and the grand schemes of Dupleix seemed to have fallen to the ground like a house of cards.

3. But Dupleix was scarcely dispirited, far less in despair. He knew that he had the support of excellent officers: and in addition to other successes the fort of Jinji, which was supposed to command the whole country, was taken by Bussy. This event

brought Nasir Jung, who was fooling away his time at Arcot, to a sense of his danger; but the proposals which he now made to Dupleix were met by demands so exorbitant that he resolved to trust his cause to the decision of the sword. The decision was to be brought about in another way. The army of Nasir Jung was disaffected, and not a few were ready to betray him for money. The fact soon became known to the busy Jan Begum; and a small French force advanced professedly to encounter the vast army of Nasir Jung, but really to aid the traitors. The disaffected troops refused to charge. Nasir Jung rode up to them and called them cowards for shrinking from a few drunken Europeans. They were his last words. In another instant a bullet laid him dead at their feet, and the soldiers proclaimed Mozuffer Jung as Nizam of the Deccan.

4. To Dupleix it seemed that the fates were indeed propitious. The Nuwab and the Nizam were both his creatures, and must remain his servants. At Pondicherry, in the midst of gorgeous ceremonies, Mozuffer Jung appeared as the representative of the Great Mogul, and in his name appointed Dupleix governor of all the countries to the south of the Kistna. Among the French officers and troops he distributed 50,000*l.*: a sum four times larger was the portion of Dupleix himself. But if he satisfied his French allies, he was less successful with his own soldiers. A mutiny among them was suppressed by the fire of the French; but a sabre stroke dealt to Mozuffer Jung a mortal wound. In this crisis, when the vice-regal army seemed likely to melt away, Bussy speedily

restored order. He took Salábut Jung, the eldest of the three surviving brothers of Nasir Jung, proclaimed him Nizam, and obtained from him a confirmation of all the promises made by his predecessor. Dupleix had now reached the height of his glory, and he resolved to raise a memorial of it to be seen by the coming ages. On the spot where, by the fall of Nasir Jung, fortune had decisively turned in his favour he built a stately column, on which four inscriptions in four languages set forth the story of his greatness. Round it rose a town bearing the name of Dupleix Fatihabad—'the city of the victory of Dupleix.'

5. The only remaining hindrance in the path of Dupleix was Mohammed Ali, and he, it was clear, could not long hold out in Trichinopoly (1751). He had even begun to make terms with his besiegers, before the English realised the full danger of their position. If Chunder Sahib should win the day, then in Chunder Sahib's name a rescript, coming really from Dupleix, might, and would, order the destruction of the English forts of St. David and St. George, and settle the question of French ascendency in the whole peninsula. It was therefore of the last importance that Mohammed Ali should be enabled to hold out. But how was this object to be attained? At Trichinopoly the English were hopelessly outnumbered; and the Hindu rajas, especially those of Tanjore and Mysore, were awaiting the issue of the conflict, prepared to join the winning side when there should be no longer doubt of the winner.

6. The problem was solved by Clive. He had just returned from Trichinopoly by the road which runs northward for 100 miles to Arcot, and from Arcot turns eastward to Madras, a distance of 70 miles. He had seen that the garrisons in the Carnatic had been drawn off for the siege of Trichinopoly, and that Arcot especially was inadequately guarded. With all earnestness, therefore, he urged an expedition to Arcot. The occupation of that city would strengthen the hands of Mohammed Ali, would determine the action of the wavering rajas, and would compel Chunder Sahib to detach a large portion of his forces for the relief of his capital. Clive's advice was taken. With 200 Europeans and 300 Sepoys he set out on the enterprise which was to decide the fate of the English in India. Of the eight officers under his command four only had received any military training, and of these only two had been in action; the other four were commercial clerks. On the road he learnt that the Arcot garrison outnumbered his own men by more than two to one: but the Arcot garrison learnt from spies that the English had marched without concern through a terrible storm of lightning and rain, and were so dismayed by this proof of their daring that they retreated to a camp at some distance from the fort, which the British force entered unopposed. In it Clive found eight guns, with a store of powder and lead. He made preparations at once to stand a siege; but the garrison which had deserted its post, now largely reinforced, threatened to storm the citadel. At the dead of night Clive sallied out, attacked the camp, slew many, dispersed the rest, and returned to the fort without any loss on his own side.

7. Dismayed at the tidings which came from Arcot, the besiegers at Trichinopoly detached an immense force for the recovery of the capital. For fifty days Clive withstood all their efforts. Having vainly tried to bribe him, and fearing that he might receive other reinforcements in addition to the Mahrattas who had joined him from Mysore, the enemy resolved upon a last onset during the great festival of the Mohurram. It was the time when the fervour of the Shiites is roused to burning pitch by the tragedy of the sons of Ali; and this fervour was heightened by large doses of bhang (Indian hemp leaves), and by the thought of the special delights promised in heaven to those who may fall in battle on this sacred day. Elephants with their foreheads armed with iron plates were driven against the gates to burst them open; but the musket balls of the besieged drove the huge beasts back in pain and terror on the masses of men whom they trampled down with their mighty feet. In an hour the enemy drew off. On the following morning they were no longer to be seen. They had raised the siege during the night, and the issue of the long conflict was virtually decided.

8. Clive's success at Arcot was followed by other successes in the field. A few months later, Chunder Sahib gave himself up to the Raja of Tanjore, who put him to death. Trichinopoly was surrendered, the French officers were put under their parole not

to serve against the English or their allies, and the French soldiers were sent as prisoners to Fort St. David. But the act which made the greatest impression on Hindus and Mahometans alike was one of destruction, which, we might be apt to think, could not easily be excused. Between Madras and Fort St. David lay the city of Dupleix Fatihabad. Clive gave orders that the column of victory and the town should be both rased to the ground. The act was not merely necessary; it was one of the soundest policy. Dupleix's monument had placed a spell on the land which could be broken only by its overthrow. Its ruins proved that the doctrine of French supremacy was not admitted by Englishmen, and that Englishmen were fully capable of contesting it.

9. Even now Dupleix was not cast down. To him and to the French Salábat Jung owed his throne, and from Salábat he received the splendid and wealthy territory afterwards known as the Northern Circars. It stretched along six hundred miles of coast until at its northern extremity it reached the shrine of Jaganath (Juggernaut) at Poree. Its revenue exceeded half a million of pounds sterling, and it had the advantage of an excellent harbour at Masulipatam. The French were thus still by far the richest of Europeans in India; but the French Company was not on this account the more satisfied with Dupleix. They charged him with wasting their resources on wars and intrigues which, if they added to his reputation and brought France some glory, brought with them no solid advantage. The English were weary of the war, wearied with incurring costs which should

be borne by the nation, if they were to be incurred at all, and wearied still more with the complications of native politics in which they found themselves entangled. The Directors of the Company in England urged that if the war was to go on, it should, as being for the interests of the nation, be at the expense of the nation, or else that it should be brought to an end.

10. In the latter conclusion both the French and English governments agreed. A treaty made by a plenipotentiary sent to Pondicherry pledged both sides to renounce all native dignities, and all governments conferred by native grandees. The conditions were never carried out, but Dupleix was recalled, 1754; and to be recalled was for him to be ruined. In the cause of his country he had spent his private funds, which amounted to 300,000*l*., and he had also borrowed largely. The French government gave him protection against his creditors; but they repudiated his debt. Labourdonnais, after the conquest of Madras, was thrust into the Bastille, and remained there for nearly two years without a trial, and being then acquitted, died of what has been called a broken heart. The end of Dupleix was like his.

11. The contest in which he could no longer take part still went on. In the Deccan Bussy maintained his footing; but Mahometan intrigue brought about in 1756 a rupture between him and the man who owed to him his position as Nizam. Bussy marched towards Hyderabad, and Salábat Jung appealed to the English for help. The opportunity for interference was eagerly welcomed at Madras, and a force was about to set off for his relief, when tidings came from Bengal which put all such enterprises for the present out of the question. The capture of Calcutta by Suraj-u-Daula seemed to threaten the very existence of the English in Bengal.

CHAPTER XI.

Clive and Suraj-u-Daula.—Battle of Plassy.

1. The Nuwab Alavardi Khan had reached his dignity in the way which custom had well-nigh sanctified in the Mogul empire,—the path of intrigue, bribery, murder, and forgery (p. 72). But in his high place he had acted for the interests of the country and had at least done something towards lessening the horrors of the Mahratta inroads; and when, in 1756, he lay, at the age of eighty, on his death-bed, he may have thought that in his favourite grandson, Suraj-u-Daula, his people would have a ruler as kindly and well-intentioned to them as himself. He was fatally mistaken. The boy had been brought up as an eastern despot, and he grew up an eastern despot of the worst type, with no other notion of life than that which makes it an alternation of sensual pleasure and wanton cruelty. Possessed by an insane hatred of the English and by the most extravagant ideas of their wealth, he lived in the hope of driving them into the sea and seizing all

their treasures. A cause of quarrel was easily found. Kishen Das, the son of a governor of Dacca, was one of the many men on whose hoards Suraj-u-Daula looked with a longing eye. He was furious when he heard that Kishen Das had taken himself and his money to Calcutta and sought the protection of Drake, the governor. The Nuwab insisted on the surrender of the fugitive and the demolition of the new fortifications of the settlement. Drake refused the former request, and denied the existence of any new fortifications; but his plea that the old fortifications had been repaired to make them serviceable in the event of an attack by the French made the Nuwab still more wroth that these foreigners should dare to make war on one another in his dominions.

2. With 50,000 men he marched, 1756, straight upon Calcutta, which was in no way prepared for resistance. The town had practically no defences, and the fort was overlooked and commanded by mercantile buildings. Had Clive been there, we should have heard of a defence as memorable as that of Arcot; but although Clives cannot be looked for everywhere, the paralysis of courage shown by some of the English in Calcutta is little to their credit. When the guns of the enemy opened fire, the governor and some others escaped with the women and children to the ships, and then, to the amazement and disgust of those who remained behind, the ships, which might have carried off the whole garrison when resistance became hopeless, dropped down the river.

3. The story is a wretched one throughout.

While some of the English fought on without flinching, some of them broke into the arrack stores and got drunk; others were spent and worn out from the natural causes of heat and fatigue. But in truth the whole European population in Calcutta had been under 600, and they had adopted a mode of defence which would have made even Clive helpless. The Nuwab sent a flag of truce, and when Mr. Holwell, who acted as governor in the absence of Drake, admitted it, the enemy rushed in at the gates and the defenders were overpowered and disarmed. The first and perhaps the only thought of Suraj-u-Daula was for the treasury, and his disappointment was bitter when he found that it contained only 50,000*l*. When the prisoners appeared before him, he assured Mr. Holwell that no harm should befall them, and having so said he betook himself to his repose without giving any orders about them. To disturb the tyrant in his hours of rest would be death, and his officers could find no other place for the detention of the prisoners, 146 in number, than a room about twenty feet square, with one window only, which had been set apart for the confinement of refractory soldiers. Into this horrible chamber all were driven at the point of the bayonet and the door was locked upon them. Words cannot describe the horrors of the ensuing hours. In a climate like that of England such a heaping together of human beings would involve death to some and fearful suffering for all; but here they were pent up in the fiery furnace of an Indian summer solstice. In their agony the victims shrieked to their guards to fire upon them;

but they were left to struggle with the poisoned air, while their guards shouted with laughter. In the morning sixteen haggard forms came forth still living. The rest were all dead. The tragedy of the Black Hole was played out.

4. For Suraj-u-Daula this only can be said, that he did not order these horrors. It is even possible that he may not have wished or intended them to take place; but to what does this plea amount? To leave his prisoners without uttering a word to insure them the safety which he had solemnly promised was infamous enough; but if any human feeling had remained with him, he must have recoiled from the results of his fatal negligence when he became aware of them. In fact, he took no notice of them whatever; and his only inquiries were for the places where the wealth of his victims might be hidden. In truth, the catastrophe excited no notice in India except among the Europeans. It was regarded as a matter of course, and native historians who relate the capture of Calcutta say nothing of the awful episode of the Black Hole. We have in this wonderful fact the explanation of the history of the East, and more particularly of the history of India. The people have no political union; and this is the cause of their depression and of the invasions and conquests which have led to that depression. It has been well said that individually the people of India are the kindest and most compassionate in the world, but that beyond the circle of their family or caste they know nothing and heed nothing. They have paid a terrible penalty for their self-imposed isolation.

5. The triumph of the despot did not last long. Six months later the English flag was flying over Fort William, and he sent an intreaty for peace, which Clive, in expectation of a war between England and France, was willing to grant. But for Suraj-u-Daula treaties went for nothing. He promised to compensate the English for their losses on the capture of Calcutta; but he wrote at the same time to Bussy, beseeching him to come and drive the English out of Bengal. He heard of the desolation of Delhi by Nadir Shah, and he sent to beg the aid of Clive against the Persian king and his followers. Rendered frantic by his terror, he gave Clive leave to attack Chandernagore, and withdrew his permission when it was too late. The French settlement, after a most gallant defence, fell into the hands of the English, 1757, and the significant comment of Clive was, 'We cannot stay here.' The British standards have advanced further north than Chandernagore: it is possible that they may have now and then advanced too far.

6. All this hateful tyranny and, still more perhaps, all this wretched weakness produced its natural harvest of hatred and conspiracy. The chief plotters in this case were the Nuwab's general, Mir Jafir, and Jagat Seth, of Murshedabad, the wealthiest banker in India. These men invited Clive to take part in their scheme, and Clive consented. The truth is that Clive, who in his dealings with his countrymen and with other Europeans would have scorned even to equivocate, had by some strange process convinced himself that in dealing with Orientals any-

thing was fair, and anything that was politic was justifiable. Habitual lying could be met only by well-considered falsehoods; and the traitor must be foiled by his own weapons. So we find Clive, who abhorred the deceitfulness of Suraj-u-Daula, writing to him affectionately, while he assured the men who were bent on murdering him that he would stand by them as long as he had a man left.

7. It is not easy to touch pitch without being defiled. We need not, therefore, wonder that Clive was led on from one dissimulation to another. The agent employed between Mir Jafir and the English commander was a Calcutta merchant named Omichand, whose great wealth had been materially diminished by the recent capture of Calcutta. Conspirators are seldom disinterested; and Clive must surely have supposed that Omichand would expect something for his pains and trouble. Indeed, if there is to be any honour among thieves, it was but fair that he should have something: but Clive was, or pretended to be, amazed when he learnt that Omichand's demand was for 300,000*l.* with a commission of 5*l.* per cent. on all payments between the two parties, and that, unless these demands were granted, he should bring the whole matter before the intended victim. This stipulation, he insisted, should be inserted in the treaty between Mir Jafir and the English; and Clive met the needs of the case by having two copies of the treaty drawn up, the one on white paper, the other on red, the latter being fictitious. How the real treaty was to be distinguished from the fictitious one, it might be

hard to say, for it was intended that both should have the genuine signatures of Clive and his colleague, Admiral Watson. There was, in truth, no distinction except in the guilty consent of the two, who were both determined that the sharp practice of Omichand should be defeated, and that the treaty guaranteeing Omichand's compensation should be null and void. This consent Watson could not prevail on himself to give. He refused to sign the false treaty. Clive forged his signature, and, having done so, wrote in altered tone to the Nuwab, setting forth the wrongs of the British, offering to submit the matter to the arbitration of Mir Jafir, and telling him that he and his men would in person come for the Nuwab's answer.

8. Suraj-u-Daula perfectly knew the meaning of the last phrase, and joined his army at Plassy, while Clive remained at Cossim Bazaar, expecting that Mir Jafir would, according to his promise, meet him with the division under his command. But Mir Jafir did not know yet how the day would go, and he prudently shrank from any act which might compromise him with the Nuwab, if the Nuwab should after all be the victor. Clive was therefore left to face an army twenty times as large as his own, with the possibility that Mir Jafir might take an active part against him. In his anxiety he called a council, and the council decided against fighting. It was dangerous to cross a river which would cut off their retreat if the day went against them. This was the only council ever summoned by Clive; and he used to say afterwards that if he had taken its advice, the English would never have been masters of Bengal. After a few moments' thought he resolved to reverse their decision, and gave the order for crossing the river. A long day's march brought his little army of 3,000 men to a mango-grove, within a mile of the encampment of the enemy, where 40,000 infantry were supported by 15,000 cavalry and 50 pieces of ordnance of the largest size, as well as some smaller but probably more formidable field pieces served by French engineers. The result of the next day's fight was precisely that which had astounded Anwar-u-dín nine years before (p. 77). In one hour the headlong flight of the Nuwab's troops swept away the little band of Frenchmen who alone struggled to maintain their ground (1757).

9. A few days later Clive installed Mir Jafir as Nuwab at Murshedabad; and nothing remained except to carry out the terms of their treaty. To the conference called for this purpose Omichand came with the confidence which the sustained kindness of Clive's manner towards him fully justified. The treaty on white paper was read: and then at Clive's bidding Mr. Scrafton, turning to Omichand, informed him that the red treaty was a trick, and that he was to have nothing. It is unfortunate for Mr. Scrafton that his name should appear in history only in a matter in which he ought to have been most thoroughly ashamed of himself. The story goes that Omichand, on hearing this announcement, fell back in his chair insensible, and that when he awoke to consciousness, he was little better than a drivelling idiot. This has been denied, and it may be denied on good grounds; but Omichand, if his mind had not failed him, might have contended that both treaties were valid, being both signed by both the English leaders, and that the red treaty, as supplementary, was the more binding of the two. Clive could scarcely have confessed his forgery, and Watson certainly would have refused to confess himself an accomplice in a scheme which he would not sanction by his signature.

10. But we turn with loathing from this tangled web of falsehood and deceit. It has been said that the whole history of British India enforces one great lesson. This lesson is that 'it is not prudent to oppose perfidy by perfidy, and that the most efficient weapon with which men can encounter falsehood is truth.' The path pointed out by prudence is the one towards which righteousness beyond all doubt leads us. Intrigue, shuffling, lying, and perjury might have gained us something in our dealings with those who use such weapons; but these gains are as nothing in comparison with the benefits secured to us by the impression left on the native mind that the British is the one power in India whose word may be implicitly relied on. It will be an evil day for Great Britain, it may be an evil day for the world, if this impression is removed by a return to the infatuated theory of Clive. We have been told, and rightly told, that English truth has done more to extend and preserve our empire in the East than English valour and English intelligence; and that Clive should even in that early stage in its growth have failed to see this, nay, that he should have gloried in the lies by which he cheated Omichand, is indeed astounding.

11. The victory of Plassy was followed by immediate results of a most substantial kind. The miserable wretch Suraj-u-Daula was caught a few days after the battle, brought back to Murshedabad, and there put to death by Mir Jafir; but as Clive knew nothing of this, he could not interfere to prevent it. A hundred boats conveyed to Calcutta silver amounting in value to 800,000*l.* sterling. A vast sum was further paid to Clive, and a large tract on the river Hugli was ceded to the Company, which was to pay a quit rent of 30,000*l.* yearly, nominally to the great Mogul, really to the Nuwab, in return for a revenue of 100,000*l.* Clive found that the forms of the Mogul organization were by no means inconvenient to himself; he therefore insisted on their punctilious observance. A patent of nobility described him as commander of 6,000 foot and 5,000 horse. These existed only on paper; but Clive demanded the jaghir, or revenue-furnishing district, needed for their maintenance. In his perplexity Mir Jafir could think of no other device than that of making over to Clive the quit-rent which the Company was pledged to pay to the Mogul or his representative the Nuwab; and thus Clive became a landowner to whom, as his tenants, the Company which he served was bound to pay a rent of 30,000*l.* a year.

12. But on the whole, the result of Clive's plottings and manœuvrings was not altogether happy. Mir Jafir was found to be absolutely unfit for his office. He wasted his time in chewing bhang and watching the movements of dancing girls; but he had no abilities, the cultivation of which might have been worth the trouble bestowed upon them. His follies and his fears, and more especially his abject terror of Clive, got for him the nickname of Colonel Clive's jackass. His wish to remove Hindus from all high offices excited discontent and intrigue everywhere. Clive could protect their persons, but he could not maintain them in their posts. He was therefore hated by the nobles, while the natives generally complained that the English took no thought of the wants and sufferings of the main body of the people.

13. The contest between the French and the English for supremacy was not yet ended. Bussy was about to march to the aid of Suraj-u-Daula when he heard of the fall of Chandernagore. By way of retaliation he drove the English out of Vizagapatam, and took three of their factories on the coast of the delta of the Godavari. In 1758, a French fleet reached Pondicherry, with a large force under the command of the Count Lally. This officer had a strong dislike of the English, and a distrust, not less strong, of the rectitude of his countrymen in India. Recalling Bussy from the Deccan, he placed the Marquis of Conflans in charge of the Northern Circars (p. 99). The latter was confronted by an English force under Colonel Forde, who recovered the factories along the coast which had been seized by Bussy. Lally's attempt to besiege Madras was not successful, and the news of its failure was received with expressions of hearty satisfaction by the French merchants at Pondicherry. Nor were his efforts happier elsewhere. In 1760, he was defeated by Colonel Coote at Wandiwash, a town near the coast between Madras and Pondicherry; and before the year was ended, Pondicherry itself had been starved into a capitulation, and its fortifications rased to the ground. The surrender of the fort of Jinji (p. 94) put an end to French military power in the Carnatic. Lally, unlike Dupleix, had acted with complete unselfishness; but he had been foiled by the indifference of merchants who cared only for their own interests. Like Dupleix, he was thrown into the Bastille; but he was brought out of it only to be condemned to instant execution. He died the third martyr of the French East India Company.

14. Towards the close of the year 1759, a Dutch fleet of seven ships appeared in the Hugli, and some vessels of the English company were seized; the Dutch colours were hoisted upon them, and the storehouses of Fulta were burnt. England and Holland were at peace; but Clive rightly held that these acts left him free to take his own course. The Dutch fleet was attacked, and every ship was taken. But 700 Europeans who had landed from them with 800 Malays made their way to the Dutch settlement at Chinsura. Colonel Forde, who had followed them thither, was in perplexity, and asked directions from Clive. The answer was that he should fight them at once, and that the authority for so doing should be sent the next day. The engagement ended in the severe defeat of the Dutch; and the sudden appearance of Meerun, the son of Mir Jafir, with 7,000 cavalry immediately after the action, seems to show that the whole enterprise was the result of intrigues at Murshedabad, and not of any deliberate purpose on the part of the Dutch government of Batavia to set up a counterpoise to English influence in Bengal.

15. With the downfall of the French military power Clive's work in India was, in substance, done. Yet he was anxious for an administration which should permanently secure the results thus far attained. The whole country was full of marauding bands of Mahrattas and Afghans, and it was out of the Company's power to maintain a force adequate to withstand or repress them. He proposed, therefore, to Pitt, that the nation should take over the sovereignty of Bengal, Behar, and Orissa, and pointed out that the surplus of revenue and expenditure would be not less than two millions sterling annually. The proposal was rejected on the ground that such an acquisition might render the British Crown too powerful, and endanger the liberties of Englishmen. The decision can scarcely be regarded as a fortunate one, whether for England or for India. To say the least, acquisitions on a far larger scale have been added to our Indian empire without any ominous effects on the constitutional freedom of the British nation.

CHAPTER XII.

Relations of the English with the Mogul Empire.

1. The empire of Baber and Akbar had but a shadowy existence in the days of Mohammed Shah. The story of its decline and disruption after his death is soon told. It is a tale of intrigue, and of shifting alliances and combinations in the vain effort to prop a falling house, or for the more practicable purpose of sharing in the plunder of its wealth. It was thus that Sufder Jung, viceroy of Oude, who had been appointed vizier by Ahmed Shah, the successor of Mohammed Shah, 1748–1754, called in the Mahrattas to aid him against the Rohillas, a warlike tribe whose country lay to the north-east of Delhi, stretching onwards to the heights of Kumaon. The Rohillas were for the time repressed; but the Afghan chief Ahmed Shah, the Durani, had again left his mountains, and was insisting on the cession of the Punjab. The disgust of Sufder Jung, when on his return he found that the cession had been actually made, irritated the emperor, who called in the aid of Ghazi-u-dín, a grandson of Asof Jah, against his vizir.

2. But Ghazi-u-dín was not more tolerable than the man whom he had displaced, and after a short time he deposed and blinded the emperor, and raised one of the royal princes to the throne under the title of Alamgir II., 1754–1759. The tyranny of Ghazi-u-dín drove the army into mutiny. The mutiny was suppressed by massacre; but Ghazi-u-dín made the blunder of seizing the governor whom Ahmed Shah Durani had left in the Punjab. The Afghan chief presented himself at the gates of Delhi to avenge the insult. Before he went back to his own land, the emperor prayed that he might not be eft at themercy of his vizir, and the Durani prince accordingly left the Rohilla Najib-u-Daula as his commander-in-chief at Delhi, 1757.

3. But Alamgir could not thus escape the toils. Ghazi-u-dín called on the Mahrattas. A Mahratta army took possession of the Punjab, and the Afghan Ahmed once more came down to recover it. But Ahmed might act as the emperor's friend. Alamgir was therefore murdered; but the prince set up by Ghazi-u-dín was never acknowledged, and the sequel exhibits a struggle directly between Mahrattas and Afghans. The former seized on Delhi, but on the approach of Ahmed they withdrew, and entrenched themselves at Panipat, the field of so many memorable fights. The inferiority of his forces compelled Ahmed also to throw up lines round his army; and so the two hosts faced each other, while each day told against the Mahrattas. Cut off from their usual method of foraging, they soon exhausted the country round, and ate out the town of Panipat. Their sufferings at length became intolerable, and the Mahratta leader made ready for the fatal conflict which ended in the annihilation of his host. Two hundred thousand men which he had led into action were left, it is said, dead upon the field; and those who were not slain were fugitives who made their way across the Nerbudda, 1761. For the time at least, Hindustan was rid of these indomitable and insatiable plunderers. The Afghan chief was once more master of the empire. He would have placed the son of Alamgir on the throne; but that prince, who, after his father's murder, had assumed the title of Shah Alam, was absent in Bengal which he hoped to reconquer, and his son Jewun Bakht was placed as his deputy on the throne of Baber under the guardianship of the Rohilla chief Najib-u-Daula.

4. Shah Alam, meanwhile, had learnt that the methods of Mogul government had brought into the field an enemy destined to supplant all the contending factions, and to set up a government under which subordinate officers should have something better to do than to make war upon each other or upon their sovereign. Shah Alam had laid siege to Patna, 1760; but it suited the English to fight in the name of Mir Jafir, and a force of 200 Europeans, with a small body of Sepoys, crossed the river and defeated him. Shah Alam fled; but his baggage and artillery were captured by Colonel Calliaud and Meerun, son of Mir Jafir. The tent of the latter was struck by lightning, and Meerun himself was killed. This man was a cruel and licentious tyrant, but he had shown ability as an administrator of Bengal. His father was in his dotage, and Mr. Vansittart, now governor of Calcutta, with the consent of his council, called on Mir Jafir to abdicate in favour of his son-in-law, Mir Cossim. The new Nuwab assigned to the Company the large districts of Burdwan, Midnapur, and Chittagong; and 200,000*l.* were set aside for the members of the council.

5. Thus, while the lawful sovereign of Bengal was seeking to assert his own right to it, the English resisted him in the field, and sold the country to one who had not even the shadow of a title; and this was done by men who, under cover of the Company's interests, gave little heed to any but their own. If it was needful to have a puppet ruler

at all, it would have been better to choose the representative of Akbar, from whom they would, it has been well said, have obtained more favourable terms and more extensive grants than those which they exacted from Mir Cossim. They short-sightedly chose the less, when they might have had the more; and the most unseemly squabbles arose between those who had received a share in the plunder, and those who found themselves as poor as they were before. Their conduct was neither straightforward nor honourable: in the sequel it was seen to be blundering. Mir Cossim was willing to be placed in power by the English; but his one desire was to exercise it without their interference. To get beyond their reach, he left Murshedabad and took up his abode at Monghyr, where he began to cast cannon and make muskets for his troops. His protests against the system of passes issued by the Company's officers, exempting merchants from the payment of customs duties, led to an open breach.

6. The system, there is no doubt, had been extravagantly abused. Before the battle of Plassy the privilege of exemption had been confined to foreign goods belonging to the Company. It was now extended to goods of all kinds conveyed under the Company's passports; and any servant of the Company now claimed the right of issuing them, as well as of trading with the products of the country, in which his own exemption from duty enabled him to undersell the native dealers. The result was not merely a serious loss to the Nuwab's revenue in a country where the transit of goods was carried on chiefly by water, toll-houses being set up at the important turns of the rivers; but Bengalis, many of them men of indifferent or bad character, went about as agents of the English, compelling the people to sell at half, and to buy at double the value of goods, and insulting the Nuwab's officers. Among the few who saw the evils of the system were Vansittart the governor, and Warren Hastings, now a man of thirty and the youngest member of the Calcutta council. Both these men insisted that this trade in the goods of the country was not within the province of the Company's servants; but they spoke to deaf ears. Many of the council were vehemently opposed to Vansittart, who had been brought from Madras, in breach of the custom which had thus far secured promotion by seniority.

7. To settle the matter, Mir Cossim, in 1763, abolished all duties; and the Company's passes became useless. The one question was whether the Nuwab had the right to remit duties to his own subjects; by a singular process of reasoning the majority of the council decided that he had not. The arrangements made with Mir Cossim, as with Mir Jafir, were intended to bestow exclusive privileges on the servants of the Company; and these privileges Mir Cossim had now taken away. The answer of Warren Hastings was clear and conclusive. 'The Nuwab,' he said, 'has granted a boon to his subjects; and there are no grounds for demanding that a sovereign prince should withdraw such a boon, or threatening him with war in the event of refusal.' But his opponents might retort that this sovereign

prince was a creature whom they might set down as they had set him up.

8. The tidings now came that a boat, laden with fire-arms for the factory at Patna, had been seized by the officers of the Nuwab. As a condition for surrendering them, Mir Cossim demanded the removal of Mr. Ellis, the chief of the factory at Patna; and when this was refused, ordered that all the English should be apprehended. The English, as though nothing could be done in India except in the name of phantom princes, retaliated by restoring Mir Jafir, in spite of his age, his leprosy, and his imbecility, to the office of Nuwab. Enraged by a double defeat, at Cutwah and at Gheriah, Mir Cossim, 1763, ordered the slaughter of all the English prisoners at Patna. The native commanders refused to act as the executioners of unarmed men. The horrible task was undertaken by Walter Reinhardt, who had spent most of his time in deserting from the French to the English and back to the French again. He had enlisted in an English regiment under the name of Somers; his forbidding face led his comrades to call him Sombre. When he deserted to the service of Mir Cossim the natives called him Sumroo. A few weeks later the army of Mir Cossim was again defeated, and the fort of Monghyr taken. Mir Cossim now formed a league with the vizir of Oude. Having been joined by the emperor Shah Alam, they made an unsuccessful attempt on Patna, and withdrew to Buxar, where they remained during the rains, 1764. Major Hector Munro, appointed to command the English army, found the Sepoy portion

of it mutinous. Some firmness and severity were needed to suppress the rebellion, which was grounded on a demand for large donations and higher pay. When at length, with an army of seven thousand, of whom not one thousand were Europeans, he reached Buxar, he completely defeated the enemy, and but for the breaking down of a bridge must have become master of all their treasure, which was supposed to amount to 3,000,000*l.* sterling in value.

9. The whole of Bengal was now at the disposal of the Company, and they were virtual masters of Oude; but the negotiations with the emperor for the partition of that territory were for the time without result, and active operations were hindered by want of money. It would in fact seem that the English had introduced no better system than that which had disgraced the Mogul government. The Company were defrauded of their profits by the private trade of their officers; and these, receiving only a nominal stipend for their services, held themselves justified as well as constrained to increase their means by presents and claims of compensation for losses, real or supposed, from native governors. To such private claimants Mir Jafir had paid a sum of more than half a million sterling; and when his death made a new appointment necessary, these claims and demands for gifts, which were taken as of right, were renewed. In this way the senior officers of the Calcutta council received nearly 140,000*l.*; and when to such payments are added those for 'restitution,' the disbursements from the

Murshedabad treasury approach closely a sum of six millions.

10. It was not likely that the Court of Directors could feel much satisfaction in a system which impoverished them for the benefit of their servants, and Clive, who had returned to England, and been made an Irish peer, was requested to resume the government of Bengal. On the very day of his landing, May 3, 1765, the vizir of Oude was again defeated by General Carnac, and besought the indulgence and favour of the English. The tide of fortune had indeed changed. Ten years ago they had been simply merchants, summarily expelled from Bengal; now they were possessed of a power more solid in its foundations than that of the Mogul empire in its palmiest days.

11. Clive expressed great indignation at the state of things which he found on his return. 'The whites and the blacks,' he declared, 'had conspired together to empty the public treasury.' His words were just and true; but in spite of all that may be urged in palliation for himself, he was living in a house of glass and throwing stones at others. He said, indeed, that when he looked back upon the vast wealth which lay ready for his acceptance at Murshedabad after the fight of Plassy, he was beyond measure astonished at his own moderation. It was also true that if he had reaped a golden harvest, he had also done great service to the State; but the vice and corruption which he now saw everywhere was that of men who had done no service at all; and lastly, it was true that, while the practice of receiving presents was permitted before the battle of Plassy, it had since been strictly prohibited.

12. He addressed himself sedulously to the task of reformation. The license for private trade was the result of the merely nominal salaries of the civil officers. Until other arrangements should be made, he ordered that the proceeds of the monopoly of salt, which had been treated as a perquisite of the Nuwab, should furnish a joint-stock sum, to be divided amongst all in proportion to their rank. For military officers, also, the extraordinary and irregular allowances and additions to pay must cease, and all must be reduced to one system, which must involve for them a considerable reduction of income. The officers pledged themselves to each other to resign in a body rather than submit to the change. Clive ordered that those who resigned should be sent to Calcutta. At the same time he summoned from Madras every officer that could be spared. The English soldiers at Monghyr appeared in arms to support their officers: they were overawed by Sepoy regiments. Some officers were tried and dismissed from the service; others expressed regret and were restored to their rank, and a serious danger thus passed away.

13. But Clive was bent on carrying out his great scheme for double government in India. By this he meant that the English should rule in the name of the Great Mogul; in other words, that their real sovereignty should be concealed from the British parliament and from the world. In this plan there would be, he held, the further advantage that, while the English administered and regulated the finances, they would be free of all responsibility for the civil government of the people. In the Mogul empire the finance was in the hands of the minister, known as the Dewan; the military authority, and with it the administration of justice and police in that of the Nizam. The Company, for the payment of a certain tribute, was to be nominally Dewan; by the very necessity of the case they became Dewan and Nizam combined. The external or foreign policy of the Company was to follow the same course. They were vassals of the Emperor, and allies of his Nizam; but they were to have no relations with any other princes or chiefs in the peninsula. They would thus be clear of the complications of Eastern intrigues, while the dominions of the Nizam would be interposed between themselves and the tribes who might be especially troublesome—the Mahrattas and the Afghans.

14. The scheme was dazzling and full of promise. To the mercantile minds of the Directors there was something very attractive in an arrangement which made the people of India pay for all that they bought, and left to themselves as profit the gross receipts of sales in England. The revenues of Bengal, amounting to at least four millions sterling, would suffice, it was thought, not only for all military and civil salaries, and all the expenses of the settlements, but also for all investments in Indian and Chinese goods. But there were some drawbacks which made themselves unpleasantly prominent as time went on. In the better days of the Mogul empire there was a real, and in the worst there was a nominal, check on oppression and extortion. The revenue was collected by Zemindars, who had to pay a block sum to the Nuwab; and the profit of the Zemindar lay in the excess of the amounts paid to him by the ryots or farmers, and cultivators, and the lump sum due from himself. The Zemindars were, therefore, always under temptation to exact more than what was fair; and, as they were mostly Mahometans, religious animosity might lead them on into exactions altogether illegal. Against such tyranny there was at least the right of appeal to the Nuwab; but the conditions of Clive's double government swept this and every other safeguard away. So long as the revenue was punctually sent in, Nuwabs and Zemindars were left to deal with the people after their will. The one care of the English was for their money; and they chose to forget that the power which takes the people's money is responsible for their welfare.

15. Whatever it may have been in its working, there can be no doubt that for the people of India this method of government was in theory far worse than the worst forms of Mogul despotism. So far, therefore, they were worse off under their new lords than they had been before. They were also poorer. The main revenues now went to men who were in haste to be rich in order that they might go as soon as possible and spend their gains elsewhere. Their own princes and nobles may have squandered vast sums on idle pageants and selfish luxuries; but the money which supported their extravagance was spent in the country, and multitudes who had subsisted on it were now left in beggary. There was, further, a not unnatural wish on the part of the native officials to cheat the white men; and the successors of Clive became fully aware of their roguery and of the ingrained dishonesty of all employed by them. The lessening of their resources was a matter of pain and grief to the Directors in England. They were still more indignant when they found that the expenditure rose as the receipts fell, and that in spite of this ominous change, their servants still returned to Europe with vast, and even princely fortunes. Four years after Clive's final departure from India a fearful famine brought matters to a crisis. Some of the English, like some of the native gentlemen, kept thousands alive by feeding them at their own expense; it was reported that others had combined to buy up large stocks of grain and sell them at exorbitantly increased rates. The Directors became convinced that a radical reform was vitally necessary, and they resolved to entrust the task to Warren Hastings.

16. Nor was adherence to Clive's policy of non-intervention a task as easy as he had supposed that it would be. A Mahratta army had been destroyed at Panipat; but the Mahratta people had not been annihilated. They were fast regaining strength, and Clive himself had suggested that it might be well to have an alliance with the Nizam, which should serve as a check on these indomitable horsemen. Nor was this the only difficulty. Clive had obtained from the puppet emperor, Shah Alam, a firman or rescript assigning the Northern Circars in full sovereignty to the English. The act was an utter violation of the hereditary rights of the Nizam; but Clive would, probably, have cared nothing for the Nizam's resentment had he remained in India. The Madras government was of a very different temper; and, on hearing that the Nizam was raising an immense army for the invasion of the Carnatic, they sent General Calliaud to arrange a peace with him on the best terms which he might be able to obtain. From the Nizam the English received possession of the Circars, on condition of paying a yearly tribute of 70,000*l.*; and it was agreed between the two parties that they should assist each other against any enemy. The first potentate against whom they turned their arms was Hyder Ali, the founder of the Mahometan dynasty of Mysore.

17. Hyder Naik is said to have been originally a sepoy in the service of the French, and beyond doubt he was a man whose education was on a par with that of Sivaji. He could neither write nor read. After leaving the French service, he gathered around himself a body of soldiers, much resembling the Greek Klephts, or bandits, who pledge themselves to obey a certain leader, who, in his turn, promises that all shall share alike the produce of their robberies. Hyder's men would indifferently sack a town, or plunder a village, or strip men of their clothes. With such a troop Hyder followed the Hindu Raja of Mysore to the siege of Trichinopoly. For each soldier he was to receive a

certain amount in money and an extra gift for each man wounded. Hyder turned the agreement to good account by false musters and by bandaging sound limbs. But the Hindu Rajas of Mysore were no better than the later sovereigns of the house of Baber, and in due time Hyder put aside a symbol which for him had no value, and assumed the title, as he already had the power, of king. But although he had many enemies he made no alliances, unless we are to regard as such his alleged relations with the French of Pondicherry.

18. The history now brings before us a series of rapidly shifting scenes in the career of Hyder. He became the ally of the Nizam, and then found that the step which he had taken was a blunder. He fought against the English with varied but on the whole with marked success, and then invited them to become his allies under the threat of bringing up the Poona Mahrattas against them in case of their refusal. At length he approached Madras itself with an army of 6,000 horsemen. Madras was in no state for undergoing a siege; and no one within it had the genius or the wish for playing there the part which Clive had played at Arcot. A treaty was accordingly entered into, by which each agreed to restore all conquests and to help each other against the Mahrattas, 1769; but the English had to bear the whole cost of the war, while the presence of Hyder's horsemen in a suburb of Madras lessened the authority of the English not less than it added to his own.

CHAPTER XIII.

The Administration of Warren Hastings.

1. When Mir Cossim abolished the customs duties throughout his jurisdiction, the foremost of those who insisted that he had a sovereign right to do so was, as we have seen (p. 118), Warren Hastings, the most remarkable and in some respects the most illustrious of British governors in India. We have now to see how far his subsequent conduct was in accordance with the principles which he laid down with clearness and force. As we read the wonderful story of his public life, it is sometimes hard to repress a feeling of indignation amounting almost to loathing; but the very strength of the feelings thus stirred should make us the more careful that we do him justice. His great task was to carry on the work of Clive; he achieved success by seeming to undo it. The double government, which to Clive appeared so marvellously convenient, proved in its working to be the greatest curse that could befall a land. It produced anarchy in many places and misery everywhere. It deprived the people of all hope of getting justice; it impoverished the revenue and emptied the treasury. There was no paramount authority to repress the evil doing of men in the highest places, and to convince the people that their true interests lay in the maintenance of good order and honest dealing. Throughout the country there was an imposing hierarchy of political

ranks; but the title in no case corresponded with the power. The representative of Baber and Akbar was nominally the supreme lord of all, the master of all kings, viceroys (Nizams), deputies of viceroys (Nuwabs), and deputies of these deputies (Naibs). In reality he was their servant, and often their prisoner and their victim. These, again, in some instances maintained their power; in others they became phantom princes like Mir Jafir. The monarchy of Sivaji (p. 62) had followed the same course. His successor was a puppet in whose name his Peshwa, or minister, reigned as king; and the Peshwa in his turn was fast becoming a mere instrument in the hands of others. Hastings, it may fairly be said, had to begin from the beginning, and he left behind him an organized system which, with large changes of outward shape, has lasted in substance to the present day.

2. This great work he accomplished without any greater advantages of political training than had fallen to the lot of Clive. He was, indeed, very unlike Clive in the character of his mind and in his habits. He had been taught first in the village school at Daylesford, and his companions remembered in after years how kindly he had taken to his books. At Westminster School he gave high promise of future distinction in the world of letters; and when his guardian resolved on accepting for him the offer of a writership in the service of the East India Company, the head-master expressed his deep regret at the loss of a pupil who must have taken a very high place in the ranks of English scholars. He

was not yet eighteen years of age when he landed in Calcutta. After two years spent there at a clerk's desk, he was sent to the factory at Cossim Bazaar, where he remained with occupations similar to those of young Clive at Madras, until, on his declaration of war with the English, Suraj-u-Daula sent him as a prisoner to Murshedabad. Hastings made his escape, and when Clive came from Madras on his avenging mission, offered himself as a volunteer in the ranks; but Clive saw that the young soldier would be more useful in other ways, and when Mir Jafir was set up as Nuwab, Hastings was sent to reside at his court as the agent of the Company.

3. Four years later he became Member of Council at Calcutta; and, to his credit, he remained poor while all around him were winning wealth at the cost of their honour and fair fame. So keen is the scrutiny which has been applied to every part of his career that any attempt on his part to obtain money or gifts of any kind from the natives or their rulers must have been laid to his charge. It was, in truth, the most discreditable period of English rule. Every Englishman was living for himself, and the thought that they owed duties to those who were subjected to them seems not to have dawned upon their minds. Against the strength of European civilisation the inhabitants of Bengal were helpless, and the new-comers abused their strength to the uttermost. In 1771, Hastings, who in the interval had spent some years in England and had then served as Member of Council at Madras, was appointed to the government of Bengal. In later years the governor became,

with regard to the executive, absolute. Hastings had only one vote in the Council, which became a casting vote in cases were the division was equal. He at once set about his work, looking into the modes in which the system of collecting revenue affected the people, abolishing many of the illegal or extra-legal demands or impositions termed cesses, leasing out the lands for five years at fixed rates, and establishing in each district a civil and a criminal court, in which the European collector sat as judge assisted by Mahometan and Hindu officials. By a strange custom in India, a fourth of the amount in dispute in all civil cases was invariably taken by the judge. Hastings abolished this practice, together with many other glaring abuses of the old system.

4. But he was more intent on destroying the double government which had so much charm for Clive. The Nuwab had already passed into the rank of *fainéant* or do-nothing princes. The Naib or deputy of the Nuwab was Muhammed Reza Khan, who had given twenty lakhs of rupees (200,000*l.*) for his high office. The government of Behar was in the hands of Raja Shitab Rai, a better and not less able man. Hastings had them both arrested and brought down to Calcutta for trial; but he was more anxious for the abolition of their office than for their punishment, and the change was quietly effected, while their trial was put off on a series of pretences. When there was no need for further delay they were tried. Shitab Rai, honourably acquitted, and clad in a robe of state, was sent back to his government at Patna; but his spirit was

broken by treatment which he felt that he had not deserved, and he went only to die. In the case of Rheza Khan the issue was the negative verdict of 'Not Proven;' but Hastings absolutely refused to restore him to office.

5. The Nuwab was now a mere pensioner, and his pension was fixed at one-half of the allowance thus far set aside for him. The yearly saving was 160,000*l*. But this was little in comparison with the needs and the liabilities of the Company. A steady pressure was applied to the governor from England, and it was applied in a way which led him into almost irresistible temptation. The despatches of the Directors were full of most excellent advice for the good government of India, or of any other country. They hated oppression, they desired no wrongful dealing with neighbouring powers. Good order and efficient justice were the great objects to be aimed at; but money was indispensable. These counsels resolved themselves into two distinct and contradictory precepts. One only could be obeyed, and it was for Hastings to determine which kind of obedience would be most to the liking of his masters. In the words of Lord Macaulay, 'he correctly judged that the safest course would be to neglect the sermons and to find the rupees.'

6. Some help towards this end was furnished by the flight of Shah Alam, the great Mogul, from Allahabad to Delhi. Besides leaving to him the districts of Allahabad and Korah, the Company had pledged itself to pay him yearly 300,000*l*. as tribute for the government of Bengal. But his departure to

Delhi was not a sign of his independence. He had sojourned at Allahabad, virtually as the pensioner of the English; he had gone to Delhi as, to all intents and purposes, the prisoner of the Mahrattas. To the Mahrattas, therefore, and not to the emperor, would the Company be paying their tribute; and this, Hastings declared, had never been a condition of the bargain. The decision was a bitter disappointment to the Mahratta chief, Mahadaji Sindia. He had seated Shah Alam on the throne of his forefathers, chiefly because he hoped to rule over Bengal in his name, and in his name to receive the tribute; and all that he had brought about by his act was the enrichment of a company of European merchants. He might treat the decision of Hastings as a declaration of war; but only by force could he recover the wealth which had passed away to another.

7. But the prospect of aggrandisement on a larger scale was furnished by a quarrel between Suja-u-Daulah, the Nuwab Vizir of Oude, and the Rohilla chief, Hafiz Khan. Vexation at the loss of the Bengal tribute led the Mahrattas to lay a pressure on the Nawab of Oude, since they dared not to attack the English. Their hands fell first on the Rohilla country on his north-western frontier, but they agreed to spare it if they should be allowed to march through it unmolested into Oude. Suja-u-Daulah anticipated them by making a treaty with the Rohilla chief, who promised to pay him 400,000*l.* for his aid against the Mahrattas. These, however, were drawn away by the internal disputes which ensued on the death of Mahdu Rao Peshwa at Poona. Freed from

the danger of Mahratta invasion, the Nuwab demanded the forty lakhs from Hafiz Khan, who denied the obligation.

8. The Rohillas were the descendants of some of the hardy Afghan mountaineers who followed the standard of Baber in his career of Indian conquest. They were rewarded with settlements in the rich plain through which flows the Ramgunga from the range of Kumaon, until it falls into the Ganges. Retaining their old bravery, they had learnt to value the benefits of order; and their country, free from the plagues of war and extortion, became rapidly more fertile and more wealthy. They belonged also to the pestilent sect of the Shiahs; and this was a sufficient reason why this inviting region should be added to the domain of the orthodox Sonnite, Suja-u-Daulah. The refusal of Hafiz Khan to pay the forty lakhs set him free to act; but he dared not to enter on the contest single-handed. There was one power which could wrest for him all that he wanted, and that power was the British. It was true that the Rohillas had done him no wrong; but Suja-u-Daulah had an abundant revenue, and it was possible that his money might be of material importance to the English. The issue was what he had expected. Hastings agreed to lend him an English army for the purpose of enslaving a free and unoffending people, at a cost of 400,000*l.* to be paid down, in addition to the maintenance of the troops so long as they remained in the field (1773). He knew that the condition of the Rohilla government was fairly good, and that of Oude horribly bad. He

knew also the character of Eastern warfare, and he made no stipulations as to the mode in which this war should be carried on, nor did he warn the Nuwab that the troops should be withdrawn, if considerations of mere humanity should make it necessary to do so. The plea has actually been urged that Hastings was justified in making this compact because the Rohillas were not an Indian race, but invaders from lands beyond the border. So, too, were the English. The excuse is almost worse than the crime.

9. Then followed the terrible tragedy. Suja-u-Daulah led a vast army into the Rohilla land, but in the bloody battle in which the brave Afghans were beaten down they took no part. The horrible work was all done by the troops of Hastings. The Rohillas had besought the English not to hurt them, and had offered large ransoms, and, when all was vain, defended themselves bravely. The English officer, Colonel Champion, declared that with a good share of military knowledge they displayed a more obstinate firmness of resolution, which it would be impossible to describe. When the battle was decided, the Nuwab let loose his dastardly rabble to plunder, torment, and murder men whom they had not dared to face in the fight. The whole country was abandoned to their brutal cruelty. The crops were destroyed, the towns and villages set on fire, the men, women, and children tortured, mutilated, or sold as slaves. The land was ruined, but the Rohillas were not wholly destroyed. The plain of the Ramgunga has recovered something of its ancient richness; but the people still remember with bitter indignation the wrong done to them by the English.

10. The government of Bengal was now to assume a new phase. The president was to be entitled Governor-General, and Hastings was named to this high office. His Council was to consist of four members, the casting vote being with himself; and a Supreme Court, under a chief justice and three subordinate judges, was to be set up in Calcutta, independent of the Governor-General and his council. Of the four councillors one, Mr. Barwell, was already in India. The other three, sent out from England, were General Clavering, Mr. Monson, and Mr. Philip Francis, the last being (there can be little doubt or none) the author of the 'Letters of Junius.' The chief justice was Sir Elijah Impey, a man whom Hastings had known in England, and of whose character he may even then have taken the true measure.

11. Hastings had spoken in no approving tone of these changes, and with no cordial appreciation of his new colleagues, who landed with a prejudice against him,—a prejudice most persistently and sedulously fomented by Philip Francis. The agreement of the three left Hastings in a minority on every subject; and although their condemnation of the compact with the Nuwab, and of the way in which the Rohilla war had been carried on was fully justified, the division of the Council led otherwise to strange and disastrous consequences. The natives soon learnt that the sceptre had slipped from the hand of Hastings, that, in fact, he was powerless, and that his downfall would be acceptable to his colleagues. In India, accusers are never wanting to a falling man. Charges of portentous gravity are forthcoming as at the wave of a magician's wand, and a crowd is ready to swear away his life. The colleagues of Hastings were probably not fully aware of this Eastern habit, and accordingly a more abundant banquet of false witness was provided for them.

12. Foremost amongst his accusers was the Maharaja Nundkomar, a man who had encountered Hastings during his sojourn at Murshedabad. There was a strong repulsion between the two, and in Nundkomar it was intensified into hatred when he found that Hastings had preferred Mahommed Rheza Khan to himself for the golden office of Naib of Bengal. He now, 1776, came forward to say that Mahommed Rheza escaped scathless from his trial, only because he had largely bribed the Governor-General, and moreover that Hastings had been in the habit of selling offices and allowing criminals to go unpunished, if they were but rich enough to pay him. Francis read the paper in Council, and when Hastings denied the jurisdiction of his colleagues and refused to be confronted with Nundkomar, he voted that the charges were proved.

13. Hastings could still appeal to the Court in England; but knowing that, if they failed to justify his conduct, his cause was lost, he placed his resignation in the hands of Colonel Macleane, under the condition that he was to produce it only in case of necessity. In the mean time Nundkomar appeared to be absolutely victorious; but he was not aware, or he had forgotten, that there was in Calcutta a court with powers of life and death wholly independent of the Governor-General and his Council, and that his own past life rendered it at least prudent not to rouse the slumbering lions. Nundkomar was a Hindu, a Brahman of the purest descent, and the most rigid guardian of his caste. He was a man of marked ability; but falsehood was to him the air which he breathed. He had tried to procure the condemnation of another Hindu by means of forged documents, and he had served as a go-between in communications between the French and the court of Delhi. But imprisonment had in no way lessened his reputation with his countrymen, who would look on forgery much as some regard a sharp bargain in selling unsound horses. Forgery to the Bengali is an offence, but it is an offence which would be classed with an act of trespass or a default in the payment of rent.

14. Hastings replied to the accusations of Nundkomar by bringing an action against him in the Supreme Court for conspiracy. The judges admitted the charge, but accepted bail. A few weeks later, Calcutta was startled by the news that Nundkomar had been arrested on a charge of forgery, and thrown into the common prison. He was brought before Sir Elijah Impey and a jury of Englishmen, and after a protracted trial was found guilty, condemned to death, and hung.

15. It is possible that the whole proceeding may have been illegal; but we may accept its legality, and we may take the charge as fully proved. Even thus the execution can be characterised as nothing less than a judicial murder. If it was legal, it was most unjust. The general sense of mankind has certainly not regarded forgery as a capital crime; nor do we Englishmen regard it as such now. The statute under which Nundkomar was convicted belonged strictly to English law, and, it may almost be said, to English law only; and this statute was now applied abruptly amongst a people in whose eyes the very theory on which it rested would be nothing less than an egregious absurdity. The Bengali may make too little of the crime, but it would perhaps be impossible to bring him to look upon it as a very serious one, or indeed as in any way worse than, or different from, common swindling and cheating. The charge in Hindu eyes was not rendered more impressive by the fact that the crime to which it referred had been committed six years before. Moreover, it was the forging of a bond, not of a paper by which the life of some innocent man was to be sacrificed.

16. The career of Nundkomar has shown that he was fully capable of the latter crime, even if he had not committed it; but his execution on the lesser charge would have been an act of undue severity even in England. In Calcutta it was a glaring iniquity. The guilt of it, some have said, must be distributed equally between Elijah Impey and Warren Hastings. But this is not the case. Hastings found himself in circumstances of almost unparalleled difficulty. He was outvoted at his own council board; his authority throughout his government, his influence beyond it, was shaken if not destroyed, and he was assailed by accusers who would not scruple to employ the most infamous falsehood as their weapon. He resolved to strike a blow which should silence them all at once; and he resolved that this blow should fall on one whose high descent, whose sacred caste and unspotted ceremonial purity, made him an object of reverence to millions. He was acting in self-defence, acting confessedly as a partisan, not as a judge.

17. But how stands the case with Impey? He knew that he was administering a law bodily imported from a distant country; he knew that he was applying a statute of that law, which would be wholly incomprehensible to all the inhabitants of the vast peninsula of India, that he was enforcing a penalty which, for the crime charged against Nundkomar, was not to be found in the codes of many nations in Europe, which Englishmen had arbitrarily affixed to it at one time, and which they might remove (as they have removed it) at another. Had Impey been a righteous judge, he would have respited the criminal, and reserved the case for the consideration of the crown; but his object was to get rid of Nundkomar, and he would not hear of delay. Some years later Hastings wrote of Impey as the man 'to whose support he was at one time indebted for the safety of his fortune, honour, and reputation.' These words, as Lord Macaulay has justly urged, can refer only to the case of Nundkomar, the inference being that he hanged Nundkomar to support Hastings, and therefore was guilty of putting a man unjustly to death to answer a political purpose.

18. Hastings was to learn a few years later that the weapon which he had employed against Nundkomar might be turned against himself. The judges who administered the new law proceeded to treat not Calcutta merely, but the whole territory of the Presidency as subject to their authority. The forms and procedure of English law were applied to a people who had never heard of either, and for whom the process of arrest familiar to Englishmen involved an intolerable insult. No place was sacred to the retainers who did the behests of the English judges, and Hindu and Mahometan gentlemen even died at the threshold of their women's apartments in the effort to protect them from indignity. It was a reign of terror. Hastings and his colleagues saw the mischief and the dangers involved in it; but if servants of the Company, acting in obedience to their instructions, obstructed the new system, they were thrown into prison for what is technically termed a contempt. The opposition of the government became more marked. The chief justice issued writs summoning the Governor-General with his Council to appear before the court. Hastings was ready to resist the summons, if need be, by the sword; but he knew Impey, and hit upon an easier method of dealing with him. Impey received 8,000*l*. a year by his appointment from the Crown. Hastings proposed to give him 8,000*l*. a year more as a judge in the Company's service, removable at the pleasure of the Governor-General. Impey understood thoroughly the meaning of the proposal. The bargain was struck, and the conflict was ended; but the wealth of the Chief Justice was not obtained without infamy (1781).

19. While Hastings was still thwarted by a majority in Council, a strong effort was made in England to remove him. Fearing the result, Colonel Macleane produced his resignation, and the Directors immediately appointed Mr. Wheler, one of their own body, to succeed him, and sent orders to General Clavering to act as Governor-General until Wheler's arrival. But before these orders could reach India, the death of Monson had given Hastings the majority in council through his casting vote. He had already reversed many of the measures carried by his opponents, when he learnt that he had been superseded. But circumstances were now changed. Hastings felt that there was nothing to hinder the great designs which he had long wished to carry out. Since he had sent the paper which Colonel Macleane produced, he had written many times to the Court of Directors, telling them that he had no intention of resigning. The imprudent vehemence of Clavering made it possible that Hastings might in the end appeal to force; but Clavering accepted the proposal that the question should be referred to the Supreme Court, and the court decided that the paper produced by Macleane was invalid. All serious opposition to Hastings came to an end; but the persistent animosity of Francis led at last to a duel in which he was wounded, and shortly after this he left India, bent still on bringing about the overthrow of the Governor-General.

20. Hastings was now free to turn his attention

to matters which might affect the very existence of the English in India. The anxieties which may have been felt about Mahratta inroads were as nothing in comparison with the danger which might be feared from the armies of Hyder Ali (p. 126), now the most formidable potentate in the whole Indian peninsula. These armies consisted of materials strangely assorted, amongst them being European deserters, runaways, and adventurers of every kind; but the whole made up a force which an enemy would do well to withstand effectually or to avoid altogether. The Madras government did neither. In 1778, they began the war against the French by the capture of Pondicherry. Their next step was to gain possession of Mahé, a place on the Malabar coast within the dominions of Hyder. Hyder had threatened that if Mahé should be attacked, he would carry fire and sword through the whole Carnatic; and from the Bhonsla Raja of Berar Hastings heard that Hyder, the Nizam Ali, and the Mahrattas had made a convention binding them to simultaneous attacks on the three English settlements in Bombay, Madras, and Bengal.

21. The threat of Hyder was soon carried out. The flames of burning villages might be seen from Madras and Fort St. George. A force under Baillie, surrounded by overwhelming numbers, was induced to surrender on a promise of quarter which was immediately broken. This disaster might have been retrieved or avenged by Sir Hector Munro, had he moved up promptly when he heard the cannonade. Hyder's army must in that case have undergone a severe, if not a fatal, defeat; but Munro, forfeiting the reputation which he had won at Buxar (p. 119), threw his heavy guns into a tank, abandoned most of his stores, and retreated hurriedly to Madras. Hastings set himself at once to meet and to break the Mysore confederacy. He detached the Nizam from it by informing him that Shah Alam had made a grant to Hyder of all the territories which he ruled as the Mogul viceroy. By a gift of money and by protracted negotiations he secured the neutrality of the Raja of Berar; and Sir Eyre Coote, who had voted for immediate action at Plassy (p. 108), and had conquered at Wandiwash (p. 112), was sent with full powers to take the command of the Madras army. Age had in some degree weakened his military ability as well as his bodily powers; but he was still a vigorous leader, and the progress of Hyder was arrested by Coote's decisive victory at Porto Novo, 1780.

22. Meanwhile Hastings was still followed by his old enemy,—lack of money. This dire want, not for himself but for the Company, had led him into injustice and cruelty against the Rohillas; it now led him into acts against the Raja of Benares, which it is difficult not to condemn as also unjust and cruel. Cheyte Sing was one of the many princes who during the breaking up of the Mogul empire had made himself independent of the court of Delhi. He could not, however, shake off his subjection to his nearer neighbour, the Nuwab of Oude; and the irksomeness of the yoke impelled him to invoke the aid of the English. The aid was cheerfully given, and in due time Cheyte Sing acknowledged himself the vassal of the Company, agreeing to pay an annual tribute, while Hastings on his part pledged himself that no further demands should ever be made upon him. Cheyte Sing's engagement had been faithfully kept; and he naturally supposed that so long as his tribute was paid, the Company would, especially after the pledge which they had given, have neither the right nor the wish to impose any further exactions. Indeed, we might be drawn to the same conclusion ourselves. Cheyte Sing was either an independent prince or a subject. If he was the former, the question was settled; if the latter, it might be said either that the subject must not be taxed without his own consent, or at all events that he should be subjected to no exactions which are not laid in the same proportion on all others.

23. But in India the distinctions which may be drawn here were blurred and confused in the days of Warren Hastings. It was impossible to define exactly what any prince or chief might be; it was easy to find in his title or his position the justification of anything which a prince or chief of greater power might choose to do to him. When the Great Mogul grants away the revenues of a province, his word and his seal are invested with an inviolable sanctity. When he asks for tribute due to himself, he is a pageant or a shadow, and a sense of duty impels the tributary to withhold money which may either be squandered on unworthy favourites, or go to strengthen a formidable neighbour. The only condition needed for thus turning words into wealth was the possession of power; and the power of the English was a fact which spoke for itself. Personally, Hastings had a further reason for laying his hand heavily on Cheyte Sing. While he was borne down by the majority of the Council at Calcutta, the Raja had paid his court to Clavering and Francis; and Hastings was not sorry to read through him to other princes a lesson as impressive as that which had been taught to men of lower station by the execution of Nundkomar. In 1778 Hastings demanded, in addition to the annual tribute, a sum of 50,000*l.* The same demand was made in 1779; and both demands were paid. When it was repeated in 1780, the Rajah tried to escape it by offering to Hastings a bribe of 20,000*l.*

24. Hastings took the money, and only after a time paid it into the Company's treasury. Having done so, he repeated the old demand yet again. Cheyte Sing protested his inability to meet it, and Hastings, adding 10,000*l.* as a penalty for delay, sent troops to enforce the exaction. These sums also were paid, and then Hastings candidly avowed his purpose of drawing from his guilt the means of relieving the Company's distresses. His guilt was to be brought into being by compelling him to do or to say something which might be construed as meaning rebellion; and the compulsion took the form of a demand that he should maintain a body of cavalry for the English service. The Raja remonstrated, and Hastings wanted nothing more. He announced his purpose of visiting Benares himself, and when, in the interview which followed, Cheyte Sing attempted to excuse himself, ordered his arrest. The order was scarcely prudent. He had come with a small force, and he was in a city teeming with a population of myriads possessed by a dislike and suspicion of the English for which they had certainly some grounds. Like the Rohillas, they had no wish for a change of masters. Cheyte Sing had not been an oppressive ruler, and the condition of his dominions was very different from that of the British territory in Behar. The wrath of the rabble brought together a vast multitude, many fully armed. The English soldiers were attacked, their officers slain, and Cheyte Sing in the confusion let himself down the steep bank of the Ganges by a rope made from the turbans of his attendants, and escaped across the river. From the other side he sent messages craving indulgence and making large offers. Hastings, with only 50 men about him, but still thoroughly self-possessed, treated them with silent contempt, and sent some men who might be trusted, to summon help from the English cantonments.

25. Meanwhile an English officer with a small body of troops had made a rash attack on the other side of the river, and the almost complete destruction of his force was the result. Then followed that strange excitement and commotion of the population generally, which have been so often caused by even the least disaster to the English arms. Cheyte Sing, carried away by the torrent of feeling, began to talk foolishly about driving the white usurpers into the sea. But the scene was soon to be changed. Major Popham, who four years before had won fame by his memorable capture of the Mahratta fortress of Gwalior, scattered his undisciplined troops, and Cheyte Sing fled from his territory, which was incorporated within the British dominions. The Company was the richer by 200,000*l.* a year; but the Raja's treasure was found to be barely more than a fourth of the sum at which it had been estimated, and the whole went as prize-money to the army (1784).

26. The sequel may be briefly told. Asof-u-Daula had succeeded Suja-u-Daula as Nuwab Vizir of Oude. His wastefulness, his vices, and his tyranny were alike horrible. He dreaded his neighbours, he trembled at the wrath of his subjects; and against both he prayed that he might be secured by English aid. It was agreed that a force should be sent, to be maintained and paid out of his revenues. Like the horse which in the fable accepts a rider in order to get the better of the stag, the Nuwab began to complain of the weight of the burden, and requested that the troops might be withdrawn. Hastings answered that the time during which the troops were to remain in Oude was not stated in the treaty, while their maintenance at his cost was set down most distinctly. He had further a conscientious scruple which withheld him from withdrawing them. A vast amount of money was yearly squandered by the Nuwab on the grossest pleasures and the basest favourites; if he were no longer called upon to pay for the troops, there would be so much the more money forthcoming for evil purposes. It was impossible therefore to accede to his request; but some settlement might be arrived at in an interview.

27. Hastings and the vizir met in the fort of Chunar, and there they agreed to rob two ladies who were called the Begums of Oude, one being the mother of Suja-u-Daula, the other his widow, the mother of Asof-u-Daula. Suja had left them, it was said, a treasure worth about **3,000,000*l*.** sterling; and of this treasure Asof had already had some excellent pickings, when the Begums, appealing to the English, obtained a treaty which pledged them to make certain payments to Asof, and bound him in return to make no further demands on their resources. But the best intentions are often frustrated. The Nuwab felt the increasing pressure of the poverty which was the natural result of his own vices; and Hastings, although for different reasons, was not less anxious to get money. The Begums were still supposed to be the possessors of vast wealth, and Hastings agreed that he would take the confiscation of the whole as a full discharge of all obligations on the part of the Nuwab to the Company. The princesses, however, were obstinate; and Hastings sanctioned measures to subdue their resistance which cannot be thought of without a deep feeling of shame. The Begums were charged, without the faintest shadow of proof, with having brought about or promoted the insurrection of Benares; and Sir Elijah Impey hurried from Calcutta to give his authority to falsehoods which convicted themselves. It is the last recorded act of his infamous career. In 1782 he was recalled to England.

28. Hastings remained in India three years longer, and they were years of singular quietness. Hyder Ali died in the same year which witnessed the departure of Impey. He had reached a great age, without bringing on himself the stroke of an assassin, although his one instrument for governing all ranks and classes of his subjects was the scourge. In 1784 Lord Macartney, Governor of Madras, made a treaty with Tippu Sultan, the son and successor of Hyder, which set free a large number of European prisoners who had struggled through a miserable captivity at Mysore. At the same time he brought to an end the farce which exhibited the Nuwab of the Carnatic as an independent ruler. It was arranged that one sixth part of the revenue should still be paid to him; and Muḥammad Ali, the son of Anwar-u-dín (p. 24), joined the ranks of the phantom princes, amongst whom might be seen the Nuwab and Nizams of Bengal. But Lord Macartney's measures were not approved in England. Muhammad Ali was loaded with debt, and his creditors had no chance of payment unless he remained master of all the revenues of the Carnatic. Orders therefore were sent out that the whole of the Carnatic should be restored to the Nuwab, and that all claims against him should be liquidated out of the revenues without any further inquiry. Unable to obey such orders, Lord Macartney resigned, 1785.

CHAPTER XIV.

Lord Cornwallis, and the Land Settlement of Bengal.

1. The treaty of Salbai, made in 1782 after the death of Hyder with Mahadaji Sindia and ratified by Nana Farnavese, the minister of the Peshwa, at Poona, pledged the English and the Mahrattas not to help the enemies each of the other. The great issue of supremacy in India now lay between these two powers and the successor of Hyder, under cover of whose influence the French were supposed to be aiming at the recovery of their lost ascendency. But the great Mahratta houses of Sindia and Holkar, of the Gaekwar and the Bhonsla, were growing into powerful and virtually independent kingdoms; and of these, Sindia, the most powerful, was seeking to make himself master of Delhi as the nominal servant of the Great Mogul. He was aided in his scheme by intriguers in the imperial palace. The Amir of Amirs, the guardian of the Emperor, was afraid of being murdered, and invited Sindia to protect him; in other words, the Mahometan sought the aid of the idolatrous Hindu. Sindia came, but it was only to bring about the death of the Amir, and obtain for the Peshwa the title of deputy of the Padishah, and to exercise the real power himself as the deputy of the Peshwa. His object was to found a new Mahratta state between the Jumna and the Ganges, and the troops which he was raising were disciplined by the Frenchman De Boigne.

2. French influence was, indeed, still a cause of apprehension to the English.. A French agent was already at Poona; but the jealousy of Sindia was roused when he heard that Mr. Malet was to appear there as the agent for the English. It was arranged that the correspondence between the Peshwa and the Governor-General should pass through the hands of Mr. Anderson the resident in attendance on Sindia, and that the two agents should arrange matters together in Sindia's camp. In the midst of the ruined mosques and shattered palaces of Agra Mr. Malet was lodged in the Taj Mahal (p. 60), the only building which still remained uninjured. The phantom emperor welcomed Mr. Malet and received his presents with stately courtesy, bestowing on him in return a tiara of diamonds and emeralds, an elephant, and a horse; but the jewels were bits of glass, and the elephant and horse were worn out with old age or disease. It was the hope of Sindia that the English would aid the Mahrattas in the war with their great enemy Tippu. But this was forbidden by the treaty of Salbai, while the treaty of Mangalore, 1783, bound them not to help the enemies of Tippu, although from this they might be absolved by the fact of Tippu's alliance with the French, who were avowed enemies of the English.

3. After a short interval, during which Mr. Macpherson was acting governor, Lord Cornwallis (1786–1791), reached Calcutta as successor of Warren Hastings, and by his position was enabled to carry out many changes which his predecessors had failed to effect. The system of perquisites was brought to

an end by the bestowal of adequate salaries, while the tone of society at Calcutta, a matter of no mean importance, was greatly improved. The private life of Hastings had not set the best of examples, and the gambling of Francis and Barwell was on a prodigious scale. But the name of Lord Cornwallis is associated especially with the question of land settlement. As the scheme was set forth, it was one for abolishing leases and granting lands in perpetuity to the Zemindars, who had thus far been merely collectors of rent, middlemen, in short, between the government and the owners or cultivators of the soil. The reason for the change was not so much a disinterested regard for the well-being of the people as anxiety for the easier collection of the Company's revenue. As a servant of the Company, the Zemindar came under the jurisdiction of the Supreme Court at Calcutta. He could be sued there, and his person and movables seized; and great practical inconvenience had been found to result from such seizures. As a landowner he would be beyond that jurisdiction, although he would remain under the control of the district courts.

4. But why an experiment so momentous should be made for all time, it might be not easy to determine. Mr. Shore, who afterwards became Sir John Shore and finally Lord Teignmouth, urged earnestly that no change should be perpetual until the value of the land had been more accurately ascertained than it could possibly be in the course of a few months or two or three years, and until the nature of the different tenures, and the rights of landlords and tenants according to existing customs should be fully and precisely known. His proposal was that the settlement should be for ten years, and then, if found satisfactory, should be declared permanent. But Lord Cornwallis and his supporters were carried away by the idea of the benefits which would accrue from their plan. That they looked upon the tax-collectors whom they wished to convert into landowners as having all along been landlords after the English type, the facts already stated sufficiently disprove. They thought that they were creating a landed aristocracy in India, and thought that this aristocracy would there have effects similar to those which it has in England, that it would apply capital to the land, clear forests, and raise the character of the peasantry, or ryots. This it failed to do. The position of the ryots was changed for the worse; that of the Zemindars was not improved. They were, in fact, quite unequal to the burden laid on them. They could not collect their rents, and they became bankrupts by hundreds. Their estates were sold, and purchased by land speculators, and in a short time two thirds of the soil of Bengal was, it has been said, in the hands of native bankers, native officials, and others, all absentees.

5. Hence arose the wretched system, known as the *ticcadaree*, or hire system. The absentee let his lands at a permanent quit-rent to anyone who might be willing to take them on the chance of squeezing a sufficient extra revenue out of the ryots. The Zemindar, who accounted to the government, was now an absentee who cared nothing for the soil and its tillers so long as he received his quit-rent, and the real owners formed a class whose one object it was to make a profit over and beyond the sums which they paid to the absentee landowner.

6. The result has been a state of terrible oppression, reproducing all and intensifying some of the evils which the peasantry endured at the hands of their Mogul masters. The man who had to make a profit on his quit rent had no enterprise, and no capital which enterprise could turn to good account. He needed money; he could get money by imposing illegal cesses (p. 131) on his tenants, and he never scrupled to do so. The ryots were reduced to a state which threw large tracts out of cultivation, and left them to the possession of wild hogs. After the lapse of nearly a century, the condition of the average Bengal ryot is most pitiable. His expenditure is from three to six shillings a month; but there are not five out of a hundred who earn ten pounds a year. The question has been carefully considered of late years, and the wide extent of the misery is beyond all doubt. Behar is the garden of Hindustan; but in a recent report the magistrate of Patna declares that had he not seen it, he never could have believed the abject poverty of the peasantry in this favoured land which has its three harvests annually. For those who look the facts in the face it is not easy to withstand the conclusion that the perpetual settlement of Lord Cornwallis was unwittingly a gigantic act of confiscation, which has fallen most heavily on the government of India. Although the expenditure has increased, and the demands on it are growing larger from year to year, the rental of land, 'the backbone of Indian revenue,' remains where it was. The government is poorer by a sum ranging from six to eight millions sterling annually. The condition of the peasantry, arising out of this settlement, scatters to the winds the notion that the people of India must be necessarily happy and prosperous under English rule, because their English rulers have acted with the best intentions. Mr. Shore saw the evils that must come of it, but his voice was raised in vain, and a system was set up which has left the ryot bound hand and foot at the mercy of the money-lender.

7. The results of the system carried out some years later by Sir Thomas Munro in Madras were not much more happy. It was impossible without much injustice and hardship to collect a revenue which was made to depend on the crops as they stood, and not on the land, and the amount taken was far too large. The old Hindu rate was one fifth or one seventh of the produce of each field; the new rate raised the demand to one third, and the whole arrangement interfered with or put out of sight the principle accepted in this part of India from time immemorial, that the land belonged to the people by right of occupation, subject only to the payment of taxes to the State. The province of Bombay was happier in having the assessment not on the crop but on the land; and the further changes introduced since the days of Mr. Elphinstone have brought about a state of things which presents a

favourable contrast to the position of the ryots in Bengal.

8. The intentions of Lord Cornwallis were good, and in the administration of justice he worked on the whole to excellent effect. Magistrates were appointed to towns and districts to deal with civil and criminal cases; and the English collectors, deprived of their judicial functions, were confined to their proper duties. Courts of appeal were established at Dacca, Patna, and Murshedabad with a final appeal to the Sudder Court at Calcutta, which was composed of the Governor-General and members of Council. Provision also was made for the speedy trial of all accused persons. It was unfortunate that with these changes the service remained closed to natives except in the most inferior positions; and the saying is but too true that 'reform in this material respect and others was only to come upon the bitter experience of years.'

9. In the regions over which the Great Mogul was still nominally ruler, things were going from bad to worse. The Mahometan party at Delhi persuaded Shah Alam that his majesty was dishonoured by his relations with Hindu Mahrattas, stirred up a revolt of Hindu Rajpúts, induced the Mahometans in Sindia's army to join the Rajpúts, and compelled Sindia himself to abandon all his acquisitions between the Jumna and the Ganges, and to fall back on the fortress of Gwalior. But Shah Alam had cause soon to rue the departure of his Mahratta protector. In 1788 Delhi was seized by the Rohilla Afghan, Gholam Kadir, who behaved like a scourge in the imperial palace, and put out the eyes of the aged emperor. At the end of two months Sindia returned, to the great joy of the tormented people, with reinforcements which he had with difficulty obtained from Nana Farnavese and Holkar.

10. The power of Tippu was now becoming formidable to Mahrattas and English alike. His father, Hyder, had not been a strict Mahometan; he therefore let the Hindus alone. Tippu was a devout upholder of Islam, and therefore a zealous persecutor; but his orthodoxy in no way interfered with the denial of all vassalage to the Great Mogul, or the open assumption of the sovereign title of Sultan of Mysore. He was known to be in communication with the French at Pondicherry, and he now demanded the submission of the Raja of Travancore. Lord Cornwallis informed him that the English would protect the Raja; and hindered by the supineness and the underhand dealings of Holland, the governor of Madras, he resolved on an alliance with the Nizam and the Mahrattas against Tippu. Mr. Pitt's Bill of 1784 had forbidden alliances with native princes; and Lord Cornwallis, to respect its spirit, if he could not obey the letter, provided that the treaties should have effect only during the continuance of the war.

11. In this war, the campaigns of 1790 and the following year produced no substantial effects. The Nizam's forces were useless except for plunder, and Sindia made conditions with which it was impossible for Lord Cornwallis to comply. The English could not guarantee to him his possessions in Hindustan, and aid him in the reduction of the Rajpúts. The campaign of 1792 was more decisive. The defences of Seringapatam were carried by storm; and Tippu, seeing that his only chance lay in immediate submission, agreed to the proposal of Lord Cornwallis that he should cede a portion of his territory, to be divided equally between the Peshwa, the Nizam, and the English, pay 3,000,000*l.* towards the expenses of the war, and surrender his two sons as hostages for his fulfilment of these conditions.

12. This war served to show the futility of the policy which enjoined on the English absolute isolation from all other powers in India. In place of this policy Lord Cornwallis thought that it would be wiser to apply the theory of a balance of power, in which the British Government should hold the scales between the Mahrattas, the Nizam, and the Sultan of Mysore. This scheme was almost as unpractical as the other. The native princes wished only to be protected each against the rest, while they insisted on enforcing their claims against them, if they should have any claims to urge; and the Mahrattas professed to have heavy claims against the Nizam, and even against the English. For the present the chief benefit seemed to be secured for Sindia, who held a strong military post in Agra, and had received from Shah Alam grants of land revenue in the Doab, the Mesopotamia or land between the two rivers, Ganges and Jumna, and had a large part of his army disciplined by the Frenchman De Boigne.

For thus extending the dominion of the Mahrattas, he demanded a payment for the costs to which he had been put. Nana Farnavese speedily silenced him by saying that his conquests had been in his hands for some time, that the territories were very fertile, and that he ought now to account for their revenues to his master, the Peshwa. In 1794 Mahadaji Sindia died, and was succeeded by his son Daulut Rao Sindia, a boy of fourteen.

13. Lord Cornwallis had returned to England the year before, and Sir John Shore had taken his place as Governor-General. War had been declared between England and France, and the English for the third time took possession of Pondicherry. Shore was scarcely equal to the difficulties of the task before him, and he candidly acknowledged the fact. The Mahrattas urged their claims on the Nizam with increasing importunity; the Nizam was, or professed to be, wholly unable to meet them. But, under the strict injunctions laid on him as to non-interference, Sir John Shore was unable to comply with his request for help, although he was well aware that the fall of the Nizam would give a most dangerous predominance to the Mahrattas. For the time the Nizam thought that he had sufficiently strengthened his position by obtaining the services of a French officer named Raymond, who disciplined for him twenty-three battalions of regular troops. But the high hopes thus raised were soon disappointed. In the battle of Kurdla, March 1795, the battalions disciplined by Raymond stood their ground; the rest were routed at the outset by the Mahratta rockets and artillery. The result was that the

Nizam ceded nearly half his territory, while he agreed to discharge all the Mahratta claims.

14. The triumph of Nana Farnavese was not much more lasting. The young Peshwa, Mahdu Rao Narain, rendered desperate by the restraint which reduced his sovereignty to a shadow, threw himself from a terrace of the palace and died in a few days; and the Nana, although unwilling to set up the nearest kinsman, Baji Rao, thought it prudent to do so on discovering that Baji was seeking to obtain Sindia's aid to seize the Peshwa's throne. The sequel brings before us a series of plots and counter-plots, ending in murder and massacre, which sufficiently showed that the Mahratta power was breaking up. The state of things in Oude was no better. Asof-u-Daula had squandered his revenues on infamous companions and infamous vices. His successor substituted hoarding for squandering, not much to the benefit of his kingdom.

15. The relations of the British power with the native states were not the only subjects for anxiety during the administration of Sir John Shore. The plan of amalgamating the local armies with that of the Crown was vehemently opposed by the officers of the Bengal army, who insisted on the re-establishment of all previous allowances. The danger was more serious than that with which Clive had to deal (p. 122). The result was regarded as showing Sir John Shore's weakness. The local regulations were modified to meet the necessities of the case; and the officers obtained even more than they looked for (1793).

CHAPTER XV.

Fall of the Mysore Sultan—Mahratta Wars—Battle of Assaye—Siege of Bhurtpore.

1. Lord Mornington, the successor of Lord Teignmouth, (Sir John Shore,) reached India, 1798, full of Lord Cornwallis's theory of the balance of power, and bent on reviving the alliance with the Nizam and the Peshwa against Tippu, and on driving the French out of India. The strong feeling which the horrible excesses of the French revolution excited in England was heightened in India by the knowledge that French officers were disciplining regiments in the service of the Nizam and of Sindia and were welcomed in the palace of Tippu. The idea of arrangements for securing a balance of power was found to be visionary. It seemed, therefore, the more necessary to carry out the other measures. A promise to mediate in the Mahratta claims, and, if need be, to protect him against them by force, removed all difficulties with the Nizam. But with the Mahrattas the Governor-General could do little or nothing.

2. This failure had no effect on the plans of Lord Mornington. Affairs with Tippu were coming to a crisis. It was known that he had sent envoys to the Mauritius, proposing to the French Government an offensive and defensive alliance against the English, and that Napoleon Bonaparte had landed in Egypt. It was reported that a French fleet was sailing down the Red Sea on its way to the Malabar coast. Lord Mornington thus felt himself justified in demanding, by Colonel Doveton, a full explanation from Tippu. Tippu evaded the main point, refused to see Colonel Doveton, and contented himself with referring to existing treaties as providing means for avoiding difficulties in the future. While he was thus seeking to gain time by fruitless negotiations, he was still begging for the aid of the French Government, and inviting Zeman Shah, the Afghan prince, who had crossed the Indus and reached Lahore, to join him in a Jehad or holy war against the infidels. An intercepted letter from Bonaparte to Tippu showed at least the possibility of an understanding between the two. Lord Mornington sent him a final warning, assuring him that the French fleet had been destroyed in the bay of Aboukir, and sending him a letter in which the Ottoman Sultan of Constantinople advised him to keep clear of any alliance with the French.

3. Tippu was inflexible, and the war began. He had desolated the country across which he thought that the English might advance upon his capital; but after the victory gained, March 27, 1799, over Tippu's forces at Malavelli, the British army kept to the south and crossed the Cauvery by a hitherto unknown ford. Tippu was now invested in Seringapatam, and the siege was pushed on with the utmost vigour. On the third day he sued for peace. The English terms now were the half of his dominions, and the payment of 2,000,000*l*. sterling. With the brief answer that it was better to die a soldier than to live as a pensioned Nuwab, Tippu prepared himself to fight to the death. After a terrible struggle the fort was stormed by the troops under General Baird, and by evening all resistance was overcome. It was not easy to repress a desire for indiscriminate vengeance on the part of the British soldiers, for Tippu had been in the habit of murdering his prisoners, and they had heard that twelve of them had been killed the night before. Tippu's body was found the next morning under a gateway, and buried amidst the crash of a fierce thunderstorm and the roaring of cannon in salute.

4. So ended after a duration of only forty years the dynasty which Hyder, the founder, forewarned his son that he would destroy. At least he died bravely in defending his inheritance; but he left behind him amongst his own people the memory of a ferocious tyrant, for whose execrable cruelties the only possible extenuation would be a plea of madness. How far the madness, if there were any, might be of his own causing, it is not worth while to ask, nor is it worth while to dwell on the details of his oppressions. Among the least of them was the system by which the richer inhabitants were compelled to buy, at the most exorbitant prices, goods which the tyrant, who had been a trader, had stored up in his warehouses. Bribery on a large scale was the only way of escaping from these forced purchases; and those who failed to bribe and would not pay were stripped of their property, and if then a balance remained, were written down as debtors for it to the

Sultan. Tippu's territority was partitioned, the nearer portions in each direction being reserved for the English, the Nizam, and the Mahrattas. The rest, forming the kingdom of Mysore, was made over to the lineal heir of the old Raja, a boy five years old, English commissioners being appointed to arrange the details of the administration during his minority, while Tippu's finance minister, Purnea, was left to carry them out.

5. The fall of Tippu involved a vast extension of British dominion. This extension included that portion of the Mysore territory which had been reserved for the Peshwa. He would accept it, he said, as a discharge for his claims of tribute on the Mysore kingdom; but he would not abate a jot of his claims on the Nizam, and his portion of Mysorean land was therefore forfeited. The other portion the Nizam ceded for the maintenance of eight battalions which by a new treaty the English agreed to provide for his protection. This treaty also bound them to defend him against all aggression, and therefore dealt a death-blow to the long-cherished schemes of Sindia. The Nizam had no reason to regret his bargain. He was safe from his ancient enemies, and he had obtained this freedom without the sacrifice of any part of his own possessions. the Raja of Tanjore and the Nuwab of the Carnatic still retained their titles, but passed into the rank of pensioners, and their domains henceforth were to be ruled by the English Company. The same fate befell Tinnevelly and Madura, while the states of Coorg, Cochin, and Travancore were reduced to a

condition of dependence and tribute. The Presidency of Madras was now virtually confined to that portion of the Indian peninsula which lay between the Kistna and the Godavari rivers and the Cape of Comorin.

6. In truth, the policy of the English in India had undergone a vast and most momentous change. It remained to be seen whether the policy would be persistently and completely carried out. But for the present the Governor-General (who, after the fall of Seringapatam, had been created Marquis of Wellesley) was acting on the principle that all the native states must surrender their independence in return for British protection. They must enter into no alliances, and make no wars, nor have any Europeans not English in their service, without the consent of the British Government. Each of the larger states was to maintain a force under the command of British officers, and for their maintenance and pay a certain portion of territory was to be ceded in full sovereignty. We have seen that the Nizam accepted and that the Peshwa rejected the new system. Sindia also would have nothing to do with it, although Lord Wellesley sent him a letter in which the Afghan prince, Zeman Shah, prayed the English to help him in driving the Mahrattas out of Hindustan. His refusal caused more than vexation to Lord Wellesley. His singularly keen military insight led him to see the practicability and to imagine the execution of schemes, which needed for their accomplishment a greater genius or more continuous good fortune

than fell to the lot of any then living. He overrated, and therefore unduly dreaded, the powers of Zeman Shah and of Napoleon Bonaparte, because he saw how much they could accomplish far more clearly than they could see it themselves. He feared the Afghans, because he knew that they had founded a great empire in Hindustan some centuries ago; but he gave no thought to the feuds and domestic wars which prevented them from repeating the exploit. So far as he knew, they might be ready to burst forth from their mountain homes, as they had done in days now long past. They might find Hindus and Mahometans ready to range themselves on their side, and Frenchmen eager to turn the tables on the English.

7. Nor were these fears altogether groundless. The Mahratta power alone was a matter for grave anxiety. It was perpetually shifting and changing its local position and its character. Tukaji Holkar, the master of Indore, died in 1797, leaving two sons, one an idiot. Sindia put the idiot on the throne and murdered the other. But there was another brother, or half-brother, who proposed to take the side of the son whom Sindia rejected; and when the latter was murdered, he betook himself to the jungles and gathered under his standard all who might be willing to join him, all who preferred war to peace, and plunder to honest industry. This was Jeswunt Rao Holkar. He soon had about him an army of 20,000 men, for whom he had no other means of subsistence than that which they might gain by violence and robbery. Meanwhile Baji Rao (p. 161) was exhibiting his profi-

ciency in tyranny at Poona. Among his victims was a brother of Jeswunt Rao, whom he bound to the feet of an elephant, gleefully listening to his shrieks as the huge beast trampled him to death. To avenge this deed Jeswunt Rao appeared at Poona, and crushed the armies of Sindia and the Peshwa. Baji Rao fled to the coast with the speed of despair, and was conveyed by an English ship to the port of Bassein. In his misery he resolved to accept the terms which the English had offered him. He declared his readiness to cede territory for the maintenance of a subsidiary British force, and bound himself to have no intercourse with any native princes, whether of the Mahratta or any other people, without the consent of the Governor-General. In short, to retain the name of Peshwa and a pension which might keep up the semblance of his ancient dignity, he yielded up all his authority, all his ancestral suzerainty over the great Mahratta houses, and brought himself to the level of men like Mir Jafir or Chunder Sahib. Baji Rao might agree to such terms in the hour of despair; it was not likely that he would adhere to them if the tide of fortune should turn.

8. It soon became clear that he had at least no wish to adhere to them. A British force brought him, in 1803, from Bassein to Poona; Colonel Arthur Wellesley, the future Duke of Wellington and brother of the Governor-General, was advancing from Madras to support him; and yet at this very time he was praying Sindia and the Bhonsla Raja to set him free from the English yoke. But these

chiefs were discouraged and perplexed by the treaty of Bassein (1802). They had no desire to join the English, and no love for the Brahman Peshwas. If Jeswunt Rao Holkar would throw in his lot with them they might see their way more clearly; but Jeswunt preferred to await the issue of the conflict and then take part with the winner.

9. The situation was grave enough; but Lord Wellesley's imagination foreboded dangers which only the same imagination in his enemies could have turned into realities. In 1800 he had sent an expedition to Egypt, which was prevented from coming into conflict with the French by the proclamation of peace between France and England. He now saw no reason why Napoleon should not again take up the design which for the time he had been compelled to abandon. French officers were collecting the revenues of the Doab (p. 159) to maintain French battalions for Sindia. The port of Baroche, at the mouth of the Nerbudda, belonged to Sindia. What was there to hinder the junction of a French army with Perron at Agra, and a French conquest of Hindustan, achieved in the name of the Great Mogul? To render such an issue impossible the English must on the declaration of war march on Delhi and occupy the country between the Jumna and the Ganges. This task Lord Wellesley intrusted to Colonel Lake; and Colonel Wellesley, having watched Sindia and the Bhonsla raja in the Deccan, and growing weary of protracted suspense, brought matters to a head by telling those chiefs that if they meant anything by their professions of goodwill to

the English they would show their sincerity by withdrawing their troops within their own borders, the English agreeing that in that case their army should be withdrawn also.

10. Sindia insisted that the English must set the example; but he forgot that only as yesterday he had threatened to invade the territory of the Nizam, and had declared himself unable to say whether there was to be peace or war between himself and the English. He was told that his refusal had broken the peace by his own act, and the second Mahratta war began. Colonel Wellesley first seized the fort of Ahmednágár as a basis of operation, and arranged with Colonel Stevenson, who commanded the new subsidiary force of Hyderabad, for a combined attack on Sindia and the Bhonsla. Sindia, it seemed, wished to get to Wellesley's rear and plunder the Nizam's land. But Wellesley's movements were too rapid. Without waiting for Stevenson to join him, he resolved to attack the enemy, whose camp lay between the villages of Bokerdun and Assaye. His whole force amounted to only 4,500 men. Sindia had 16,000 disciplined infantry, and 20,000 cavalry, without reckoning the irregular troops of the Bhonsla raja. The issue of the fight was as decisive as that of Plassy; but it was gained over an enemy vastly more formidable, and the English general lost more than a third of his army (1803).

11. By the middle of September the Deccan campaign was over; and before that time Lake, who had carried the fort of Alighur by storm, had defeated the Mahrattas under their French leader De Bourquin near the walls of Delhi, and entered in triumph the city of the Great Mogul. Shah Alam, who had spent fifteen years in blindness (p. 158), received the conqueror, seated on the throne of Baber and Akbar. It was well that he could not see the faded finery which now did service for the magnificence of the ancient kings. Lake left the aged emperor in the palace, and set off to capture Agra and defeat the enemy at Laswaree. For these services he was raised to the peerage under the title of Baron of Delhi and Laswaree. The French battalions of Sindia were broken up, and their commander, Perron, invoking the protection of the English against his former master, was allowed to take up his abode in the French settlement of Chandernagore. The Mahratta rajas were compelled to enter into compacts based on the treaty of Bassein. Sindia resigned all pretensions to *chout*, or tribute, from any princes, gave up the Doab and all but two districts in Rajpútana, together with all claims on the Nizam, the Gaikwar, or the Peshwa. The Bhonsla raja ceded the province of Cuttack and all Berar to the west of the river Wurda, giving up also all claims on the Nizam. Lord Wellesley had achieved a splendid success; but he thought it necessary to throw a veil over these conquests, and to exhibit them to the people of England as measures needed to render French rivalry in India impossible. He therefore kept Cuttack as exposing the coast of Bengal to the danger of an attack by sea, and bestowed Berar as a free gift on the Nizam.

12. The English campaigns against Sindia and his ally furnished to Jeswunt Rao Holkar a golden opportunity for plunder, and he reaped the harvest in Malwa and Rajpútana. His marauding bands were swelled by deserters after the defeat of Sindia and the Bhonsla raja; but he felt that the good old days were gone, and that the English would interfere with a repetition of the exploits of Sivaji. It was needful to obtain their friendship or their countenance; it was still more necessary to maintain his own freedom. He thought that he should attain both, if he professed his goodwill and at the same time insisted on what he was pleased to call his right of levying *chout*, and of plundering the protected tribes in Rajpútana. On being told by General Lake that no aggressions could be allowed on the British Government or its allies, he insisted on an English guarantee for his territory of Indore, under a threat of indiscriminate ravaging and slaughter if his request were refused.

13. Jeswunt Rao, it was evident, must be put down. In 1804 General Lake moved into Rajpútana; and Jeswunt retreated southwards in the direction of Indore. Colonel Monson was despatched in the same direction to keep him in check, and, fully expecting the arrival of British reinforcements, advanced fifty miles to the south of the Mokundra pass. But his supplies were being exhausted, and Bapaji Sindia, the commander of one of his bodies of irregular horse, was inviting his kinsman to turn round and fall on the English. The tidings that he could look for no help from Colonel Murray, who was retreating to Guzerat, and that Jeswunt was approaching him with an overwhelming force, made him resolve on returning to the Mokundra pass. Here Bapaji deserted him and joined Jeswunt Rao with all his horsemen; but even thus Monson beat off the whole body of the enemy, and all might have been well had he kept his ground. Unfortunately he continued his retreat. The rains had set in. His guns sank in the mud, and he was obliged not only to spike them but to destroy his ammunition. The commander of Sindia's detachment which had been sent to support him followed the example of Bapaji; and at the end of August, with a wretched remnant of his force, Monson reached Agra.

14. Lord Wellesley was astounded. The protected princes began to think that after all the English were not to be masters of India. Jeswunt Rao, whose glory was compared with that of Sivaji, hastened to Delhi with a huge throng of marauders and bandits. Foiled by Colonel Ochterlony in his attempt to seize the emperor, he sent his guns and infantry to Bhurtpore, the strongest fortress of Hindustan, which the Raja, breaking with the English government, had placed in his hands. With his horsemen he betook himself to harrying and wasting the Doab; but his bands were dispersed by General Lake, who unwisely, perhaps, laid siege to Bhurtpore, January 1805. Four months were wasted before its huge mud walls; but enough was done to counteract the efforts of Jeswunt's victory over Monson. For readmission to the number of protected princes the Raja of Bhurtpore paid 200,000*l.*;

and Jeswunt Rao was undergoing defeat after defeat in the field, when Lord Wellesley was recalled, and Lord Cornwallis was sent back to reverse his policy (1805).

15. The government of Lord Wellesley was a memorable one. He, and perhaps he alone, saw that peace in India was impossible, unless one paramount power prevented aggression, tumult, war, and anarchy among the rest. He saw that the notion of a balance of power as applied to such a country was sheer absurdity. He saw not less clearly that the continuance of anarchy and savage warfare beyond the territories of the Company must in the end and perhaps soon have a fatal effect on the interests and the existence of the Company itself; and thus seeing that of all existing powers the British alone could become paramount in India, he held it to be his duty to work for a consummation which would be an equal benefit to the English government and its new subjects. His mind was occupied with matters of wider importance than the commercial interests of a company of traders; and a consciousness of the inadequacy of merely mercantile training as an education for the administrators of a great country led him to found the College of Fort William for the special education of young civilians on their arrival from England. It was soon abolished by the Court of Directors; but the idea which suggested its foundation was carried out at Haileybury.

CHAPTER XVI.

Administrations of Lord Minto and Lord Hastings—Operations in Nepal and against the Pindharries.

1. For the present it seemed that Lord Wellesley's schemes had been finally set aside. To the Directors of the Company in England extension of territory had no other meaning than that of increase of expenditure without any corresponding profit, and conquest was little better than a road to poverty. That India could be ruled to its own benefit, as Lord Wellesley held, only by reducing all its native states to dependence on one paramount power, was to them an incomprehensible and perhaps ludicrous idea; and if the native states could be fairly compared to those of Europe, their view would have been undoubtedly right. The kingdoms of Europe for the most part represented nations. Some of them were, nearly all would have wished to be, self-governing societies, in which the action of the rulers represents the will of the people. They may have had their origin in invasion and conquest; but they had assumed their present form by a slow process which had defined the functions of all classes and orders in the state, and made the executive magistrate strictly the representative of the nation. There was nothing of this kind in India; there never had been. The conquests of Baber were not yet 300 years old; and the empire which he founded had long since crumbled

into fragments. The ministers of the Mogul sovereign had become independent princes, and had in their turn been displaced by more powerful subjects. So the strange drama had gone on, not dragging its slow length, but with marvellously rapid changes of action and scenery, with this result that there was scarcely a native power in India which could boast an existence even of half a century.

2. In such a state of things the sudden and complete reversal of Lord Wellesley's plans might have involved serious dangers and disasters. It was the purpose of Lord Cornwallis to abandon Delhi and the Doab to Jeswunt Rao Holkar, removing the emperor and his family to Bengal, and to withdraw from the Rajpút chiefs the protective treaties which saved them from the ravages of the Mahrattas. But the carrying out of this purpose was prevented by his death. He was sixty-seven years of age when he landed at Calcutta to face the damp heats of a Bengal August. In September, the most trying of all months in the plains, he was journeying northwards, and in less than ten weeks from the time of his landing he died. His successor was Sir George Barlow, a civil servant of the Company, who had supported Lord Wellesley's policy. He now practically reversed it. The inconsistency seems strange; but he had no choice between this and resignation, and he may have regarded the reaction of public opinion as justified by the circumstances of the case. According to a treaty made by Sir John Malcolm, all the territories of Holkar, with the exception of the fort of Tonk-Rampoora, were restored to Jeswunt Rao, who now insisted again

on all his old claims. Dissatisfied with this treaty, Sir George Barlow ordered the restoration of Rampoora also. Jeswunt Rao felt himself like a prisoner set free, and he refreshed himself by levying enormous sums on the Raja of Jeypur, while Lord Lake, bound by the policy of non-intervention, was compelled to look on with folded hands. Lake had further cause for vexation. He had promised protection to the Jeypur raja, if he withstood the advance of Holkar. The raja had complied with this condition; but Sir George Barlow annulled the treaty, and Lake felt that his fair fame was tarnished in the eyes of the raja.

3. The Governor-General was soon to feel the difficulties of the new policy. The Court of Directors desired the restoration of all territories acquired during the Mahratta war. Barlow replied that such a course would be only to let loose Mahratta hordes to attempt the subversion of British power in India. Nor could the Mahrattas or other chiefs see why the measure dealt to Jeswunt Rao should not be meted out to themselves. The Bhonsla raja, now known as the Raja of Nagpore, demanded the restoration of Cuttack and Berar, although the latter had been bestowed as a gift on the Nizam (p.171), and Cuttack, in Sir George Barlow's judgment as in that of Lord Wellesley, was essential to the defence of Bengal.

4. It is possible that the mutiny of the two sepoy regiments left with the family of Tippu at Vellore may have been connected with the policy of non-intervention. There seem to be good grounds for thinking that it was encouraged, if not excited, by the Mysore princes. The mutiny, which involved a horrible slaughter of the European part of the garrison while they were asleep, was promptly put down (1806); but it became known that the disaffection had spread through the sepoys of the whole Madras army, the cause assigned being the issuing of orders which interfered with national customs or religious prejudices. It was admitted that Lord William Bentinck, the governor, had forbidden the sepoys from appearing on parade with earrings or caste marks, while they were also ordered to shave their beards, and to exchange the turban for a head-dress with some likeness to the European hat, an object of great aversion to Orientals generally. The sepoys imagined, not unnaturally, that these orders were preliminary to their conversion by force to Christianity. The idea of forcible conversion was, of course, thoroughly familiar to their minds, and they could not see why this force should not be applied by an English governor as it had been applied by Tippu or Aurengzebe. It would have been well if the lesson taught by this mutiny had been more carefully remembered. Military necessities and the safety of the empire may justify interferences which would be otherwise unwarrantable; but it is not easy to see why a turban on a man's head or some streaks on his face should be a hindrance to the preservation of discipline, or how the prohibition of customs in themselves not wrong, and consecrated by religious usage from time immemorial, should render them more loyal.

5. The alarm caused by this mutiny led to the recall of Lord William Bentinck, Sir George Barlow

being sent to take his place, while Lord Minto was sent out to Calcutta. Lord Minto was more keen-sighted in discerning the results of the policy of conciliation. Bundelkund, a district lying between Behar and Malwa to the south of the Jumna, was infested with marauders who issued from its hundred and fifty fortresses to rob and murder. Lord Minto put aside the notion of non-intervention, and the country was soon brought into fair order (1807). Nor was Bundelkund the only region which sorely felt the lack of this great blessing. The daughter of the Rajpút chief of Udaipur was betrothed to the Raja of Jodhpur. The raja died, but his successor contended that the princess who had now been betrothed to the Raja of Jeypur was betrothed to the throne of Udaipur, and not merely to the temporary holder of it. On this followed a horrible and desolating war between the two rajas. The Raja of Udaipur in his distress prayed for British protection, urging, unwittingly, the very argument of Lord Wellesley, that without a paramount power there could be no peace or safety in India, that the English alone could act as such a power, and that it was therefore their duty so to act. His request was refused; but the war still raged on, and to bring its horrors to an end the innocent cause of it was compelled to drink poison. The tragedy stirred a deep feeling in Western India; but Lord Minto felt that in that part of the country he could not interfere. The Dutch settlements in Java had passed into the hands of Napoleon. Lord Minto himself accompanied an expedition to Java, which was occupied by the English to the end of the war. On his return he found himself obliged to deal with the Pindharries.

6. The Pindharries were to the Mahrattas what the carrion crow is to the vulture. Of their origin nothing is known; but a horde of them had fought as allies of the Mahrattas at the fatal fight of Panipat (p. 115). Entering the service of the great chiefs, they were known as the Pindharries of Holkar or of Sindia. But the only tie which bound them together was that of plunder. Their arms were opened to welcome Hindus or Mahometans, men of any caste or of none, so long as they were ready to leave all natural kindliness and affection behind them. Wherever they went, they swept the land like a flight of devouring locusts. The names of their two most conspicuous leaders, Chetú and Khurím, became sounds of terror for all who heard them. At their approach the men of the wretched villages would set fire to their huts and die in the flames, and the women would throw themselves by troops into the wells. Methods of torture the most fiendish and the most ingenious were applied to compel their victims to disclose their little wealth; and from their marvellous rapidity of movement they were far beyond the reach of pursuit soon after their murderous work was done.

7. The task of dealing with these loathsome savages fell to the lot of Lord Moira, better known as the Marquis of Hastings, the title which he received after the Nepalese war. Lord Minto had left India, having won the respect of the people generally; and he deserved their gratitude for his efforts to

make their lives and property secure. The administration of police still remained very defective; but much was done to suppress the Dacoits or common thieves, whose gangs infested Bengal. The improvement in the public credit was shown by the fact that he was able to pay off loans contracted at an interest of twelve per cent. by others raised at six per cent. Lastly, his encouragement of native literature was greatly to his credit, at a time when the prevailing opinion was that India would be safe only so long as the people were kept in ignorance.

8. Lord Moira, or as he may be called at once by his more familiar name, Lord Hastings, was nearly sixty years of age when he reached India. He had left England strongly convinced of the wisdom of the non-intervention policy. But he was a man of no obstinate prejudices; and the evidence of Pindharrie barbarities, brought before him soon after his landing, opened his eyes to its weakness, and he frankly declared that good government in India could only be secured by a league, the forces of which could be set in motion by one paramount power. But the merits of Lord Minto's policy were to be tested first amongst the mountains of Nepal, a region which may be described as lying between Cashmere and Bhotan, on the southern slopes of the Himalayas. Down to the time of the battle of Plassy, Nepal belonged to a people known as the Newars. This race of Hindu Buddhists had found their way thither in all likelihood after the reaction which dealt the death-blow to Buddhism in the plains of India. Their traditions still went back to the glories of the time when Bud-

dhist monasteries studded the banks of the Ganges and the Jumna, and their scholars were taught that the land of their sacred cities of Magadha and Benares still bore the name of Behar (Vihara), or the monastery.

9. With this inoffensive people of farmers and traders the East India Company had long had profitable dealings, and the imports from Nepal included large quantities of gold from Thibet. But the year which saw the final departure of Clive from India came laden with disasters for the Newars. The Ghorkas of Cashmere, a fighting race of Rajpúts (p. 67), were drawn eastwards by their lust of land and conquest. The Newars can scarcely be said to have struggled against the invaders, and perhaps their lives and their habits rendered the task of resistance hopeless. Their raja abandoned the open country, took refuge in his capital of Khatmandu, and besought the aid of the East India Company. Captain Kinloch was sent to help them; but it was the season of the rains, which fall here with terrific force. He was therefore baffled in his attempt to cross the Terai, a broad malarious belt of almost impenetrable jungle, stretching along the base of the hills which form the vanguard of the snow-clad Himalaya. The Newars were thus left to their fate, and the Ghorka chief, Prithi Narain, parcelled out the land amongst his warriors as William the Conqueror parcelled out English land amongst his barons. This conquest was accomplished with horrors astounding even in the annals of Eastern cruelty. The chief among the Newars were massacred everywhere, and

mutilations on a vast scale were more appalling even than the massacres.

10. Prithi Narain died in 1771, and of his two sons the elder died four years later, leaving an infant son. The younger became the guardian of the babe, and purposely led him, as he grew up, into every species of vice and cruelty, to make his own power more sure. During these years the bands of the Ghorkas were never at rest, and their daring led them onwards to the highlands of Thibet and the plundering of the temples of Digarchi and Lhassa. To avenge this wrong, a Chinese army of 70,000 men approached Nepal, 1792, and the Ghorkas offered to enter into a commercial treaty with the English. A duty of two and a half per cent. was arranged for all goods imported on either side; but the Ghorkas were not thinking about trade. Soon after the treaty had been signed, the Ghorkas frankly asked aid against China, and received the natural reply that the English had no quarrel with the Chinese. But Lord Cornwallis could offer mediation, and Colonel Kirkpatrick was sent on the errand. Meanwhile the Ghorkas had been thoroughly routed by the Chinese, and bound to pay an annual tribute as well as to disgorge all their plunder; and when Kirkpatrick reached Khatmandu, he found himself courteously received, but in a way which showed him that the Ghorkas now cared nothing for the English or their treaty.

11. Three years later, 1795, a revolution sent Ran Bahadur, the grandson of Prithi Narain, into exile. It would be of little use to tell a horrible tale of cruelties matching those of a Nero. It is enough to say that the tyrant made his way to Benares. Lord Wellesley, who was then Governor-General, can scarcely have been unaware of the infamy of his career; but policy seldom looks very closely into a man's private life and character. The presence of the Maharaja seemed to open a way for the revival of the extinguished trade between his country and Bengal, and money was advanced from the Calcutta treasury for his support. Time went on, and another revolution placed the infant son of Ran Bahadur on the Nepalese throne. The new government was lavish of promises to Captain Knox, the English envoy; but the promises came to nothing, and Lord Wellesley announced to them that the alliance with Nepal was dissolved.

12. The Ghorkas seem to have supposed that they were now set free to do as they pleased on English ground as well as on their own, and they used the licence so well that more than two hundred British villages were gradually included within the borders of Nepal. Thus far the English had held their peace; but the Ghorkas now seized two villages about the ownership of which there could be no doubt. After a long inquiry it was found that they had always belonged to Oude; but the Ghorkas maintained that this fact only proved their own right to them. Lord Hastings replied by saying that if the districts were not surrendered within a given time, they would be taken back by force. The time was allowed to go by, and English police took possession of the villages in dispute. The Ghorkas

had treated the threat of Lord Hastings with seeming contempt; but in fact they were sorely divided as to the course to be taken. Some talked loudly about their impregnable position. Not even Iskander (Alexander the Great), they said, could bring his arms into their mountains; and the English who had been foiled before the mud walls of Bhurtpore could do nothing against fortresses which had been raised by the hands of God. The Ghorka barons resolved on war, and they made their purpose known not by the formal notice usual amongst European nations, but by slaughtering eighteen British constables at a police station (1813).

13. The Ghorkas had reckoned without their host. They might have thought at first that they had nothing to fear, for the English achieved but little in the campaign of 1814; but the prospect was changed when General Ochterlony, who had seated the blind Shah Alam on his ancestral throne at Delhi, dragged his artillery up the narrow zigzag mountain tracks, and stormed one hill fort after another, until the only one which remained surrendered when the English guns were about to open fire upon it. The Ghorkas, convinced now that prudence was the better part of valour, surrendered the whole of the Terai, and agreed to receive a British resident at Khatmandu. But the question rose whether the word Terai meant the slopes of the mountains, or only the marshy and fever-laden jungle land at their feet. The Ghorkas treated the question as an insult, and talked of resistance to the death in preference to disgraceful concessions. The matter was soon decided. Sir David Ochterlony defeated the Ghorka army within fifty miles of Khatmandu, and the original treaty was signed. In justice to the Ghorkas it must be added that they have adhered with strict fidelity to the peace of 1816.

14. The British Government was now able to turn its full attention to the extirpation of the Pindharrie hordes. With such ruffians negotiations and treaties could answer no purpose. They were in no sense a nation; and a society of bandits cannot claim the benefits of international law. But these lawless thieves were convenient instruments or allies for such powers as Sindia and Holkar, which still retained not a little of their old marauding character; nor was there much doubt that with these powers the Peshwa was laying schemes for a general uprising against the English. He was still aiding and abetting his minister, Trimbukji Dainglia, whom he had been compelled to surrender as the murderer of an envoy from the Gaekwar, and who had escaped from imprisonment at Thanna. This man had assembled an army within fifty miles of Poona; but the Peshwa pretended to know nothing of the fact, while he himself was strengthening his forts and sending his treasures out of Poona. Mr. Elphinstone, the future historian of India, then the British resident at Poona, resolved to bring these treacherous plottings to an end; and a threat of immediate forcible interference on the part of the English extorted from the Peshwa three important forts as security for his good faith. By a new treaty, June 1817, the Peshwa bound himself to hold no communications with any power except the English.

15. It remained now to deal with Sindia, who was living in a fool's paradise, dreaming of the signal retaliation which he should bring upon the English by means of the Pindharries. He knew that a British army was moving northward from Madras; but he expected that their mission was to defend the frontiers of the Nizam and those of the British territory, and thought that the Pindharries would have no difficulty in hiding themselves or joining his own army, while the British troops made, as he expected that they would make, some attempt to drive the freebooters out of their fastnesses and their homes. But he was not prepared for simultaneous and energetic operations from both north and south; and when he was requested to issue orders for the reception of the Madras troops advancing to expel the Pindharries from his territories, he was astounded. The plans of the Governor-General were laid before him in detail; and his confusion left him speechless when, in open durbar or council, the British resident placed in his hands his own intercepted letters to the Nepalese chiefs, telling him that they contained proposals for a combined attack on the English. Like the Peshwa, he agreed to a new treaty which placed the Rajput states under British protection and bound him to active measures for the suppression of the Pindharries.

16. The rooting out of these incurable ruffians was accomplished by the campaign of 1817. Terror-struck by the tidings that Sindia had been compelled to abandon them and even to take active part against them, they strove desperately to escape without coming into conflict with British troops. They fled first with their wives and children northwards; but here the Bengal army hemmed them in. Some then turned to the south, and escaped for the time with the loss of nearly all their baggage, but were severely handled in many small encounters, and in the end completely dispersed. The rest, leaving their horses behind them, sought lurking-places in the jungle, where many or most of them came to a wretched end. Those who were found in the open country received but scant mercy at the hands of the villagers whom they had kept in constant terror. Some of their leaders submitted themselves to the English. Khurím, from their misplaced indulgence, received an estate on British territory. The body of Chetú was found in the jungle, half devoured by a tiger; and the few of his followers who still survived were mingled with the population. The Pindharrie raids were a thing of the past.

CHAPTER XVII.

The Dethronement of the Peshwa—Internal Administration of Lord Hastings.

1. When the Peshwa Baji Rao signed the new treaty at Poona, he never meant to keep it; but he thought that much might be gained by pretending to do so. He disbanded large bodies of his cavalry; but he paid their officers for half a year in advance, ordering them to appear with their men, when called for, at a moment's notice. Pointing to this proof of his fidelity, he complained bitterly to Sir John Malcolm, who was then at Poona making preparations for the Pindharrie campaign, of the unjust suspicions which had deprived him of his three fortresses. Malcolm, deceived by his falsehoods, advised and obtained the restoration of these forts, and Baji Rao, under the pretence of operations against the Pindharries, began to enlist horsemen far beyond the numbers which could possibly be needed for such a purpose; but these troops, when enlisted, were not sent forward to the Nerbudda, where they were urgently wanted. He still corresponded with Sindia, Holkar, and other chiefs, and plotted the murder of Elphinstone, the British resident, who without making any comments brought up a European regiment from Bombay, the Poona subsidiary force having advanced under General Smith against the Pindharries. European troops were a terror to the Peshwa, who thoroughly understood the reason of their appearance, and declared that he would leave Poona if they were not sent back to Bombay. Elphinstone withdrew the British force to the neighbouring village of Khirki, and the very day on which he left the residency to join them, they were attacked by the army of the Peshwa. But the subsidiary force was now approaching under General Smith; and without waiting to be attacked, Baji Rao fled from Poona, and his city was occupied by the enemy, against whom he seemed to have no other weapon than that of treachery.

2. Treason was, in truth, a favourite weapon with all the Mahratta houses. Rughoji, the Bhonsla raja of Nagpore, died in 1816. His successor, an idiot, was murdered by the regent Appa Sahib, who made a subsidiary treaty with the English, and then proceeded to hatch schemes for their destruction with the Peshwa. To Mr. Jenkins, the resident at Nagpore, he dwelt on the impossibility of his following the evil example of Baji Rao in attacking the British troops at Khirki; but at the same time he and his ministers were found sending their treasure and their families out of the city, and Mr. Jenkins posted the troops on the Sitabuldi hill between the residency and Nagpore. These troops were merely 1,400 sepoys, three troops of Bengal cavalry, and four six-pounders. The army of Appa Sahib amounted to 18,000 men with thirty-six guns. The battle began in the evening, lasted through the night, and was decided the next day by the judgment and valour of Captain Fitzgerald, the commander of the Bengal horse (1817). Appa Sahib disavowed any share in the attack, and denied that he had ordered it. But even this excuse, hollow as it was, would have been taken, if he had disbanded his troops, and if it had not been discovered that he was the murderer of his predecessor. On this charge he was sent a prisoner to Allahabad; but he made his escape on the road, and having spent years among the Vindhya mountains (p. 9), found a refuge at last with the Raja of Jodhpur. An infant grandson of Rughoji was placed on the throne; but Mr. Jenkins was charged with the whole administration during his minority, and Nagpore ceased to be a source of anxiety and annoyance.

3. In Holkar's state of Indore the disaffection of the unpaid troops had led Tulsi Bai, the queen-mother, and regent for the young son of Jeswunt Rao, to seek the protection of the English. But the troops were afterwards paid by the Peshwa, and Tulsi Bai, no longer needing their aid, openly declared herself on the side of Baji Rao. Her army encountered the forces under Sir John Malcolm in December 1817; and her officers, seeing her readiness to negotiate with the British commander, carried her by night to a neighbouring river, where they beheaded her and cast her body into the stream. The result was the destruction of the army in the battle of Mehidpúr, three days later.

4. After abandoning Poona to its fate, the Peshwa thought to strengthen his position by summoning from Satara the representative of the great Sivaji; but his hopes were fast dying away, and the splendid defence of Korygaum by Captain Staunton left him in despair. With a detachment not exceeding 800 men, the only Europeans being ten English officers and twenty-four artillerymen, Staunton defended the village until nightfall against the attacks of the Peshwa's army of 25,000 horsemen with about 6,000 infantry (January 1, 1818). The next day Baji Rao's troops refused to fight, and marched away. They were defeated again at Ashti, and the Peshwa became a fugitive.

5. The English had resolved that he should be the last of his line. The appointment of another Peshwa would only have been an encouragement to the revival of old intrigues and old pretensions: and a change of title would scarcely have extinguished in the Mahrattas the feeling that their allegiance was due to the chief who sat on the Peshwa's throne at Poona. The danger could be avoided only by having no Peshwa. In June of the following year, 1818, Baji Rao was caught in the toils of his pursuers. He might reasonably have looked for condign punishment; but he was sent to live near Cawnpore on a pension of 80,000*l.* a year. Indore was made a subsidiary state, and the British resident was the virtual ruler during the minority of Mulhar Rao Holkar.

6. The great task of Lord Hastings was thus successfully accomplished. From that day to this there has been no deliberate combination of native states against the British power. The great rising of 1857 was strictly a military mutiny, which assumed a form seriously affecting the whole country, only because it received the sanction of the Great Mogul. It is at the least likely that if the phantom prince at Delhi had shared the fate of the Peshwa in the days of Lord Hastings, that great convulsion might never have occurred, or would have done no mischief except to the rebellious soldiers.

7. But while Lord Hastings was thus compelled to extend the limits of English territory and dominion, he stood almost alone in his conviction that the real interests of the English government lay in the general well-being of the Indian people, and

more particularly in their education. He set up schools which were thronged by native children, established a society for making known to native scholars the literature and science of England and of Europe, and allowed the missionaries of Serampore to issue a newspaper which formed the foundation of the present native press. His wars against the Nepalese, the Mahrattas, and the Pindharries had been costly; but his budget nevertheless showed a surplus of two millions sterling annually, and there was always an ample reserve in his treasury. In the character and habits of the government officers, both civil and military, there was a vast change for the better. The old days of lawlessness and licence had passed away.

8. The difficulties of Lord Hastings arose not so much from Mahrattas and Pindharries as from the affairs of the Nizam, who left everything to his minister, who in his turn left everything to his deputy, Chunder Lal. Chunder was a Hindu, who thought that it was his wisdom to walk in the ways of Mahommed Rheza Khan (p. 131) in the days of Warren Hastings. He had contracted a loan of 600,000*l.* from the banking house of William Palmer and Co., which had been established at Hyderabad in 1814. Two years later an Act of Parliament declared all pecuniary dealings by Europeans with native powers illegal; but this Act was suspended in favour of Palmer's house by an order in Council which only required that they should communicate the nature of their transactions when called upon to do so. Mr. Metcalfe, the resident at Hyderabad, declared that this

loan of sixty lakhs was not straightforward; that of the sum borrowed, 80,000*l.* went as a bonus to the partners of the banking house, the remainder being devoted to the paying off of loans granted to the Nizam without the knowledge of the British Government; and that thus the real debts of the Nizam remained just where they had been before. The sanction of the order in Council seemed to implicate the Governor-General in the matter; and it was resolved that the debts of the Nizam should be paid off, and his relations with the banking house brought to an end. This was accomplished by capitalising the annual rent of 70,000*l.* paid by the Company for the Northern Circars, at a sum which represented the purchase of twelve and a half years only. For the banking house the repayment of the loan was a heavy blow, as it knocked off the high rate of interest charged for it; but at the same time all their other dealings were declared illegal, their outstanding debts, their advances for timber and cotton, and other assets were forfeited, and the house necessarily became insolvent. To Chunder Lal, also, the repayment of the sixty lakhs was no benefit. It drove him to the local banks and to money lenders whose charge for interest was vastly more extortionate. The comments on these occurrences threw a cloud over the last year of Lord Hastings's sojourn in India, which he left on January 1, 1823.

CHAPTER XVIII.

Burmese War—Second Siege, and Capture, of Bhurtpore.

1. The evil habits of centuries are never got rid of at once: and in spite of the catastrophe which had overwhelmed the Pindharries and broken up the power of the Peshwa and the Nizam, of Sindia and of Holkar, there were still thousands, it may be hundreds of thousands, who would gladly have welcomed any reverse to the British arms which might hold out a prospect, if not of expelling the English altogether from India, yet of restoring the wild licence which had been put down by Lord Wellesley and Lord Hastings. Such a reverse it was hoped that the British arms would receive at the hands of the people of Burma.

2. The country known as Burma stretches along the eastern coast of the Bay of Bengal northwards from the river Pakshan, which serves as the Siamese frontier, until it touches Assam and Thibet. Through it the Irrawaddi flows from the Himalaya range in a southerly course until it empties itself into the sea through a vast delta stretching between Cape Negrais and Rangoon. The upper valley of this mighty river is known by the name Ava, the town as Pegu. It is a country of burning sunshine and an immense rainfall. The towns and villages are built chiefly on the banks of rivers, on piles; and each village has at least one Buddhist monastery, which owns no lands

and has no endowments. The monks are supported wholly by the gifts of the people, and these gifts are never lacking, for in the popular belief they will secure to the donor a higher life in the series of transmigrations which await the human soul after death. The people have been described as Indo-Chinese. They have the slanting eyes and the features of Mongolians. As disciples of Buddha they have no caste, and with the exception of the king and his family they have no nobility which is not strictly personal and official; and as all officials are removable at the will of the king, the people have no representation whatever. Seemingly they do not greatly feel the lack of it. They go through life with the placid contentment which is the natural fruit of the systems bearing the name of Buddha, and with some advantages which are beyond the reach of the Hindu and the Mahometan. With these the betrothal of children takes place almost in their infancy, and the future bride and bridegroom have little or no voice in the matter. Among the Burmese boys and girls grow up with a natural familiarity, and are left to the choice of their affections. Their festivals are scenes generally of much quiet gaiety, and their lives are spent in utter ignorance of the world beyond them.

3. In such a country we should scarcely look for cruel and desolating wars. Yet it has been overrun by tyrants, for whom the shedding of human blood is nothing more than the pouring out of water. The history of Burma, so far as it can be said to have any history, is a tale of sickening horrors. The narrative

of the siege of Martaban by the Burmese warrior, Byeen-noung, in the sixteenth century, with the catastrophe which followed it, can be surpassed in fearful colouring only by the doings of a Genghiz (p. 22) or an Attila. In the middle of the eighteenth century, the English in the factory of Negrais were massacred by Alompra the hunter, an adventurer, who shook off the yoke of the Talain kings, and made Rangoon his capital. Like him, his successors shed blood like water. But massacre provokes murder, and it is the common lot of Burmese kings to be slain themselves, and have their wives and children slaughtered with them. Hence the frequent movings of the capital from Amarapura to Ava, from Ava to Mandalay, and from Mandalay, it may be, back to Ava.

4. In the reign of Bhodau Phra, the third son of Alompra, some fugitives from Arakan, which he had conquered, escaped into British territory, and Sir John Shore gave them up on the request of the Burmese governor. Lord Wellesley was less complaisant. He refused to surrender political exiles who would only be tortured to death; but every effort was made to secure the friendship of the Burmese government, and to make a treaty with them. The offers were rejected with an air of immeasurable superiority; and the Burmese studied their dignity by claiming an island on the English side of the frontier, and threatening to invade Bengal if it should not be given up. The conquest of Assam and Munipore by the Burmese general, Bundula, in 1822, was followed by an irruption into

Bengal, in which the Burmese cut off a detachment of British sepoys. Lord Amherst, who had succeeded the Marquis of Hastings, declared war, sorely against his will, and an expedition was despatched by sea to Rangoon.

5. The sight of the ships disconcerted Bundula, who was preparing to obey orders by setting off for Bengal and bringing back the Governor-General in golden fetters. The British forces on their side were not less astonished at the miserable materials which the Burmese dignified with the name of an army. The contest could not be called a war. The throwing up of a stockade summed up the whole military skill and science of the Burmese; and when, in December 1824, Bundula threw up stockades round the whole ground in which the English troops were encamped, he fled on the first onset of the enemy, and solaced himself by sawing one of his officers asunder for disobeying orders. Bundula was killed by a shell fired at the town of Donabew, to which he had retreated, and the advance of the British from Prome on Ava filled the king and his court with terror. But a peace was concluded in 1826, by which the territories of Tenasserim, Arakan, and Assam were ceded to the English, and the king pledged himself to pay a million sterling for the expense of the war, one fourth part of it being laid down at once. The cost of the war was not much less than 13,000,000*l.*; but the provinces gained have been estimated as cheap at the price. The tea of Assam is equal, perhaps superior, to that of China; its cultivation is capable still of being vastly ex-

tended; and the city of Moulmein, on the Tenasserim coast, has a trade of nearly a million sterling yearly.

6. But the war had never been popular with the Bengal sepoys. They had nothing to dread from the enemy; but the march of General Morrison with 10,000 men from Chittagong was accompanied by a terrible mortality from the pestilential fever of Arakan. Three sepoy regiments became disaffected; one mutinied openly. All three were paraded and ordered to ground their arms. On their refusal the artillery opened fire, and eleven men were killed. The mutiny was thus suppressed, and the name of the forty-seventh regiment was struck out of the list of the army. It may be some excuse for the sepoys that they dreaded the sorcery of the Burmese far more than they feared their muskets. For not a few of the natives of India the thought of the power of Burmese magic carried with it a strange illusion. The charms of the Burmese witches would, it was supposed, be fatal to the grasping conquerors who had crossed the water to Rangoon, or led their troops along the fever-stricken jungle-track to Ava. An omen of final victory for the natives of the peninsula, of final ruin for the strangers from the far west, was still to be seen in the virgin fortress of Bhurtpore. Its mighty ramparts rose as proudly as in the days which had gone before the unsuccessful assaults of Lake, and, if any parts showed signs of weakness, these had been diligently strengthened. In the belief of the Jats who held it, it would bid

defiance to all attacks as safely as the eternal bastions of the Ghorkas in Nepal (p. 185).

7. This proud vaunt was now to be put to the test. Here, as it so often happened at the most critical times in so many states, there was a boy raja, who was set aside and imprisoned by his cousin, Doorjun Lal, who usurped his throne and set himself at the head of the troops. But the boy, at the request of his father, the raja who had concluded the peace of 1805, had been recognised by the British Government, and Sir David Ochterlony issued orders for the immediate attack of Bhurtpore. The order was countermanded by Lord Amherst, and the indignity broke the heart of the old general, who, with a handful of men, had defended Delhi against a host of sixty thousand horse and well-nigh two hundred guns.

8. But Lord Amherst's eyes were soon opened to the fact that Ochterlony was as right in policy as he was in his strategy. The order which withdrew the troops from Bhurtpore convinced the natives that the English were afraid to attack it. The whole country was in commotion. The Mahrattas of Sindia and Holkar, the chiefs of Bundelkund and Malwa, the scanty relics of the Pindharries, all indulged in bright hopes that the old days of free-booting and private war would soon return. Sir Charles Metcalfe, the resident at Hyderabad, assured the Governor-General that it was fully as much his duty as his interest to scatter a delusion which might light a dangerous flame throughout the whole peninsula. Twenty thousand men, with a hundred

pieces of artillery, advanced under Lord Combermere to the attack of the mud walls, on which Lake could make but a feeble impresssion. The balls now, as in the former siege, buried themselves harmlessly in their sun-baked slopes, and it was resolved to try the effect of mining. Ten thousand pounds of powder were exploded under the main bastion and counterscarp of the ditch, and in a few hours the fortress was in the hands of the English. Their loss was 1,000, as against 6,000 of the enemy, who died defending the last stronghold of Hindu independence.

9. Under the care of Mr. Jenkins (p. 191), the territories of Nagpore had made a wonderful advance in prosperity and wealth. But the young raja was now of age, and the government was placed in his hands. The wealth which he thus attained seemed to furnish a reason for folding the hands in sleep, and in a short time things were as they had been of old. The fact was one which must be taken into account in answering the question whether, and how far, the evils under which India has suffered, or is suffering, are the necessary result of English conquest.

CHAPTER XIX.

Administration of Lord William Bentinck, 1827–1835.

1. Lord William Bentinck had been recalled from Madras after the mutiny which some ascribed to unwise acts of interference with the religious prejudices and customs of the sepoys (p. 178). Twenty-two years later he returned to India as Governor-General, and his second administration proved not only that the orders issued in Madras could have been prompted by no feelings of indifference for the population which he had to rule, but that no one had their well-being, in the highest sense of the word, more deeply at heart. His sojourn in Bengal was a time of comparative tranquillity between the rapid march of English conquest under Lord Wellesley and Lord Hastings and the fierce struggles which agitated north-western India after his departure. He had to deal with native states; and he dealt with them on a principle which he can scarcely be said to have carried out with complete consistency, and which in the opinion of many was the cause of grave evil and mischief. He had to deal with the condition of the people in British territory; and he dealt with it in a spirit of justice, generosity, and mercy, which rose higher even than that of Akbar, for the simple reason that he was not hampered by the system against which Akbar was driven to rebel. The inscription on the pedestal of his statue at Calcutta, written by Macaulay, speaks of him as one 'who, placed at the head of a great empire, never laid aside the simplicity and moderation of a private citizen, who infused into Oriental despotism the spirit of British freedom; who never forgot that the end of government is the welfare of the governed; who abolished cruel rites; who effaced humiliating distinctions; who allowed liberty to the expression of public opinion; whose constant study it was to elevate the moral and intellectual character of the government committed to his charge.' Nor can it be said that this high tribute was undeserved, or that there is still no need for English rulers in India to keep steadily before their eyes the standard at which he aimed.

2. It was natural that the establishment of British sovereignty should carry with it for Indian princes a strong temptation to carelessness and inactivity. With many of them decent government, where decent government was found, sprang from the fear of rebellion on the part of their subjects. Now there was a power in the land which could put down such opposition, as it had already put a stop to the freebooting habits of their rulers. The succession of minors to a throne was one of the most fruitful sources of intrigue and violence. In most cases the British government found itself compelled to interfere when the evil became intolerable. Had it interfered at first the mischief might have been nipped in the bud. Thus in Gwalior Sindia's widow set her mind on retaining supreme power for life. The result was a civil war between those who fell in with her plans and the party of the raja her adopted son. The Governor-General visited Gwalior, but refused to interfere, although both parties professed their readiness to abide by his decision. The raja besieged the queen in the palace; the queen escaped and advanced at the head of another body of troops. A battle was prevented by the personal interference of the resident, who obtained from Lord William Bentinck the recognition of the raja. The step which might have been taken at first was taken in the end. In Bhopal a like quarrel ended in bloodshed and anarchy; but the Governor-General held his peace, and order was restored by his successor, Sir Charles Metcalfe. In Jeypoor one of the two rivals for the office of minister laid a plot for the assassination of the British resident. The fact of this rivalry was well known; but nothing was done to repress it, and the unsuccessful competitor attacked the resident and his assistant in the street. The former was seriously wounded, the latter murdered. The Governor-General now interfered to inflict punishment, and the country soon became both peaceful and prosperous. Even in Oude he contented himself with warning the king that if the horrors of his misrule were suffered to go on unchecked, the British government would take the management of his dominions on itself.

3. In this unfortunate country the miseries which are the natural fruit of Eastern despotism were increasing in appalling measure, and the English were responsible for maintaining in his seat a profligate wretch who thought of nothing but his own vicious pleasures. By the instructions received from England the Governor-General was authorised, if he thought fit, to place Oude on the same footing with the Carnatic. Had he acted on these instructions, this harassed and exhausted land might soon have been made a flourishing and wealthy territory. The same results might have been obtained with equal ease in Mysore. Here Tippu's minister, Purnea (p. 165), failed in his efforts to make his position as minister

the foundation of an hereditary power like that of the Peshwa. The young raja was placed at the head of affairs, and it was his pleasure to live the life of Suraj-u-Daula (p. 101). Purnea had left in the treasury no less a sum than seven millions sterling. Within three years the resident reported that this vast sum had been squandered by the most disgraceful means. In a few years more the state was overwhelmed with debt; the army was unpaid; the land was let to the highest bidders, who ground the cultivators to powder, while the raja went on with his horrible debaucheries. At last in 1830 the people broke out into rebellion, and the English Government was compelled to interfere. The resident became a Commissioner, and Mysore was reduced virtually to the condition of a British province. The people breathed freely, and the revenue was more than doubled.

4. Two annexations only are recorded during the whole of Lord William Bentinck's government. The one was that of the little raj or state of Cachar, now a rich tea-growing district, on the north-east frontier of Bengal; the other that of a small territory which Hyder Ali and Tippu had vainly sought to conquer. The mountaineers of Coorg, whose little state on the western Ghats lies between Mysore and Malabar, had been ruled from the sixteenth century by the dynasty of the Vira rajas. To the demand of Hyder Ali for tribute the Vira raja of the day returned a refusal; but Hyder succeeded only in taking two or three forts and giving to Mahometans the lands of some whom

he dispossessed and carried away. Greater efforts to subdue this hardy people were made by Tippu, who brought the raja to Mysore. After four years the Coorg prince escaped, and during the wars which ended in Tippu's ruin remained in alliance with the English. Time passed on. His wife died, leaving some daughters but no son; and the raja requested that one of these daughters might be recognised by the British government as his successor to the exclusion of his brothers. The recognition was given under the impression that the raja, who was independent, had made the request merely as a matter of form, and from the wish of showing his loyalty to the English. It turned out afterwards that he had done so only in order to get their sanction for a breach of the immemorial custom which gave a preference in the succession to brothers over daughters. But a change had come over the raja much like that which came over Nadir Shah after his departure from Delhi (p. 90). He murdered one of his brothers, and would have murdered the other, had he not resigned all claim to the throne and professed to become an ascetic. At length the raja died, and the ascetic, who had been taken to be a fool, showed that he had sufficient wit and a superfluity of cruelty. He seized the throne and worked his will on the people for more than ten years. Then followed the reign of his son, whose actions were those of a tiger; and, like a tiger, he took care to hide them from those who were able and might be willing to punish him. But his sister escaped with her husband, and told the awful story to the English, who warned him that his iniquities could not be allowed to go on. The raja bade them defiance as being an independent prince, insisted on the surrender of his sister and her husband, and, when this was refused, declared war. After overcoming severe resistance in the mountain passes, General Fraser occupied the capital, Merkara; the raja was sent to Benares; and the Governor-General desired that his subjects should choose a new ruler. The people declared unanimously that that ruler must be the British government, praying only that their raja might never be allowed to come back (1834).

5. The true glory of Lord William Bentinck rests on his internal administration. It was upright and it was fearless. He scorned the notion that reforms imperatively demanded on considerations of mere humanity were not to be made because they might offend certain classes of people; rather, he felt sure that in their moral sense he should have a power which would soon disarm all opposition. Whatever may have been the origin of the rite known as the Suttee, or Sati, it was beyond doubt maintained by the Brahmans on the authority of a text in the Rig Veda, which they gave forth in the following form:—

'Om! let these women, not to be widowed, good wives adorned with collyrium, holding clarified butter, consign themselves to the flames. Immortal, not childless, not husbandless, well adorned with gems, let them pass into the fire.'

6. It has been said that this is perhaps the most flagrant instance of what can be done by an

unscrupulous priesthood. Lord William Bentinck did not know that the verse was garbled, and that it was addressed not to the widow but to the other women who are present at the funeral, and who have to pour oil and butter on the pile. The text really runs thus: 'May those women who are not widows but have good husbands draw near with oil and butter. Those who are mothers may go up first to the altar, without tears, without sorrow, but decked with fine jewels.' And it is actually preceded immediately by one which orders the widow to leave the body of her husband. 'Rise, woman, come to the world of life; thou sleepest nigh unto him whose life is gone. Come to us. Thou hast thus fulfilled thy duties of a wife to the husband who once took thy hand.' But to Lord William Bentinck it mattered nothing whether the authority alleged for it was real or fictitious. The practice was an abomination and must be put down. In 1829 an Act was passed which declared all who were implicated in the ceremony to be chargeable with murder, the assistants being liable to prosecution as accessaries. It was an Act which would have called forth the enthusiastic approval of the great emperor who mounted his horse and rode off to prevent the commission of one of these horrid crimes (p. 46). For righteousness and humanity the names of Akbar and of Bentinck may well go together. As we might expect, the Brahmans threatened resistance; but the moral sense of the country was against them, and the rite was soon a thing of the past.

7. Lord William Bentinck's legislation could not

indeed fail to bring into clear light the duty of statesmen in reference to religion. The Court of Directors had been nervously afraid of offending Hindu or other prejudices, and shrank with horror from anything bearing the most distant likeness to persecution; but they forgot that in order to appear forbearing and tolerant a man need not speak or act as if he were ashamed of his own faith. Thus far troops had been paraded and offerings presented to idols at great festivals in the name of the Company. This useless and most pernicious bowing down in the house of Rimmon went on until it was abolished by Lord Auckland in 1840.

8. From the days of the first Mahometan invasions, perhaps from times far earlier, India had furnished a congenial home for plunderers and marauders. The robbers on a large scale founded kingdoms like those of the Mahrattas; those who failed to reach this high eminence grew up into hordes like those of the Pindharries. There were lower ranks still which were not so prominent, but whose powers for mischief were sometimes vast. What the Pindharrie was to the Mahratta, that the dacoit and the Thug were to the Pindharrie. Roving bands of dacoits might swell almost to the size of an army, and were always prowling about in the hope of filching from villagers and reaping a richer harvest from wealthy travellers. Over the whole length and breadth of the Indian peninsula the secret society of the Thugs had flourished from times immemorial. The Thug looked down on the dacoit as a freebooter would look down on a burglar; but

both dacoit and Thug plied their task as a religious calling.

9. Banded together under a name which signifies deceit, the Thugs devoted themselves with solemn ceremonies to the worship of the goddess Bhowaní, in whose eyes the most proficient murderer was the greatest saint. The traveller, as he rode on horseback, or was borne along in his palanquin, fell in with a calvacade which accosted him with courtesy, and whose agreeable companionship made him grateful for the chance which on unsafe roads had given him the benefit of their protection. For two, three, or four days they might journey on together, each day being enlivened by recreations and entertainments more cheerful and light-hearted than those of the days preceding. For the traveller and his servants, or escort, there seemed to be not a cloud in the sky; but the graves were ready dug to receive their bodies, and as they sat in gay merriment eating the noontide meal in the shade of the mango grove, or resting by the banks of the nullah or stream, the handkerchief of each Thug was round the neck of his victim, and in a few seconds the grave-diggers were covering their corpses with the earth. No class among the people was safe from their artful toils. The rich bunnea, or banker, fell in with a company of merchants as rich, seemingly, and as well versed in business as himself. The merchants were Thugs, and his bills of exchange were soon in the hands of his murderers, who with unbounded assurance would present them for payment at the bank on which they were drawn. The

soldier going home on furlough met other soldiers who were full of the memory of exploits, in some of which he may perhaps have himself had a share; but the military knowledge of his informants was got at secondhand, and their business was done when their fingers were griping his throat. On women they never laid hands, if they could help it; and the men of some few trades, such as carpenters, tailors, oilmen, were forbidden prey.

10. To the English the existence of this system was scarcely known before the year 1810; but the disappearance of large numbers of sepoys absent on furlough gradually roused both anxiety and suspicion; and possibly the consciousness that the eyes of the English were upon him may have supplied the motive to the leader of a band of Thugs, who on the evening of a day in 1829 saluted Major Sleeman, the deputy commissioner of the Saugor district, as he sat at his tent door. The man confessed his calling, and told him that the bodies of many murdered travellers lay in the grove in which his tent was then pitched. On the following day the bodies were found on the spots which he pointed out. The gang was taken, and a search was begun throughout the country which proved the wide extent of the league and the maintenance of a common system of signs and passwords from one end of India to the other. Lord William Bentinck at once organized a new department for its complete suppression, placing Major (afterwards Sir William) Sleeman at its head. Within six years more than three thousand Thugs were brought to justice; many turned approvers, and the system was brought to an end within the limits of British territory, although it is supposed still to linger on in some of the native states.

11. The Governor-General was as anxious to bring India nearer to England as the Court of Directors seemed eager to prevent it. It was his great wish to set up steam communication by way of the Red Sea; but the Directors vetoed the scheme on the score of its expense, and nothing more was done for twelve years. But steamers built at Calcutta and fitted with engines from England ascended the Ganges in 1830, and began a new era for river navigation in India.

12. Thus far India had been a sealed country except to the servants of the Company. But the Company's charter, extended in 1813 for twenty years, came to an end in 1833; and its renewal was obtained at the cost of some sacrifices. The Company was deprived of its monopoly of trade to China, and the Court of Directors became an administrative body, subject to the Board of Control in England. The prohibition which made it impossible for Englishmen generally to reside in India or to hold lands there was withdrawn; and it was now lawful for them to apply their capital and their enterprise to the development of its resources. A still more important change was the admission of natives of all castes and creeds (and this would, of course, include the native Christians) to the public service. Thus far it had been held that such admission must be fatal to English predominance in the country; but in spite of this notion native judges were appointed in 1831 with a primary jurisdiction in civil suits. The result of the experiment was found to be eminently satisfactory, although the regulation that Europeans as well as natives were to be subject to their jurisdiction was vehemently resented and reviled as the Black Act. At the same time the usage of Hindu law that no one abandoning the Hindu faith could inherit property was set aside. This usage had rested on the old Aryan idea which is seen in the legislation of ancient Greece and Rome as clearly as in that of Manu, and which regarded inheritance as depending on the discharge of the religious duty owed by the heir to his ancestors; and it was held that he could not discharge this duty unless he were the legitimate son and worshipped at the same hearth. A further reform of the greatest importance was the substitution of the vernacular dialects for the Persian in the law courts. The use of the Persian was a benefit to the Mahometans alone. But, while the use of the local dialects was permitted in judicial proceedings, the regulations which withheld from natives a knowledge of the language and literature of England were done away; and the school of the Scotch mission did much towards extending the benefit of this great change throughout the country. The last restrictions on the press of India were removed by Sir Charles Metcalfe during the brief interval between the departure of Lord William Bentinck and the arrival of his successor, Lord Auckland.

13. Another measure of the highest advantage was the land settlement of the north-western provinces, which was made in 1833. It is enough to say of it that it differed from Lord Cornwallis's settlement of Bengal in these special particulars, that all lands were surveyed and all fields defined according to their quality as tilled or as waste land, that the rights of all proprietors were registered, and that the lands were assessed at a rate which was to be maintained for thirty years.

14. Lastly, a medical college was established in Calcutta shortly before Lord William Bentinck left India. Thus far, apart from traditional theories, whether Hindu or Mahometan, there was no medical knowledge in the country. The anatomical study of the human frame was unknown. The physicians were no better than gatherers of simples, and, as in old English days, the barber was the surgeon. The college at once attracted a large number of students, and the whole range of European medical science was brought within the reach of the people of India.

15. When to all this it is added that successful measures were taken for reclaiming some of the aboriginal tribes (p. 11), who retained much of their ancient savagery, we shall see how impartially Lord William Bentinck's care was extended to every part of the country. The Kohls, who had been irritated into acts of rebellion by the operation of laws to which they had never been accustomed, were placed under a special commissioner with happy results. The Mairs became quiet cultivators of the soil, and the Khonds were made to give up their horrible human sacrifices to the great goddess of the earth.

CHAPTER XX.

The First Afghan War.

1. A magnificent spectacle was seen in 1831 at Roopur on the banks of the Sutlej. With a small escort Lord William Bentinck advanced to greet Runjeet Singh, who appeared at the head of a splendidly equipped force of 16,000 men. This chief, who had won for himself the name of the Lion of Lahore, had welded into a compact body the loose military confederacy of the Sikhs (p. 79). He was now in middle life, and the continuance of his marvellous energy was threatened only by his horrible vices. Of these, however, the world saw not much; and from the first stage of his career circumstances had made him a personage whose good will the British government thought it prudent to secure. In 1807, Runjeet was seeking to establish his supremacy over the Sikh chiefs of Sirhind, between the Sutlej and the Jumna; and these chiefs asked for the aid to which their compact with the English entitled them. But there was the fear that Napoleon might still attempt to carry out his gigantic schemes of Eastern conquest; and the dominions of Runjeet included the ground on which Alexander the Great had encamped his army, when he still hoped to find his way to the banks of the Ganges.

2. This difficult task of protecting the chiefs of Sirhind and of avoiding offence to Runjeet Singh was entrusted to Charles Metcalfe, by whose tact

Runjeet was led to withdraw his troops beyond the Sutlej. By the treaty of Amritsur this river became the boundary of British territory, and a small English force was stationed at Ludhiana. The compact may not have been altogether to the taste of Runjeet, but to the day of his death, a period of more than thirty years, he adhered to it with scrupulous fidelity; and only after his death was it known to how large an extent its maintenance had depended on himself alone. During these years he had succeeded in raising an army of 80,000 men, with 300 guns, under the discipline of two Frenchmen, Allard and Ventura, who joined him as military adventurers in 1822, and who in the work of training native soldiers proved to be officers more efficient and successful than the Frenchmen who had drilled the troops of Sindia, Holkar, and the Nizam.

3. The death of the great Afghan conqueror, Ahmed Shah Durani (p. 114), preceded the birth of Runjeet by six or seven years only. His grandson Zeman Shah thought it well to put a cloak over his own weakness by appointing the young Sikh leader viceroy of the Punjab; but the act converted Runjeet into a sovereign as really independent as the Nizams of the Mogul emperors or the Peshwas of the Mahratta kings. Henceforth the Afghans were kept more within the limits of the wild highlands which had been their ancient home. This region of rugged and savage mountains, enclosing some valleys of wonderful richness and fertility, contains four important cities, the westernmost being Herat, the easternmost Peshawur, Cabul to the north,

and Candahar to the south, with the celebrated fortress of Ghazni on the road between these two.

4. These cities, with their territories, have sometimes been united under a single head; more often they have been ruled by princes who spent their time in making war upon each other. The subjects of these chiefs have been described as hardy mountaineers, for whom freedom is of more value than life, and who have no favour to ask of other nations or powers but that of being left to themselves; or again as ruthless savages, delighting in the tortures and death of those who have been lured into their nets by falsehood and treachery. There may be truth in both these pictures; but their dealings amongst themselves must not be allowed to affect our judgment of the modes in which others with whom they had no quarrel, and to whom they had given no offence, have chosen to deal with them.

5. The two most prominent tribes among the Afghans are the Abdalis and the Ghilzais. The former are known also as Duranis, and thus Ahmed Shah is called indifferently the Abdali or the Durani. The Barukzais are, it is supposed, an offshoot of the Abdalis; but a common origin has not prevented the outbreak of feuds and wars amongst them. The story of the Mogul and the Mahratta is repeated here, as everywhere else in the East. On the assassination of Nadir Shah the Afghan Sirdars or chiefs resolved to throw off the Persian yoke and choose a Shah for themselves. After much strife and debate, Jemal Khan, a Barukzai dervish, brought about the election of Ahmed Shah Durani, and Ahmed Shah

chose the dervish as his hereditary minister. In a few decades of years the minister became the master, and the monarch the puppet of the minister. Ahmed's grandson was the Zeman Shah, who lost the Punjab by making Runjeet Singh its viceroy; and another grandson was Shah Shuja, who was appointed by his brother Zeman Shah governor of Peshawur.

6. To recount the feuds, fights, and massacres which kept the land in constant convulsion would be both wearisome and unprofitable. It may be enough to say that Mahmud, the son of Zeman Shah, was a mere instrument of his minister Futih Khan, the Barukzai, who had placed him on the throne, and that the course of events in the almost incomprehensible revolutions which were constantly taking place drove Shah Shuja into exile in 1809. Mahmud at length contrived to bring about the death of Futih Khan, whose brother, Dost Mahommed, advanced with an army from Cashmere to avenge him; and thus in Shah Shuja, the exile at Ludhiana, and in Dost Mahommed, the conqueror of Cabul, we have two of the most prominent personages in the terrible drama of our first Afghan war.

7. Dost Mahommed, elected Amir in 1826, found himself in a position which made the good-will of the English a matter of the first importance; and he was ready to enter into an alliance with them, if he could be assured, first, that they would not attempt to restore Shah Shuja to his throne, and secondly, that they would aid him in driving the troops of Runjeet Singh from Peshawur. In the issue the English refused this aid, and brought Shah Shuja

back to Cabul; and the issue was laden with disasters and woes of which, perhaps, we have not yet seen the end. In 1831, Alexander Burnes, the ablest of the Oriental linguists of his time, reached Cabul as the envoy of Lord Auckland. Dost Mahommed had found out that the English, who had been more than a match for all the princes of India, were terribly afraid of the shadow of the Russian Czar; and he resolved to make use of this fear to further his own purposes. He therefore put before Burnes wonderful pictures of subtle and widely spread Russian intrigues, in the hope that he should thus secure the English as his own permanent allies.

8. The fears of the English envoy were heightened when, towards the close of 1837, the Russian Captain Vicovich arrived at Cabul with a letter from the Russian ambassador at Teheran. To play off the two envoys against each other seemed the most obvious plan; and in proportion to the scant encouragement which Dost Mahommed received from the Englishman was the large encouragement which he gave to the Russian. His policy was followed by momentous results; but these results were precisely the opposite of those which he looked for or intended. In the long series of events which now follow we have to remember that the conduct of the English was determined by considerations of a very different kind from those which had generally shaped their policy in India. Thus far they had, rightly, dealt warily and boldly with problems arising out of the conditions of the several states and powers of India. Now they were about to enter upon undertakings which would strain their resources to the uttermost, in order to baffle supposed schemes which might possibly be carried out some generations hence by a power separated from India by waterless deserts and impracticable mountains. With this end in view Lord Auckland resolved on the restoration of Shah Shuja to the throne of Cabul. It was necessary to have an independent, orderly, and friendly Afghanistan as a barrier between India and Muscovite aggression; and the bringing back of the Ludhiana exile seemed to be the best mode of obtaining it.

9. At the same time, without declaring war against Persia, he sent an expedition from Bombay to Karrack, an island in the Persian gulf. The Persian king understood and heeded the warning which it was intended to convey, and pledged himself to make no attempts upon Herat. The Russian scheme for the invasion of India, if there were any scheme, was thus foiled, for without the aid of Persia it could not be carried out; and as it was impossible that Dost Mahomed should fail to see this, it would be no hard matter to settle all difficulties by mediating between him and Runjeet Singh, nor could it be doubted that this friendly intervention would be welcomed by both. But Lord Auckland's mind was made up, and on October 1, 1838, he published at Simla a manifesto which, from its consequences, is one of the most important state papers of the present century. It has been described as being as weak in argument as untrue in its assumptions. It has been pronounced unfair to Dost Mahommed and unjust to the Afghan people, on whom it forced

a sovereign long since expelled from his kingdom and unsuccessful in all his attempts to regain it. The object of the expedition has been characterised as not less delusive than it was dangerous and inexpedient. By all statesmen in India whose judgment should carry weight it was steadily disapproved; by Lord William Bentinck, by the Duke of Wellington, by Lord Wellesley and Mr. Elphinstone, it was emphatically condemned; and as the ages pass along, that condemnation will not lose its force in the eyes of all who regard the question in reference to the eternal distinction between right and wrong.

10. To the army which was to execute Lord Auckland's orders Runjeet Singh refused a passage through his territory. It was compelled, therefore, to go through Sinde to Quetta, where it was joined by the column from Bombay. A false step generally makes other false steps necessary; it was not otherwise in the present instance. Greatly against their will the Amirs of Sinde had accepted the treaty of 1832, which prohibited the passage of troops and stores along the line of the Indus. They were now told not merely that this prohibition must be removed in favour of the English, but that they must pay arrears of tribute. This tribute had not been demanded of them for thirty years, and for the tribute itself they had the formal acquittance of Shah Shuja, who had released them from the obligation for a sum of 30,000*l.* paid to him some five years before. They were also compelled to choose between complete political extinction and the signing of a subsidiary treaty binding them to pay 30,000*l.* annually for the maintenance of a contingent in their territory. By the same threat Sir Alexander Burnes wrested from them the fort of Bukkur on the left bank of the Indus. But if our military ascendency in the country was thus secured, we can scarcely resist the conclusion that the means employed have, in the words of Colonel Meadowes Taylor, 'left these transactions under a stigma which they will never recover.'

11. The difficulties of a British army will probably never begin with the actual invasion of Afghanistan. The whole difficulty lies in the task of permanent occupation. From Quetta to Candahar, and from Candahar to Ghazni, the capital of Mahmoud the idol-breaker (p. 20), the march was unopposed. The northern or Cabul gate of this great fortress was blown open by the explosion of 300 pounds of gunpowder; and the stronghold of the kings who conquered Hindustan was in the hands of the English. The approach of the invading army convinced Dost Mahommed that it would be well to make terms, and he offered to recognise Shah Shuja as king if he himself were permitted to retain the post of Amír or prime minister. The offer was refused, although the sequel proved that it would have been wise to close with it. Dost Mahommed fled, and Shah Shuja took possession of the throne after an exile of thirty years (1839).

12. At Calcutta and in England the prevalent feeling was that of satisfaction on achieved success. But the prospect was soon darkened. The Cabulese

began to complain that Shah Shuja was not an independent ruler, and to chafe under the restraints of British political and social order. The rise of prices caused ill-will and discontent among the poor; and the king himself was irritated by the relations of nominal superiority, but of real subjection, in which he stood to the English envoy. There were elements of disturbance and signs of danger everywhere. Kharrak Singh, a contemptible wretch, weak in mind and body, sat in the place of his father, the Lion of Lahore, while the state was administered by Nao Nihal Singh and Dhyán Singh of Jummoo. The effects of the change were soon evident. The passage of British troops and stores through the Punjab called forth expressions of strong resentment, and Afghan chiefs were consulted about schemes for the destruction of British power. A Russian expedition to Khiva was a cause of much deeper alarm, but no one cared to heed the lesson taught by its miserable failure. Dost Mahommed was labouring for the recovery of his lost dominion; but all anxiety on this score was removed by his voluntary surrender after the fight at Parwundarra to Sir Robert Sale. Little, however, seemed to be gained by the departure of the Amír to Calcutta. Shah Shuja, with strange blindness, had insisted on the surrender of the Bala Hissar to his own use. This fort and palace commanded the city, and here the British army had been posted; but the king wanted it for the reception of his harem, and the forces were sent to open cantonments some three miles distant from the city. More alarming than all was the cost of the occupation. The revenues of Cabul were far from answering to the glowing descriptions given of them by Shah Shuja in the days of his exile. It was necessary to cut down subsidies and allowances, and the economy naturally excited deeper discontent. The Court of Directors urged that the scheme should be given up altogether; the counter argument was that Shah Shuja could not be abandoned without dishonour, until his authority had been established. The Ghilzai chiefs affected by the financial reductions proposed an attack on the house of Sir Alexander Burnes.

13. Burnes was entreated by his native friends to seek safety elsewhere; but he could not be convinced of his danger until his dwelling was surrounded by a furious mob. For six hours Burnes and his attendants held out, and then the crowd, bursting in, soon finished their work of slaughter. The whole country was now in insurrection. Armed men were swarming into the city. The Afghan winter had set in with its full severity. The roads, blocked with snow, were watched by the orders of Akbar Khan, the son of Dost Mahommed, who had placed himself at the head of the people. Cold, hunger, and want of food were arguments for retreat which were daily becoming more imperious. A treaty must at once be signed for the safe departure of the English troops, with the king if he chose to accompany them, and for the return of Dost Mahommed and his family from Calcutta. Sir W. Macnaghten met Akbar Khan for this purpose; but at the same time he was negotiating with the

Barukzai chiefs for the continuance of the British troops in Cabul, and of Akbar Khan as Amír on a British subsidy of 40,000*l.* a year. The victim had fallen into the trap laid by the wily Afghan; and the contradictory treaties were exhibited as a comment on the good faith of Englishmen. For himself Macnaghten could only plead that he had done the best he could for the lives which were at stake. It was necessary to have another interview with Akbar Khan. The envoy thought of signing covenants; the Afghan was intent on securing his prisoner. Macnaghten's companions were seized; he himself struggled with his captor, and Akbar drew a pistol and shot him (1842).

14. At length, after more negotiations with the chiefs who had now raised their terms, the army set out on its fatal retreat on January 6, 1842. At starting it numbered more than 16,000. Of all these, Dr. Brydon, a medical officer, was the only one who reached Jellalabad to tell the story of the terrible catastrophe. The Khúrd Cabul defile should have been passed before their first halt, but the snow and the cold made this impossible. On the next day they were unable to advance more than four miles. On the third morning they had scarcely moved into the pass, in many places a few feet only in width, when from the heights on either side the Afghan muskets poured down a murderous fire on the crowded throng beneath. Within four days there remained not one-third of the number which had left Cabul. At Gandamak these poor survivors were again attacked. A few were taken prisoners: the rest were killed, except the solitary fugitive who told the tale at Jellalabad. The unspeakable horror of the woeful story becomes even blacker if it be true, as some good judges have thought, that had the troops remained in the Bala Hissar they might have undergone some privations, but could easily have been not merely safe but triumphant in the face of any local efforts to dislodge them.

15. The appalling tidings brought by Dr. Brydon failed to shake Sale's resolution to hold out in Jellalabad. He had taken possession of the place in the middle of November, when he had only two days' provisions left; he kept it, although he knew that the whole country was in arms against the English, and although demands for its surrender and for his return to British territory came not only from Akbar Khan but from Shah Shuja also. He could see before him nothing but signs of failure everywhere; but his spirit would not have been shaken had he known that the disaster of the Khurd Cabul pass had tempted the Emir or Amír of Bokhara to break the law of nations by slaying two English envoys sent to ask for his alliance and friendship. He had already thrown Captain Conolly and Colonel Stoddart into his dungeons; but when he learnt that things were going against the English at Cabul, he had them publicly beheaded in the market place.

16. But the direction of affairs at Calcutta had passed out of the hands of Lord Auckland into those of Lord Ellenborough, and Lord Ellenborough was resolved that no pains should be spared to repair the mischief of past crimes and blunders, so far as it might be possible to do so. General Pollock was sent to the rescue of Sale and his men at Jellalabad; and in spite of the virtual mutiny of some of the native regiments, who refused at first to enter the Khyber pass, he reached it in the middle of April, 1842, to learn that Akbar Khan had been foiled in a determined attempt to take the city. The garrison had sallied out, had routed his forces, seized his guns, baggage, and ammunition, and burnt his tents.

17. Before Akbar returned to Cabul, Shah Shuja had been shot as he was going from the Bala Hissar to the city, to take the command of the army which was to drive the English out of the land. He had been writing to Sale, assuring him that his loyalty to the British had undergone no changes; but the readiness which he professed to the Ghilzais to take the field availed not to save his life. The Afghan chief who enters into alliance with the English is, it would seem, a doomed man. The murder of the old king greatly smoothed the way for Akbar Khan, who occupied the Bala Hissar, and then, having paid his homage to the son of Shah Shuja, ruled in his name as the Nizam ruled in the name of the Great Mogul.

18. The minds of the English generals were set on the reconquest of Cabul. But Akbar thought that they would give up the idea if he offered to restore the hostages which he had taken before the invaders set out on their fatal march through the Khurd Cabul pass. To his surprise the offer was refused, and Akbar had no choice but to march out for the defence of the city. For a time it seemed as though the storm which he dreaded might be averted. Lord Ellenborough, who had said that the infliction of due punishment on those who break their word was the condition necessary for the evacuation of Afghanistan by the English, sent instructions soon afterwards for the direct withdrawal of the forces into India. It was natural that such an order should be in a high degree distasteful to officers like Sale, Nott, and Pollock; and their strong protests led to a modification which left the decision to their judgment, and therefore made them responsible for the result.

19. The English army encountered that of Akbar Khan at the pass which had witnessed the great catastrophe of the preceding winter. The tokens of that fearful massacre were still strewn about the ground, and the British forces, roused to fever heat by the sight, charged with an impetuosity which carried everything before them. The victory which scattered the army of Akbar Khan was won almost without loss on the English side. Two days later the British flag was again waving on the Bala Hissar. The only task now remaining was to rescue the hostages whom Akbar Khan had sent off to Bamian. Happily the officer in charge of them could not resist the seductions of an offer which guaranteed to him an immediate payment of 2,000*l.*, and a pension of 200*l.* a year; and the captives were soon brought back to Cabul.

20. If history be not a truthful record of facts, it is nothing; and if it would do its work, it must set down the good and the evil on every side. The slaughter of the retreating army in the Khurd Cabul pass was indeed infamous, even for Afghans; but it must be remembered that when the British force broke into the city, the requital was to the full as awful and merciless. The mangled body of Sir W. Macnaghten had been exposed to the public gaze on the walls of the Cabul Bazaar, one of the noblest stone buildings in all Central Asia. It was the act of savages. The British troops blew up the bazaar with gunpowder; but it may be questioned whether magnanimity would not have been better shown by leaving the building in its ancient grandeur. From Ghazni General Nott brought away the gates which the idol-breaking sultan (p. 20) is said to have taken from the temple of Somnath. It was, perhaps, a matter of indifference where the gates might be; but the interest of their recovery was somewhat lessened by the likelihood that the original gates had perished long ago, and that these were but imitations.

21. Unjust schemes seldom, perhaps, redound to the dignity of those who devise them; and assuredly nothing was added to English dignity when the Governor-General welcomed the troops returning from Cabul with a procession of painted elephants, and issued a proclamation declaring that the bringing back of the gates avenged the insult of 800 years. The gates had been taken away by a Mahometan conqueror; their restoration to an idol temple could not, therefore, be agreeable to Mahometans, and for the same reason the gates themselves would be impure in the sight of the Hindus. But the recovery of some Hindu bronze gates was not the errand on which the British armies crossed the Afghan frontier; and it may have seemed, to say the least, prudent to hide the real issue from the public gaze. Twenty thousand lives had been sacrificed on the English side, and fifteen million pounds sterling had been spent in the effort to secure a barrier against Russian aggressions, without gaining an inch of ground, and at the further cost of stirring up in the breasts of all Afghans a deadly hatred of the English. Before the war the solitary English traveller might have moved with perfect safety from one end of the land to the other; after its close he would have been slain with as little compunction as men feel when they kill noxious vermin. But time has a marvellous power in quieting the most hateful passions; and as the years passed by, another generation grew up which had not the same temptation to keep up a useless feud. Not many, perhaps, would then have supposed that the wounds were to be torn open afresh just when they were healed.

CHAPTER XXI.

The Sikh Wars.

1. The fears of Russian invasion had already led to some injustice towards the Amírs of Sinde, when the British troops were on their way from Bombay to

Cabul. The injustice then done led to more injustice when the designs on Afghanistan came to nothing. It could not be supposed that the Amírs would feel much gratification in a treaty which had been forced upon them; but they had done nothing contrary either to its letter or to its spirit. Their patience was now still further taxed by a demand for the surrender of a certain amount of territory in place of the annual payment for a subsidiary force; and by a strange carelessness the amount of territory named in the new treaty was far larger than what was needed to raise the necessary revenue. They were charged with writing treasonable letters, and it was discovered that the letters produced by Major Outram were forgeries. They were prohibited from coining money, and enjoined to find wood from their plantations for steamers plying on the Indus. In most eastern societies there is a traitor. The traitor among these Amírs was Ali Murad, and this man extorted from the chief Amír, who was known as the Turban, lands to the value of 60,000*l.* yearly; and this was done under the authority of the name of Sir Charles Napier.

2. The whole revenue of the Amírs' territory was twenty lakhs of rupees; only six were now left to them. The Amírs complained; but the only answer vouchsafed to their protests was the capture and destruction of the fort of Enamgurh by Sir Charles Napier without a declaration of war. The execution of the new treaty was still insisted on, and the Amírs signed it; but the Beluchee chiefs, holding that their rulers had been dishonoured and disgraced,

were irritated beyond endurance. This quarrel was decided, February 17, 1843, on the field of Meeanee, where the proportion of killed and wounded on the two sides was much as it had been whenever, from the days of Clive downwards, Asiatics encountered Europeans. The Amírs were now made poorer still. Their capital, Hydrabad, was taken; their treasures yielded prize-money to the amount of 70,000*l.*; but Outram refused to receive his share of 3,000*l.*, and relieved his conscience by declaring that the whole business was without excuse.

3. In truth here, as in Cabul, the British Government was not merely acting in a way unworthy of itself, but it was spending millions in a vain chase after thousands. Sinde was conquered, but it was not worth a tithe of the money spent on its conquest, and the dearly bought acquisition led in no very indirect way to the great mutiny of 1857. Among the sepoys both of Madras and Bengal, service in Sinde and service in Aghanistan were almost equally unpopular; and it was clear from their disposition and their language that they could not be trusted with the task of guarding the new territory. This task was therefore handed over to troops from Bombay. But the fire was not put out; it was only smothered.

4. The course of events seemed to show a widely extended antagonism between Europeans and Asiatics. The two races were oil and vinegar poured into one vessel. They might push the one against the other, but they would not combine. The death of Jankoji Rao Sindia without a male heir led to the

usual course of intrigue and rivalry. The queen-mother dismissed the minister recognised by the British Government, and in the present condition of things it was thought highly dangerous that such a slight, or rather such an insult, should pass unnoticed. The prospect in the Punjab was not encouraging, and there were reasons for suspecting that the Sikhs were plotting with the men of Gwalior. The conspiracy was effectually suppressed by the British victories of Maharajpur and Punniar. The Sikhs could have no further hope of help from Gwalior. The queen-mother was deprived of her regency. The splendid army which had been disciplined by De Boigne was reduced to 9,000 men, and, as in the dominion of the Nizam, a contingent force of 10,000 men was placed in the charge of officers from the British army, a certain portion of territory being set aside for their maintenance.

5. The settlement of the Gwalior Mahrattas came in good time. Had it been delayed, there might have been a very different issue for the struggle between the English and the strange military society set up by Guru Govind (p. 80). Sooner or later this conflict must come. The army of the Khalsa had grown into a power which overshadowed such civil power as could be said to exist in the Punjab; and as the rulers cared little for anything so long as they preserved their own powers, the result was virtual anarchy as soon as the strong hand of Runjeet Singh was withdrawn. The narrative of events after his death brings before us a series of plots, counterplots, murders, and revolutions, which are peculiarly base

and disgusting. His first successor, Kharrak Singh, died a few months after Runjeet; and Kharrak's son was killed by the fall of an arch as he came back from his father's funeral. Then came Shere Singh, another son, or supposed son, of Runjeet, who found the army so heavy in numbers that he besought English aid in the task of keeping it down. His request was refused. Shere Singh was shot on the parade-ground of Lahore, and the army, having executed his murderer, placed Dhuleep Singh, another son of Runjeet, on the throne. But Dhuleep was a child, and Heera Singh acted as regent. More murders followed, and more revolutions, and the army became from day to day a heavier incubus. Means were lacking for paying them; and it was impossible to provide them always with refractory governors, like Mulraj of Múltan, from whom they could extort huge sums as fines.

6. One desperate venture alone remained. The whole strength of the holy brotherhood of the Sikhs might be thrown upon the English. If the Sikhs were victorious, there would be nothing to prevent them from founding an empire more splendid even than that of the great Mogul; if they were defeated, still more if they were crushed, the dastardly representatives of Runjeet would be rid of their masters and left to the peaceable practice of iniquity. Such was the policy of the mother of Dhuleep Singh, and her colleagues, Lall Singh and Tej Singh; but their motives were too clearly seen by the army, and the Sikhs at first refused to stir. But the remonstrances of Sir Henry Hardinge, now Governor-General in

place of Lord Ellenborough, furnished them with the means for stirring up their military pride, and by the middle of December, 1843, the Sikh army, 100,000 strong, with 200 guns, had crossed the Sutlej, and was encamped at Ferozepur. The Sikhs were at war with the English; and nowhere in India had the English encountered such enemies as they were now to encounter in these hardy warriors. But they could face them with a clear conscience. The strife was none of their making, and it was forced upon them by a people whose peculiar organization made it impossible for them to remain at peace, unless a stronger power compelled them to do so.

7. It was manifest that the Sikhs must be rulers in India or subjects; but two wars were needed to decide the controversy, and each war was marked by terrific battles, in which they showed wonderful discipline, skill, and bravery. The discipline and the skill they owed in no small degree to European officers, like Allard and Ventura, Court and Avitable; their bravery had been fostered into fearlessness by the institutions of Guru Govind. The records of these two campaigns are, down to their minutest details, full of interest and instruction for the students of military history; but we can do little more here than name the great conflicts which convinced the Sikhs that it would be no disgrace to them to obey an English master.

8. The battle of Moodkee, the first of these great struggles, was fought by the British army immediately after a march in which they had moved 150 miles in six days; and in it fell Sir Robert Sale, the

defender of Jellalabad (p. 226). From Moodkee Sir Henry Hardinge advanced to attack the Sikh intrenchments at Ferozeshahar. The arrangements for the assault might have been more judicious, and it was scarcely prudent to make it at a late hour in the afternoon of the shortest day in the year. Night had come before the camp could be carried; and it was remembered by those who had to go through it as the 'night of horrors.' For many hours they had had neither food nor water; and there was a hard frost. Early in the morning the battle began again, and the forces of Lall Singh had been defeated, when Tej Singh came upon the ground with another splendid army of horse and foot and seventy guns. The moment was critical; but the charge of Tej Singh's soldiers was suddenly arrested, and they drew back as quickly as they came. It was said that the leader had received an English bribe, but the story has never been proved; it is more likely that he saw that he had come too late to save his superior, Lall Singh, and that he felt bound to follow him. The combination of the two forces earlier in the day might have made things go very hard with the English. The next position of the Sikhs at Aliwal threatened the British outpost of Ludhiana; and here again after a fierce struggle they were defeated, multitudes being lost in the Sutlej as they hurried across the river on their bridge of boats.

9. But even after these three great blows the Sikhs were not subdued, and Gholab Singh, who had succeeded Lall Singh as minister, confessed himself helpless in their hands. Under the direction of a

Spaniard named Huerba some singularly powerful defences had been raised to cover a bridge of boats thrown across the Sutlej river at the village of Sobraon. From day to day the British army had to look on the progress of the work, while they were compelled to await the arrival of heavy guns and ammunition from Delhi. As soon as these were received, the preparations for the fight were made under cover of a fog. The battle began at seven o'clock, when the mists suddenly parted off; by eleven not a Sikh soldier, unless wounded or dead, remained on the south bank of the river. The fight had been fierce and the carnage fearful; and the horrors of the flight were made tenfold greater by the purposed or accidental breaking of the bridge by Tej Singh.

10. The road to Lahore now lay open to the conqueror; and the Governor-General, advancing to the capital of Runjeet, announced that a new treaty was being prepared which should secure the British from a repetition of outrages such as those which had provoked this war. The army was to be reduced to 20,000 foot and 12,000 horse; a fine was to be paid of 1,500,000*l.*, and the Sikh territory to the west of the Sutlej with the Jullunder Doab (p. 159) was to form part of the British dominions. The fine was raised partly by the sale of Cashmere to Gholab Singh, who had been the governor and who now became an independent prince. The sale seemed to be a necessity of the time; but it fastened on Cashmere a yoke which has bowed the necks of the people under a crushing weight. Two hundred and fifty magnificent guns were carried away to Calcutta to convince the incredulous that the victories over the redoubtable Sikhs were not a fiction.

11. It had been arranged that a body of British troops should remain for one year only at Lahore, while the new government was taking shape; but the new shape gave no promise of improvement on the old, and as the year drew to its close, the Sikh chiefs besought the Governor-General not to leave them to themselves, and confessed their inability to control their soldiers. Nor could the Governor-General deny that the only alternative for anarchy was British prevention. The new covenant therefore placed the council of regency under the direction of the British resident, and fixed twenty-two lakhs of rupees, 220,000*l.*, as the yearly allowance for the maintenance of the British troops. When Lord Hardinge left India in 1848, he regarded the arrangement as in all likelihood a permanent one; nor did his successor, Lord Dalhousie, imagine on his landing that a second Sikh war was almost an immediate certainty.

12. The storm broke first in Multan, where with wanton and causeless perfidy Mulraj murdered two Englishmen who had been sent to take charge of the provinces, the government of which he had resigned. His resignation was a sham, a mere pretext for avoiding the payment of any portion of the fine imposed upon him (p. 234). To punish this great crime, Lieutenant Herbert Edwardes advanced with such forces as he could gather, and defeated Mulraj in the open field. With his army greatly increased he appeared before Multan. General Whish soon arrived with large reinforcements, and with 32,000 Sikhs under the command of Shere Singh. But the task before them was scarcely less formidable than that of Lake at Bhurtpore; and the desertion of Shere Singh, who openly joined the enemy, made it necessary to interrupt the siege. It was resumed when fresh troops came up from Bombay, and on the 29th of January, 1849, Mulraj surrendered the fortress without conditions. He spent the rest of his life in imprisonment.

13. The Sikhs had been again seized with the spirit of the Jehad or holy war (p. 234). The Ranee at Lahore talked of a confederacy which should drive the English into the sea; and her intrigues in various courts were carried on with untiring zeal. Not a few of the chiefs were ready to break faith with the English; but the only one thus far in open revolt was Chutter Singh, the father of Shere Singh, and under his standard the soldiers of the old army hastened to take their places. It is hard to find any excuse for this wholly unprovoked defection; and it was not wonderful that Lord Dalhousie should with some vehemence declare that the Sikh people had called for war, and that they should have it with a vengeance.

14. The first action took place at Ramnugger on the south or right bank of the Chenab, November 1848. It was indecisive, and Lord Gough was scarcely warranted in claiming it as a victory, and certainly mistaken in saying that it had broken up the Sikh army. Shere Singh had crossed the river.

and taken up a far stronger position at Chillianwalla on the southern bank of the Jhelum, about thirty miles nearly due north of Ramnugger. In the awful battle which followed, January 1849, both armies assuredly encountered foemen worthy of their steel; and here, too, nothing more could be said than that the Sikhs were not the winning side. Night closed in before the wounded could be carried off the field. Under cover of darkness the Sikhs returned and murdered all whom they found alive; and in this fierce savagery lay their doom as an independent nation.

15. The battle which left the Sikhs hopeless of success was fought on the 27th of February, 1849, at Gujerat, a place which marks the apex of a triangle of which the line between Ramnugger and Chillianwalla is the base. In the previous fights Lord Gough had made so small use of his artillery as to excite the surprise of the enemy. At Gujerat, following with some reluctance the counsels of most of his brother officers, he placed eighty-four guns in the centre of his line. In less than three hours the enemy's guns were almost silenced, and the strength of the Sikh army was irretrievably broken. In this fight less than 100 were killed on the British side, and less than 700 wounded; at Chillianwalla the loss had been upwards of 2,400, including 89 officers killed and wounded.

16. At Manikyala, on the 12th of March, Shere Singh surrendered himself with the fragment which remained to him of his once magnificent army. They had fought with astonishing bravery for that which to them may have been freedom or independence, but which really meant the right of conquering, slaying, and plundering others. But although they had done savage deeds, they were not savages; and from the day when they laid down their arms at the feet of General Gilbert, their good faith to the English has never failed. Had it been seriously shaken during the time of the great sepoy mutiny, the result might not impossibly have been the extinction of British power in India.

17. The conduct of the Sikhs had settled the fate of their country. They had provoked, and most wantonly provoked, two wars in which blood had been shed like water, and money thrown away like dust. The penalty was paid in the annexation of the whole Punjab, and the penalty has long since proved to be a blessing. Runjeet Singh, for instance, had extorted from his subjects one half of the produce of the soil; the exaction was now reduced to one fourth, and payment in money instead of in kind was rewarded with a further reduction of ten per cent. Runjeet's custom-houses faced the people at almost every turn; they were now all swept away. The country was cleared of robbers, and intersected with roads; slavery was abolished, and other causes of misery and suffering removed, which but for the white-faced strangers might have retained all their powers of mischief unimpaired for centuries.

18. The British power now embraced the whole peninsula of India, from the Indus to the Himalaya, and from the Himalaya to the ocean; and this mighty work, barely attempted by Alexander, and scarcely half achieved by the Great Mogul, had been done by the servants of a Company of Merchants in less than a hundred years. With the completion of the century it was to undergo an ordeal, which was to tax its strength to the uttermost.

CHAPTER XXII.

The Policy of Annexation.

1. The dealings of Lord Dalhousie with the native states have furnished matter for controversies which can scarcely be said even at the present time to have died away altogether. The equity or the injustice of his acts can be measured only by examining impartially the circumstances which called them forth; it cannot be measured by the offhand application of principles which even in England have sometimes to be taken with limitations. These questions arose from disputed successions, from the exercise of the right of adoption, and more particularly from the excesses of a tyranny not more tolerable because in some cases it may have sprung from ignorance or recklessness.

2. At the close of the Mahratta war of 1819 the powerless representative of Sivaji was placed by British compassion on a throne at Satara. In a few years it became clear that the Mahrattas troubled themselves very little about the do-nothing prince, in whose veins the blood of Sivaji was flowing; it

was likely that they would care not at all for a boy, which this prince might adopt from another family to keep up an empty name. The state, moreover, was an English creation, and it was argued that the Raja had no right to adopt without the consent of the paramount power. In this case the necessary consent had not been obtained, and the territory had therefore lapsed to the giver. To such territories Lord Dalhousie held that the government was bound to extend the benefits of English sovereignty, present and prospective.

3. Questions of a more serious nature were connected with the abode of the Great Mogul at Delhi. The successor of Baber and Akbar was still in theory the sovereign of Hindostan; the Nizam was still his viceroy, and the Nuwabs his viceroy's deputies; and among these Nuwabs was the East India Company. The theory, it is true, was but an empty shell; but so long as the shell remained, the hope that it might some day be filled again was cherished with stubborn pertinacity. The wretched intrigues of the palace were sometimes extended to distant lands, and the emissaries of a Ranee from Delhi might be found stirring up the Persian Shah to undertake or to join in the destruction of the English. The dreams of the palace became in like manner the excitement of the faithful who dwelt in the crowded alleys of the imperial city. The mob of Delhi had not lost the restlessness and violence which brought about the great catastrophe with the soldiers of Nadir Shah (p. 89). It would be well, therefore, if the imperial pageant could be placed elsewhere, and it

was arranged that on the death of the aged emperor, Bahadur-Shah, his successor should surrender his ancestral home at Delhi and spend his days in the palace named after the emperor Kootub (p. 21). But there were two or three claimants; and the heir with whom the covenant was made might disappear before the infirm old king should pass away. That the pageant would come to an end long before the death of this poor old man was known to none.

4. In the territories of the Nizam things were going from bad to worse. Chunder Lall had obtained loans at a high interest from the house of Palmer and Co. (p. 193). When that house was ruined, he obtained loans at a far higher interest from native bankers, and squeezed the wretched tillers of the soil in order to provide that interest. Talookdars indulged in the luxury of private war; thieves and bandits plied their craft on the roads and byways. Law and justice had disappeared; there was no police; and the state was loaded with debt, most of which was owed to the British Government. In 1853 Chunder Lall resigned, and for a time the Nizam pretended to carry on the administration with the help and advice of Suraj-ul-Mulk, the grandson of Mir Alam, a former minister. But Suraj was too tightly hampered to be able to do anything. He was put away, and the farce was carried on in other names, until the Governor-General demanded a cession of territory as an equivalent for the payment of debts and for the maintenance of the contingent force. The Nizam was sorely perplexed. He could not bear the thought of parting withthe contingent,

which protected him from his mercenaries, and he had no means for maintaining them or paying his debt. Cession of territory was the only other course open to him. A new treaty, accordingly, assigned three districts, Berar being one, for the support of the contingent. This treaty was modified seven years later, 1860, not long before the death of Suraj-ul-Mulk, whose son, Sir Salar Jung, the appointed minister, had won for himself a high place in the ranks of European and Asiatic statesmen.

5. The year 1853 witnessed the extinction of two great historic names in the history of India,—the Nuwab of the Carnatic, and the Peshwa. The former died childless, and his uncle claimed the throne; but the Governor of Madras opposed the succession as not within the terms of the treaty, and the claim was disallowed, although provision was made for the family of the prince whose title had passed away.

6. The case of Baji Rao, the last of the Peshwas, was perhaps the clearest of all which were submitted to the consideration of the British Government. The ex-Peshwa had been sent to Bithoor with a life pension of 80,000*l.* a year. He, too, died childless, having adopted an heir, Dhondu Punt, notorious and infamous subsequently as Nana Sahib, who inherited his personal property. Baji was a man of miserly habits; his private hoards were acknowledged to exceed a quarter of a million sterling; they amounted really to half a million. This vast wealth descended to Dhondu Punt, who also received for his life the town and territory of Bithoor. This, however, was nothing, unless Baji's pension were continued to him

also. He besieged the Indian government with complaints as one of the most injured of mankind; he sent an agent to London to obtain redress of his grievous wrongs. In each instance the result was the same. He had no case; but the rebuff, which he thoroughly deserved, led to serious consequences.

7. About the same time with Baji Rao died the Raja of Jhansi. The succession was claimed for his adopted son, a child of five years old; but the claim was disallowed, and the state was forfeited. Here the case was somewhat complicated. The claim was grounded on the alleged fact that Jhansi had been an independent state long before the coming of the English. The counter-argument denied the fact of its independence, and declared that it was strictly a dependency of the Peshwa, and that the forfeiture of the territories of the latter carried with it the lapse of the former, whenever the government chose to assert their right. But even if this view be taken (and it can scarcely be rejected), it was a blunder to sell the private property of the raja, in spite of the fact that the proceeds were funded for the benefit of his family. The property realised less than half the sum expected; and the interference excited a bitter feeling which brought about fatal results in the days of the mutiny.

8. The name of Rughoji, the Bhonsla Raja of Berar or Nagpore, must be added to the catalogue of princes who died childless in 1853. Nagpore, unlike Jhansi, was an important state with a population of not much less than six millions. Rughoji

died without having adopted anyone; and the court determined that no one else should exercise the right for him. No choice, therefore, was allowed to his widow, who in this case could have brought forward only kinsmen on the female side. In law the decision held good; but it created anxiety and alarm amongst the native princes generally.

9. Tired out with the monstrous abuses which rendered all idea of government a mockery in Oude, the Court of Directors resolved on the annexation of that kingdom, and Lord Dalhousie remained in India until this task should be done. The wretchedness of this country, which under any decent management would have been one of the richest in the whole peninsula, can scarcely be described; nor is much gained perhaps by heaping up particulars of the great total of oppression, extortion, and ruin on the side of the people, and of foul vice and determined selfishness on the part of the ruler. The truth of the horrid picture is allowed by every one; but it is still urged that in times past the princes of Oude had been the friends and benefactors of the English, and that the extinction of the dynasty came with an ill grace from those who but for the Oude princes might have failed to reach their present pre-eminence in India. The theory of gratitude is surely somewhat strained when it is argued that a wicked man should be allowed to inflict misery on all around him, because his ancestors had been decent men with a fair character in the eyes of their fellows. The Government failed to see the force of this plea, and the country was therefore annexed, the mistake made

at Nagpore of selling the private property of the prince being repeated. The king was sent to Calcutta, to live upon an allowance of 120,000*l.* a year (1856).

10. In March 1856, Lord Dalhousie returned to England. He was still only forty-four years of age, and he lived but four years longer. His toil had worn out a body physically not strong; and none can doubt that his toil from first to last was honestly given for the bettering of all classes and ranks in India. Beyond all question, the rule of the native princes was at that time at least miserably bad. The corrupt means by which power was acquired could be matched only by the extortion and tyranny with which it was abused. Lord Dalhousie felt very strongly that the British Government could not shake off all responsibility for the continuance of this terrible misgovernment or rather anarchy; and feeling this, he went on to the natural conclusion that the extension of British power was the greatest boon that could be conferred on the people of India.

11. It was no difficult task to represent the policy which sprung out of these convictions as one of systematic annexation; nor can we say that the picture so drawn was altogether a fiction. Lord Dalhousie saw that in many of the states the people might be vastly richer than they were, if placed under a system which would yield to the state thrice the revenue now drawn from them; and it might be urged that he had before him but the one object of using India as a field for reaping golden harvests,

In a certain sense the charge would be true; but in that sense Lord Dalhousie might face it without fear and with the approval of the vast mass of his countrymen. He left India with the full assurance that, in spite of some disturbing causes, a steady growth in all the essential conditions of civil prosperity might fairly be looked for.

12. His successor, Lord Canning, on taking office, saw no reason for questioning the grounds of this assurance. But both these statesmen were mistaken; and in the case of Lord Canning a heavy responsibility rests on those who saw the clouds gathering on the political horizon, and yet hesitated to point out to him the signs of a coming storm. The new Governor-General was, we are told, a cold and impassive man, little likely to suspect that an outward calm merely veiled a slumbering fire, and little likely to give credit to those who might bring before him the true state of the case. The people of India, we are also told, were carried away at this time by an excitement not very far removed from the borders of madness, and were eager to swallow down the most absurd reports and to accept the most monstrous falsehoods as indisputable truths. But the most ridiculous fancies, if they are turning the heads of a whole nation and driving them on into sedition and treason, become matters of the gravest moment; and if the Indian people were in truth carried away with the idea that the British intended to make them sooner or later walk on their heads, and were becoming stubborn and rebellious in consequence of this idea, the absurdity of the delusion could furnish not the slightest excuse for disregarding it. The great calamity was close at hand. That its approach should have been so dimly foreseen, and that so little should have been done to guard against or to prevent it, is one of the most astonishing features in the history of British India.

CHAPTER XXIII.

The Great Mutiny, 1857–58.

1. The rebellion which broke out the year after the arrival of Lord Canning has received its name from its military character. It is called a mutiny, because soldiers in the pay of the British Government were throughout the chief actors in it. But the disaffection which led to it was not confined to sepoys only. The changes introduced by Lord Wellesley, Lord Hastings, and Lord William Bentinck, had in most instances improved the condition of the people; those of Lord Dalhousie might possibly bring with them even greater benefits. But the sowing of the seed is not the same thing as the reaping of a crop; and for the natives of India the results of these changes were still in the future.

2. It was not, however, pretended that every act of the British Government was for their benefit only. The English found themselves charged with a gigantic task, which even in quiet times sufficiently taxed their powers; and in this work it was abso-

lutely necessary to avail themselves of all the resources which an advancing civilisation might place in their hands. These resources have during the present century been so multiplied as to astonish even the nations amongst whom they have been produced. To the natives of India this strange exhibition of new powers was simply bewildering. For centuries the Hindu had served a Mogul or a Mahometan master; but they had seen nothing in their sovereigns who ruled at Delhi but men who had vast armies and could use them at their will. Now they had to look on a very different sight. No human eye had before seen ships move without oars or sails and without heeding wind or current, or beheld the fire chariot speeding on its iron pathway. To minds full of superstitious fears it seemed that the English were a mysterious people endowed with unlimited resources which they kept hidden until the fit time for using them, and which were then applied to the conquest of Hindustan. What other purpose could there be for the poles and wires set up along the roads, which in some incomprehensible way revealed instantaneously to their rulers what was happening at a distance of hundreds of miles? These were all devices for fastening on the nations of India a yoke which they could never hope to shake off—a yoke which would compel them to yield up their ancient customs, their caste, and their religion. To this end everything seemed to be working. In the Government schools, it is true, nothing was said which directly assailed the hereditary faith of the pupils; but they were filled with a learning which their parents could not understand, and which left them with impressions at variance with their old ideas. In addition to this there were now schools of missionaries, who went about with the avowed design of rooting out the religions of the land and of inducing or constraining all to become Christians. In short, everything was changed or changing. The English of to-day were not like the English even of the days of Warren Hastings. It was impossible to understand them; it was intolerable to live under their sway.

3. Such notions, expressed in the talk of villages throughout the country, could not fail to react on the sepoys, who had, or thought that they had, their own special grievances. They had never received with a good grace the orders which sent them to military service beyond the Indus. They had hated the thought of piercing the gloomy defiles and scaling the barren mountains of Afghanistan; and for following their British leaders into this unknown land they had been terribly punished. The bodies of thousands who were their kinsmen remained unburied on the soil of the infidel, where no son could perform for them the funeral rites needed for the repose of the dead; and for this tremendous sacrifice they were to have no recompense. The conquered country might be included within British territory, and thus for service in the Punjab they were to receive little more than for service on the banks of the Jumna or the Hugli. Of the existence of great discontent in the Bengal army Sir Charles Napier, who succeeded Lord Gough as commander-

in-chief, was thoroughly convinced. The Governor-General was more incredulous; and the result of this difference of opinion was that little or nothing had been done, when the year 1857 completed the century from the defeat of Suraj-u-Daulah at Plassy. For that year astrologers had long since announced a conjunction of planets which would be fatal to the British *raj*, or rule. For the year before they had predicted terrible outbursts of cholera and flood. The cholera and the floods came, and left assurance doubly sure of the speedy downfall of the English. Their power seemed indeed to be more firmly established than ever; but destiny was invincible, and their ruin was certain.

4. Still, means must be used for bringing about the end; and here the inherent weakness of all political movements in the East showed itself. In reality the genuine Hindu wished to return to the condition of things which marked the time of the Aryan conquerors of India. The Mahometan longed to revive the imperial magnificence of Baber and Aurengzebe. The great Mahratta princes were watching the opportunity for recovering the power which they had exercised as representatives of Sivaji, and the lesser rajas were anxious only for the overthrow of a system which checked them in their tyranny and deprived them of the luxuries of plunder. All could not have what they wanted, and some one therefore must give way. The greatest power in India had been that of the Great Mogul. What other standard than his could be held up as a rallying point for all who were determined to

shake off a foreign yoke? The Mahometans, no doubt, made it known that they would fight under no other. The fact is indeed proved by the speed with which the mutinous regiments at the outset of the revolt hurried to Delhi. For many years the princes of the imperial house had been wandering over India in the hope of rekindling the flame of loyalty to the old man who was in theory absolute master of Hindustan. The intrigues of the queen Zeenut Mahal were extended to distant countries; and proclamations from the Shah of Persia urging the people of India to revolt were scattered throughout the land. The agents of Nana Sahib (p. 245), who had his own special ends in view, returned from Europe with wonderful stories of the exhaustion of England in the Crimean war; and with some little inconsistency Mahometans exulted in this result of an enterprise which, as they said, the Queen of England had undertaken as the vassal of the Turkish sultan.

5. The whole country was infected with a fear which shut out all reason; and the English would have done well, if, when the signs of general disturbance became unmistakably clear, they had taken up strong positions throughout Bengal, and refrained from issuing proclamations which came too late to be credited. The passing of *chupaties*, flat cakes of flour, from village to village may have answered to the sending of the Fiery Cross over the Scottish Highlands; at the least it was a sign that grave troubles were impending, and almost every incident of the day added fuel to the smoking fires.

The cartridges of Enfield rifles are in England greased with beef and pork fat; the order was unfortunately given at Calcutta that they were to be greased in like manner in India. But the pig is an abomination to the Mahometan, and the cow is sacred in the eyes of the Hindu. The order involved defilement to both, and no further proof, it was thought, could be needed that the greased cartridges were to be the means of making everyone a Christian. At Barrackpore, a military station near Calcutta, a Lascar, it is said, asked a Brahman to let him drink out of his brass pot. The Brahman replied that he could not do so without defilement, and received the retort that he need have no scruple on that score, seeing that he was sufficiently defiled already by the touch of the new cartridges.

6. The retort was not true. The new cartridges had not yet been given out to the troops; and had this been made known at once, the horrors of the revolt might have been lessened, if, as is most likely, they could not even then be prevented. But nothing was said until the whole country was passing through a paroxysm of terror; and then the explanation, regarded simply as a trap for catching the unwary, could only increase the prevailing fever. Incendiary fires broke out at Barrackpore, and a detachment of native troops going from that place to Berhampore, near Murshedabad, served as a means of communication between the troops in Southern Bengal and the regiments of the interior. The sepoys at Berhampore made some attempt at open revolt; but their plans were not yet matured,

and they laid down their arms and were soon afterwards disbanded. A sepoy at Barrackpore wounded two officers, his comrades doing nothing to help them; but he was taken, convicted, and hanged.

7. The chief danger, it was now thought, had passed away; but the lull was only for the moment. Sir Henry Lawrence, residing at Lucknow as chief Commissioner of Oude, heard a few days later that some of the Oude irregular infantry were threatening their officers. With the European regiment then stationed there he quelled the mutineers; but he heard afterwards that but for these English troops the sepoys, whom he took with him, would have joined the rebels. The storm broke in earnest at Meerut. To the story of the greased cartridges was now added the more horrifying news, that the public wells, the *ghee* (clarified butter), and the flour sold in the markets, in short, everything, had been defiled by bone-dust, and that the salt had been polluted with the blood of swine and cows. The disposition of the sepoys became known to their officers, who called on them to use ungreased cartridges of the old sort. Many refused, and having been tried were sentenced to imprisonment. They were stripped of their uniforms, ironed, and placed in jail under the charge, strange to say, not of a European but of a sepoy guard.

8. The next day was Sunday (May 10, 1857). The native servants, it was noticed, disappeared from the English houses at an early hour; but between the European barracks and the sepoy lines lay a large tract of ground filled with houses

surrounded by gardens. The English, therefore, could not see what the sepoys might be doing. At five in the evening they were about to go to the evening service, when the native troops burst in upon them. With them were the convicted mutineers and the other prisoners let loose from the jail. They were in panic terror from the suspicion that the English troops were to be slipped on them like dogs from a leash, and resolved to anticipate imaginary onslaughts by real massacre. Every European whom they met, man woman and child, was shot at, struck down, wounded or killed; and when at length the English forces, after many unaccountable delays, reached the native lines, it was found that the sepoys were gone.

9. The mutineers had hurried off in hot haste to the old imperial city; and before the sun was up they crossed the river over which the road from Delhi to Meerut is carried. A telegraphic message had brought the tidings of their flight from the station. At this time Delhi had no English troops. It was held by three native regiments, one in the city where lay the magazine with its immense store of powder and ammunition, the other two in the cantonment on the Ridge which overlooks it. The officer in command of the place was Brigadier Graves. Lieutenant Willoughby had charge of the magazine.

10. Time had failed to place cannon on the bridge of the Meerut road before the mutineers reached it; but large detachments of sepoys were sent from the Ridge to aid the regiment in the city. The English officers, confident in the speedy arrival of help from Meerut, ordered the sepoys to charge. Some refused, others fired into the air; but still sepoys and Englishmen both looked to the immediate coming of the European troops, and the former hesitated to rebel, while the latter were prepared to stand out to the last. The hours passed on and no succour came. At length the sepoys joined the mutineers, shot down their officers, and went to salute the emperor, on whose behalf they had defied the English. The whole city was in revolt, and the temper of the populace was as furious as when they fell on the soldiers of Nadir Shah. The crowd surged about the magazine. For the maintenance and extension of the rebellion its contents were of priceless value; but it was in the hands of men who knew their duty and were ready to do it. Messengers, speaking in the name of Bahádur Shah, the pensioned Mogul, demanded its surrender but received no answer. The defenders held out as long as they could; and when their ammunition was exhausted, and none could leave the guns to bring more powder, Lieutenant Willoughby gave the command; the train previously laid was fired; and with the contents of the magazine some fifteen hundred rebels were blown into the air.

11. But the heroism of Willoughby and his companions could make no change in the lot of the English then at Delhi. Those who could fly fled; many more were shot down by the sepoys or the populace; and those who were taken prisoners were put to death under an order bearing the king's name, but extorted from him in all likelihood by

the vindictive Zeenut Mahal. The rebels soon cut the telegraph wires; but these had carried the fatal story to many stations, and hampered or defeated the plans of the mutineers. There were vast magazines at Ferozepore and Phillour. The former was attacked, but the rebels, although defeated, were allowed to make their escape to Delhi; the latter, by timely precautions, was saved without a struggle.

12. The conflagration, repressed in one spot, broke out in another. The disarming of regiments in one place seemed to lead only to the revolt of more regiments elsewhere; but in the fact that these outbreaks came in succession lay the main hope of ultimate safety for the English. This running fire of mutinies had clearly been no part of the plan of the rebel leaders. The sepoys of Meerut threw down the gauntlet three weeks too soon. It was proved afterwards that a simultaneous rising over the whole country had been fixed for the last day of May Had this intention been carried out, the crisis for the British government would have been well nigh desperate. The truth is, that almost from the first the most prominent actors in the horrid drama began to pull in different directions. There was no master-mind to direct the mass, and the plausible proclamation addressed to the whole world by Bahádur Shah was the work probably of some European renegade. This clever paper succeeded even in England in exciting some feeling of sympathy for a sovereign who professed to have set up his standard for the delivery of his country from an oppressive foreign yoke, and to win for them the power of exercising their inalienable right of self-government. The claim was urged in language well fitted to describe the motives of Servians, Bulgarians, or Greeks; but in India it was nothing less than an impudent fiction. The Hindu sepoys had no wish to restore the Great Mogul to his ancient power. The Mahometans had no intention of extending to Hindus the benefits of an equal law. The Mahrattas had no thought of setting anybody free but themselves.

13. But so far as the movement was political, so far were its horrors aggravated; and the treachery of the soldiers was outdone by the treachery of princes. The Ranee of Jhansi held herself aggrieved by the decision which deprived her of all hope of ruling that state as regent for her adopted son (p. 246). Fifty-five Europeans were sojourning in the place with the sepoy garrison, and when the troops revolted, took refuge in the fort; but they had no store of food, and their surrender was a mere question of hours. Whether aware of this fact or not, the Ranee pledged herself by a solemn oath that she would have them all taken safely to some other station, and the soldiers joined in giving the same assurance. But they were to leave the fort, it was agreed, two by two. As each couple came out, they were murdered.

14. At Lukhnow Sir Henry Lawrence had an English force of 570 foot, with sixty artillerymen. But he had to keep down four native regiments and a civil population, of which the hangers on of the late court formed no small part. These Lukhnow conspirators kept their time. They rose on May 30,

and rushed to the bridges which they must cross from the city to reach the Residency, where Sir Henry Lawrence had placed all the English non-combatants. The steady fire with which they were received convinced them that their wisdom lay in flight, and they hurried off to Delhi. For the present they were safe, for pursuit was impossible.

15. At Bithoor the claimant of the Peshwaship was biding the time when he might strike a blow for himself; and it was perhaps owing to him that the sepoy regiments at Cawnpore remained quiet till the beginning of June. During the terrible days which had passed since the first great outbreak at Meerut Nana Sahib had been lavish in his professions of friendship. These protestations were received with a slight incredulity by Sir Hugh Wheeler, who of his threescore and ten years had spent fifty-four continuously in India. While others seemed to think themselves safe, he ordered that some barracks, then not in use, should be intrenched and filled with ammunition and stores for undergoing a siege. Unhappily his orders were very inadequately carried out, if they were not neglected altogether.

16. At length, on June 4, the sepoys broke into tumult, and having set the cantonments in flames, rode away for Delhi. But thither the Nana resolved that they should not go. He was but waiting for the collapse of British power, which he felt sure that the Delhi rebels would be able to bring about, and then he would seize the prize for which he had yearned since his childhood. The outbreak of the sepoys may have taken him in some measure by surprise; and he might have been better pleased if they had postponed it for some weeks. Now, however, there was nothing to be done but to bring them back; and the bait by which he lured them was the abundant plunder which, according to his description, would be furnished by the sack of the British cantonments. The return of the sepoys disconcerted Sir Hugh Wheeler. Had he expected this change of plan on their part, he might have made a still greater effort to escape with the wives and children of officers and with the merchants of the place to Allahabad; but there also a mutiny had broken out, and lack of transport would have made the flight a desperate enterprise. The siege for which he had wished to be prepared began on June 5, and for nineteen days the little garrison bore up against almost incredible sufferings. It was the hottest time of the year, and the heat was fearful. A barrack which sheltered the sick and the wounded was burnt, and day and night they were assailed by an incessant fire from the enemy. Their food ran short, and the hearts of the bravest failed as, helpless themselves, they looked on the misery of starving and fever-stricken women and children.

17. On June 25 Nana Sahib promised to convey safely to Allahabad all who should lay down their arms. It is hard to say that Sir Hugh Wheeler deserves blame for trusting his word. He might or might not have heard of the massacre at Patna by the orders of Mir Cassim (p. 119); but the loud professions of friendship which preceded the Nana's attack furnished sufficient proof of the traitorous nature of the man. Still the lengths to which he could go could not be known beforehand; and the condition of the women and children seemed to leave no room for deliberation. Such precautions were taken as the circumstances of the case allowed. Each man was to go out with his arms and sixty rounds of ammunition; and the voyage to Allahabad was to be made in boats provided by the Nana, who had also given them safe conduct to the river's bank. The boats were filled and were ready to start, when a murderous fire was opened on them from both banks, and in a few minutes their thatched roofs were in flames. Many were murdered in the water or drowned. Of those who were dragged ashore the men were shot down at once, the women and children were carried off to a house near the Nana's quarters, June 27.

18. Dondhu Punt thought that his success was now assured. Hastening to Bithoor, he went through the coronation ceremonies which were to mark the restoration of the Peshwa's office, July 1, and then hurried back to Cawnpore, because the Mahometans were already plotting against him. Here, while he tried to bribe his opponents into submission, he won fresh fame by murdering all the men belonging to a party of English fugitives from Futtehgurh and by sending the women and children to share the captivity of those whom he had already seized. The number of his prisoners was now somewhat over two hundred.

19. In the hope that with strenuous exertions he might be in time to save these prisoners, General

Havelock was hastening on with a force of 2,000 Europeans and Sikhs, all included, from Allahabad. He won victory after victory on the road. On the afternoon of July 15, he had chosen his camping ground for the night, when he heard that the Nana's prisoners were still living. Rising instantly, he marched fourteen miles more, and was thus only eight miles from the city. But the tiger temper of the Nana was now roused to frenzy. That night his victims were hacked and hewn almost limb from limb; and in the morning the whole mangled mass, dead and dying together, were thrown into a well. At two o'clock in the afternoon of this fatal day Havelock came up with the army of the Nana. The battle was fiercely contested; but the terrible charge of the British bore the enemy down; and when they had once taken to flight, they were for the time safe, for Havelock had no cavalry. It was not until he entered the station the next morning that he saw the reason which had brought the Nana's forces away from Cawnpore. The signs of the great tragedy carried them step by step to the well, where all was still in death. The well is now enclosed within a rich screen carved in stone, and on it the figure of an angel in the attitude of perfect rest signifies the joyful hope of resurrection to eternal life.

20. Having destroyed the Nana's palace at Bithoor, Havelock left General Neill in command at Cawnpore, and hastened to the rescue of Sir Henry Lawrence and his beleaguered garrison at Lukhnow. Here, for nearly two months, the English had held out against an overwhelming host of rebels, whose

numbers had been swelled by troops of disbanded sepoys, and by crowds of marauders and thieves, who suddenly made their appearance like flies with the sunshine of spring. But the fearless and conscientious Sir Henry Lawrence had died, as he had lived, in the discharge of his duty. On July 4 he was killed by the bursting of a shell in the room where he was lying severely wounded. To the last his counsel was a strict charge that in no case should the place be surrendered. But the brave defenders may well have hoped, when they heard of Havelock's advance from Cawnpore, that they might soon be freed from a strain almost beyond the power of human endurance. Unhappily heat, fever, and cholera were enemies which fought against Havelock as fatally as against the English who were shut up in Lukhnow. On August 4 he had only 1,300 men and thirteen guns to face an army of 20,000. Even thus he won a victory; but six and thirty miles were yet to be traversed before he could reach the city, and without reinforcements the task was manifestly impossible. When Havelock returned to Cawnpore he had little more than 700 men fit for active service in the field.

21. But before the heroic defenders of the Residency at Lukhnow could be rescued from their peril, the issue of the great struggle had been virtually determined by the storming of Delhi and the catastrophe which ended the phantom empire of the Great Mogul. For nearly a month after the mutineers from Meerut had rallied round the standard of Bahádur-Shah, their prospects might have seemed

to them not altogether unhopeful. General Anson, the commander-in-chief, had hurried from Simla to undertake the siege of the imperial city; but nothing was ready, and much time was wasted before he could set out from Umballah with such forces as he could get together. At Kurnal he died of cholera. By June 4 his successor, Sir Henry Barnard, was within twenty miles of Delhi, and being joined by Brigadier Wilson from Meerut, had nearly 4,000 English soldiers under his command. Four days later (June 9) the English standard was again floating over the Ridge which overlooks the town.

22. The scene was one never to be forgotten by those who witnessed it. In the dazzling glare of the Indian summer sun, the city with its houses nestled amongst gardens, and the great structures which spoke of the grandeur of a fallen dynasty, rose from the vast plain on the right bank of the dark-watered Jumna. High above the other buildings, the massive walls of the imperial palace led the eye to the graceful minarets of the Jumma Musjid, or great mosque, a structure not unworthy to be compared, for the harmony of its forms and the majesty of its proportions, to all but the grandest works of European Christendom. In the rear of the English position the ground was covered with all the ammunition of war, baggage-waggons, artillery, camels, bullocks, and horses, while from the batteries within the walls wreaths of white smoke rose into the burning air, as the echoes from the shotted guns died away.

23. The weary soldiers who had gained the Ridge had little leisure, and could have but little

heart, for admiring the magnificent prospect before them. They were facing an enemy who had never withstood them in the open field, but who could now, if they pleased, stand on the defensive and fight under the shelter of bastions and ramparts. Against the 4,000 English under Sir Henry Barnard the Mogul king had 30,000 men, and the number of his followers was swollen almost daily by the arrival of sepoys from regiments tempted into rebellion by the comparative success of the mutiny. The city was amply supplied with food and with military stores of all kinds, and except on the side held by the small British army the country lay open to the rebels. To the English any serious prolongation of the war must in itself be a grave disaster; to the mutineers each day and each week, as it passed by without actual defeat, brought virtual victory. From one end of the land to the other the troops which had not yet broken faith were waiting with feverish impatience the result which would ensure their loyalty or justify their revolt. In the Punjab Sir John Lawrence had the bravery and the prudence to make use of the Sikhs in the furtherance of his own plans; but even these were intently watching the movements of the game, and could be trusted only so long as they saw that in spite of desperate difficulties the English were slowly but steadily gaining ground.

24. Still, though the mutineers were fully aware that the mere retention of the imperial city must tend to inspire the whole country with a confident hope of their ultimate success, they were not content to leave their enemies to themselves. Assault followed assault on the English lines, and on June 23, the hundredth anniversary of the fight at Plassy, they attacked the British position with a pertinacity, bravery, and skill which they had not thus far displayed. But their utmost efforts were vain; and they must have returned into the city with a gloomy conviction that the prophecy which had stirred them up to rebellion had not, to say the least, received a literal fulfilment.

25. For two months longer, however, the tidings might be carried over India that the imperial city had not fallen, and that the English would in the end be foiled in the attempt to storm its walls. But the long expected siege train arrived from Ferozepore on September 6, and on the following day the troops in the city learnt, not without misgiving, that the conditions of the conflict were changed. In spite of the incessant fire from the walls three batteries of heavy and light guns were brought to bear on the doomed city. But if the hopes of its defenders were damped, their courage was not shaken for a moment. All that brave soldiers could do they did unflinchingly; but even the discipline of British-trained sepoys was of little avail in the long run against the sterner resolution and the unattainable military genius of those who had trained them. Within a week the English engineers reported that the breaches in the walls were practicable, and long before dawn on September 14 the assaulting columns were formed in the trenches.

26. Then began the fiercest struggle ever known in Indian warfare. The mutineers, however vague

might be their notions of the usages of Europe, yet knew that by the massacre of their prisoners they had furnished counts for a heavy indictment, and must expect to pay a heavy reckoning. Their assailants were roused to a deadly hate which cast all thought of mercy to the winds. The Kashmere gate was blown open; but the stormers rushed in only to find themselves in narrow streets, exposed to the fire of sepoys posted on every house-top. Thus far the success of the English was but partial. They had failed to take the Jumma Musjid; the right column had been compelled to retire, and the enemy still retained some of his strongest positions. But each day brought fresh disaster and discouragement to the revolted sepoys. The magazine was breached and stormed, the guns were turned against them, and the line of attack advanced steadily over the city. On the 19th Captain Hodson forced the gates of the palace; but the vast building was almost empty. The mutineers had fled in two main bodies, of which one followed the line of the Jumna, while the other hurried to the Doab.

27. The orders given by General Wilson were that no quarter should be given to any who might be found with arms in their hands, and that no harm should be done to non-combatants. The former order was obeyed with sufficient strictness; the latter, perhaps, was not disregarded. On the 21st the aged Bahádur Shah was found with his family in the tomb of the Emperor Humayun (p. 42) and brought into the palace. On the next day Captain Hodson arrested his two sons within its precincts.

As the carriage which was taking them to the city approached the gates, the mob gathered round with gestures which seemed to portend a rescue, and Hodson at once drew a pistol and shot them both. They had taken part in the murders of English prisoners, men, women, and children; and he, therefore, ordered their bodies to be exposed to the gaze of the awe-struck crowd. It was said that Hodson had promised the princes their lives, and that only a very strong reason could justify the real or seeming breach of faith.

28. Some months after the great catastrophe the sovereign to whom the mutineers had plighted their faith was brought to trial before a military commission (January 27, 1857). He was charged with ordering the murder of English men and women within the walls of his palace, with issuing proclamations inciting the people to rebellion, and with levying war against the British Government. It was an indictment to which no answer could be made. Success might have placed him at the head of a splendid empire; but failure left him to bear the burden of sins which perhaps were not his own. The massacres were the work of his vindictive wife; the proclamations were certainly not drawn up by a hand trembling with age, nor could their stirring and dignified eloquence be ascribed to a mind already stupefied with the lethargy of second childhood. It was impossible for his judges to acquit him; but his helplessness might be pleaded in mitigation of punishment. The sentence was banishment for life; and Bahádur Shah, without even the title of king, went forth as an exile to Burmah. So ended the great drama of Mogul sovereignty, magnificent even amongst the most splendid of earthly empires in the days of its glory, gaudy and flaunting in its season of decay, and despicable in the long ages of its impotent decrepitude.

29. On the very day on which the English soldiers burst open the gates of the royal palace at Delhi, Havelock crossed the Ganges into Oude. He had with him 2,500 men; and of these more than half had joined him four days before, under Sir James Outram, who, as senior officer, might have assumed the command. But the relieving of Lukhnow was the work which lay nearest to the heart of Havelock, and Outram generously refused to take it out of his hands. Two battles were fought before they could reach the city, and then they had to run the gauntlet of a deadly fire from loop-holed houses and garden walls as they struggled on towards the Residency, where for four months the beleaguered garrison had received from the world without no other tidings than that Havelock had already tried to rescue them, and had been foiled in his attempt.

30. On September 25 the mutineers knew that the delivering army was at hand, and they poured a still more furious fire on the besieged. But slowly and steadily, in spite of the desperate efforts of rebels fighting under the cover of narrow and crooked lanes and of houses turned into military strongholds, the English troops came on. At each step their numbers were thinned, and before they entered the British intrenchments Colonel

Neill was amongst the dead. With killed, wounded, and missing the numbers of the relieving force had been lessened by about one-fifth; but the great work was achieved, and Brigadier Inglis could feel thankful that he had been enabled to carry out the dying charge of Sir Henry Lawrence to hold his ground to the last.

31. The garrison was rescued, and the women and children were safe, but they could not yet be removed; and the rebels were not scattered, and perhaps not much disheartened. For two months longer the siege went on; but the English were no longer fighting at fearful and desperate odds, and they could await with confidence the more effectual succour which Sir Colin Campbell brought in November. But even with his larger force Sir Colin Campbell could not recover the city, and he resolved to abandon the position, and to carry the garrison with the women and children to Cawnpore. So skilfully was this work of evacuation done that the mutineers went on firing at the entrenchments long after they had been deserted. Outram remained in the neighbourhood with 4,000 men to act against them, whilst Havelock was to march with Sir Colin Campbell to Cawnpore. But the fervent spirit had in him outworn the body, and on the day after leaving Lukhnow he died, having won for himself a reputation as pure as it was glorious (November 24).

32. Even in the eyes of the revolted regiments and their supporters the tide had turned in favour of their English rulers; but there were yet to be two or three incidents answering to the Pretender's

victory at Falkirk after the retreat from Derby before the fatal catastrophe at Culloden. As Sir Colin Campbell approached Cawnpore, he heard the firing of heavy artillery, and soon received the astonishing tidings that the city was in the hands of the sepoys. General Windham, who had been left in charge of the station, had been out-manœuvred by the genius of Tantia Topi, the one general produced by this war on the side opposed to the English. The cold intellect of this wonderful Brahman exulted in the retrieving of the most terrible disasters by new and unlooked-for movements and combinations. In the greatest straits he was never at a loss; and though he never won a victory in the field, he prolonged for months a struggle which, if he had been dealing with better materials, might after all have ended in success. He might have been a rival of Moltke in the direction of campaigns from a distance; in India he failed because he lacked, not the military genius, but the personal bravery and audacity, of Clive.

33. Tantia Topi was now the leader of the Gwalior contingent (p. 233) which, having thus far held itself neutral, had at last openly joined the rebels under Nana Sahib and his brother Bala Rao. With this magnificent force of 20,000 men and 40 guns, Tantia outflanked Windham, seized his camp, his equipage, and his stores, and in a few hours more would have destroyed the bridge of boats, and thus cut off the retreat of his enemies across the Ganges. Sir Colin Campbell came up just in time to prevent this great disaster. The non-combatants and the wounded, whom he had brought from Lukhnow, were sent on to Allahabad, and there was fought the battle of Cawnpore, which for the time frustrated the strategy of Tantia Topi. The Nana's army fled to a ferry twenty-five miles above Cawnpore; but before they could cross the river they were severely defeated by Brigadier Hope Grant, and the Gwalior contingent retained only six of its forty guns.

34. The memorable year, to which Hindus and Mahometans alike had looked forward with eager hope and expectation, was drawing to a close. Much still remained to be done; but this was chiefly owing to the vast extent of country over which the rebel forces were scattered, and the task of hunting them out was in many cases a work rather of vengeance than of warfare needing both skill and endurance. If the conquerors smote with a rod of iron, it may at least be said that they had received provocation of the most terrible and maddening kind. At their worst they must be judged as we judge Hastings for his dealings with Nundkomar (p. 139); but history may hereafter speak in sterner language of the furious cry for indiscriminate revenge raised in this country even by those whose duty it was to still the passion of natural resentment. Bishops and clergy were carried away by the storm of indignation which for the time hardened their hearts while it confused their minds. Of those who were charged with the work of suppressing the mutiny it may not be our duty to speak harshly; but assuredly it can never be said that they were too slack in the task of retribution. Rather, it may be feared that they were hurried on into excesses, the memory of which may not yet have passed away. Happily, Lord Canning was not one who could ever be seduced or stirred into the temper of merciless revenge. He was assailed with virulent abuse by men who, if left to themselves, would have made the English name a byword in India and throughout the world; but he withstood the storm unmoved, and by summarily preventing the burning of towns and villages, and the slaughtering of a helpless and unarmed population, did as much to save and to strengthen our empire as was done by those who fought their way through the streets of Delhi and rescued the beleaguered garrison of Lukhnow.

85. The first month of the new year, 1858, was marked by a series of decisive victories at the Lukhnow suburb of Alumbagh, in which the body of Havelock was resting, and elsewhere in Oude and Central India. In March, with 16,000 English troops, the largest number ever brought together in India, and 9,000 sepoys, Sir Colin Campbell advanced to the final attack of Lukhnow. Here, as at Delhi, the defenders of the city may deserve to be called ruthless wretches; but it cannot be denied that they fought with desperate courage and unwearied energy. The struggle was as fiercely sustained as at Delhi; but at last the sepoys were beaten out of their fastnesses, and had to fight for their lives as they fled towards Sitapore, cast down indeed yet not utterly dismayed, and resolved that the English should hear of them yet again. But the toils of the hunters were closing round them,

and when they were gathered at Bareilly under Nana Sahib and Prince Feroze of Delhi, with the Rohilkund chief, Khan Bahádur Khan, the antagonism between Hindus and Mahometans was already leading the former to regard the latter as oppressors more hateful even than the English.

36. In spite of these evil omens, the Nana and his colleagues carried on their schemes with marvellous tenacity of purpose, and the siege of Jhansi by the Bombay troops and the Hyderabad contingent under Sir Hugh Rose called for efforts as severe as those which had brought about the fall of Delhi and Lukhnow. Within the walls was the Ranee, ready to fight and die as a sovereign at the head of her followers; and without them was Tantia Topi with 20,000 men, hoping to find the means either of entering the city or of compelling Sir Hugh Rose to raise the siege. In both these hopes he was doomed to disappointment. His army was routed, and the Ranee was left to her own resources. On April 3, the breach in the walls was stormed; and the undaunted queen, seeing that all hope of saving the city was gone, escaped by night to fight again on other fields. Six weeks later she fell, dressed as a man, in the battle of Morar. The trooper who cut her down knew not that he had slain the brave Lakshmi Bai, whose cruelty rivalled that of Zeenut Mahal (p. 259). During those few weeks she took part in every engagement which had been fought since her escape from Jhansi, and in the last she might have hoped that the genius of Tantia Topi was destined at length to achieve success.

37. The conquest of Jhansi, followed by another defeat of the rebels at Kurch, convinced the Mahratta Brahman that he must again change the scene of the struggle. Hurrying to the old rock fortress of Gwalior he stirred Sindia's men to revolt, and received their promise to join the rebels as they came in from Kurch. Sindia discovered the plot and against the earnest advice of his minister resolved to meet his enemies in the open field. He met them at the head of an army which would not fight or which went bodily over to the enemy, and his only resource was in flight. His city and fortress with all their contents fell into the hands of the mutineers, who once more proclaimed Nana Sahib under the title of Peshwa. The move was the most striking and able of all that had been made by Tantia Topi; but the splendid advantage which it seemed to insure to him was lost, when the Gwalior troops were surprised in the cantonments of Morar. It was but a passing gleam of success. In three or four days Sindia was again seated on his throne; but his treasury had meanwhile been plundered of property amounting to half a million pounds sterling. On the following day the Gwalior contingent underwent a crushing defeat at Jura Alipore, and Tantia Topi was once more a fugitive.

38. The rebellion had now assumed the character of intermittent outbreaks; but there were elements of serious danger still in some parts of the country, while others had passed through periods of the gravest peril. At Bombay, Poona, Kolhapur, and Kurrachee, regiments had shown signs of disaffection or had mutinied openly. Symptoms of rebellion were seen also in a portion of the Nizam's cavalry; but his infantry and artillery remained faithful, and the efforts of Mahometan fanatics who strove to seduce the population of Hyderabad into insurrection were promptly repressed by Salar Jung, the eminent statesman who still administers the Nizam's dominions to the admiration of all who have seen the results of his wise and beneficent rule.

39. It was natural that the southern Mahratta country should share the disturbance of the rest; but the back of the rebellion was now broken, and though in November a sepoy army, numbering, it was said, 20,000 men, was still in the field, their dispersion was a matter rather of days than of weeks. Before the year was ended, Nana Sahib had taken refuge with his brother Bala Rao in the Terai jungles of Nepal; and here it cannot be doubted that they died, although the story went that the Nana was still living, and impostors were found willing to earn notoriety at the cost of their necks by representing one who could scarcely expect much mercy at the hands of English judges. The last dying embers of the mutiny were seen in the junction of the Mogul prince Feroze with Tantia Topi; but their condition was little better than that of the hunted hare. Tantia was caught during sleep in a Malwah jungle, April 1859. The remembrance of his schemes of subtle and consummate leadership might make us regret that he could not be treated as a prisoner of war; but he had placed himself in the ranks of murderers by superintending in person the massacre of the English by the river side at Cawnpore. His trial and sentence were followed by immediate execution, April 1859; and so died the man who, had his schemes succeeded, would assuredly have taught Nana Sahib that the Peshwa must henceforth be the subject and puppet, if not the victim, of the Peshwa's minister.

40. If the British Government in India had been honestly bent on ruling the country for the good of its people, the great mutiny was a terrible breach in the orderly progress of their beneficent work. On the whole, the honesty and sincerity of their purpose cannot be doubted. The Governors-General had made some mistakes and blunders, and had been guilty of some wrong doing, into which they had been betrayed chiefly by idle and groundless fears. These terrors had led to the fatal enterprise which was to make the Afghan king the passive instrument of English policy; but the failure of that miserable scheme had been virtually admitted by the withdrawal of our troops from his barren and worthless mountains, and since that time it may fairly be said that in no country and in no age has the rule of foreigners ever been so beneficial to their subjects as was that of the English in India for more than thirty years after the disasters in Cabul. On the Sikh wars we may look back with a clear conscience; and the Sikhs themselves can look back upon them only with feelings of thankfulness that the victory remained with a people under whom they have been enabled to turn their spears into ploughshares and their swords into pruning-hooks.

41. But although the rule of the East India Company had been of immense advantage to the natives of India, the great rebellion of 1857 was held to furnish conclusive proof that it ought to give place to the direct government of the Crown. The Act which ordered the change became law in August 1858, and on November 1 the people of British India were informed by proclamation that they were henceforth subjects of the sovereign of Great Britain, who would respect all existing rights, titles, dignities, and treaties, and who would repress all attempts to interfere with their religion or their caste. The Company's *raj*, or rule, thus passed away, and in this sense only was the prediction which precipitated the mutiny fulfilled. It was well, indeed, for India that it should be so; but it is absurd to suppose that this fact really represented the meaning of the men in whose minds the prophecy had taken shape.

42. From that time to the year 1876 disturbing causes have from time to time interfered with the quiet advancement of the country in industry and wealth. There have been military enterprises some of which might by careful forethought have been avoided. There have been famines, some of which might by a more provident statesmanship have been prevented, or at the least, greatly mitigated. But, after all due deductions have been made, the fact remains that the country has been ruled steadily, wisely, and well. The civilisation of one nation is not necessarily fitted for another; and some mistakes have beyond doubt been made by bringing European laws and customs to bear on a people who like the Hindus are now much what they were three or four thousand years ago. At the beginning of this prodigious period, when our forefathers were among the rudest of savages, the Hindus stood in the front ranks of mankind. With such a race sudden and trenchant reforms are likely to do far more harm than good; and summary interference with long-established usage can never be justifiable except where, as in the case of suttee (p. 207), the custom is in itself inhuman, and rests on falsehoods maintained from interested motives by a dominant priesthood.

43. But on the whole the work done by the Aryans from Europe (p. 1) among the Aryans of the East has been marvellously beneficial. The face of the land is changed. The plains of Bengal, the table lands of the Deccan, the hills and valleys of Mysore and Bombay, are no longer at the mercy of invaders following each the other in close succession, like flights of devouring locusts. We in our island of Great Britain, on whose soil no invader has set his foot for more than eight hundred years, can scarcely realise the condition of a country swept by storms of foreign enemies almost as frequently as by their physical tornadoes and cyclones. The history of the old Aryan dynasties in India, so far as it can be said to be known to us, is little more than a dismal catalogue of acts of aggression, violence and murder. The inroads of Turks, Saracens and Afghans brought into the land the more deadly and merciless fanaticism of Islam; and although one magnificent empire was established by men who called themselves followers of the prophet of Mecca, we have seen how weak were its foundations and how loosely put together was its superstructure. It rose indeed to something like real greatness in the memorable reign of Akbar; but it did so only because Akbar threw off the yoke of the Koran, and won from Mahometan bigots the evil reputation of an apostate. But even in the days of Akbar there was nothing which could fairly be called a national administration. The Great Mogul and his princely vassals might build massive forts and splendid palaces, and when they died their bodies might rest in sepulchres on which Eastern art lavished all its dazzling splendour and all its exquisite grace; but with the wealth and resources of India at their disposal for six or seven centuries the Mahometan dynasties of India did little or nothing in the way of making roads, of forming harbours, of cutting canals and building bridges. They had wide and wealthy dominions; but the arm of the law was not seldom powerless to smite down the wrongdoer, and side by side with their wealth and their glory was a grinding and crushing poverty to which they can scarcely be said to have paid any heed at all. There was, in fact, no real security anywhere. Mahratta and Pindharrie hordes might at any time sweep over the country like hailstorms across the sky; while dacoits, Thugs, and other societies of robbers reaped their harvest under cover of the prevailing lawlessness, much as the lesser beasts of prey are supposed to follow in the track of the lion and the tiger.

44. The subject which these thoughts bring

before us is vast indeed, and may well be made the study of a lifetime. It is a matter of no slight moment to ascertain the relations of Mahometans and Hindus to the new system which with something like the rapid growth of tropical vegetation has sprung up in their midst, to mark the passive resistance of the Hindu and the fiercer and more determined bigotry of the Mahometan. It is a great but not an easy task to judge fairly of the capacities for self-government possessed by Hindus and Mahometans severally, and to measure the progress made by the native independent states as compared with the condition of the country under the immediate sovereignty of the British. It is useless to ascribe to them faculties for improvement if the signs of their existence are not forthcoming; it is unjust to deny or to keep out of sight the least evidence which shows that they are advancing in all that constitutes a well-ordered state; it is cruel to throw a veil over any wrongs which they may be suffering at the hands of their European masters. There is no reason for thinking that their English rulers are guilty of wilful and wanton injustice anywhere; there is every reason for believing that on the whole they are honestly striving for the good of the people everywhere. Twice within the last fifty years the British Government has allowed unreasonable fears to lead them astray from the path of their manifest duty; but between these two disastrous enterprises there was a long interval of conscientious administration on which we may look back with more than satisfaction. The lesson taught by the results of these fatal schemes has been sharp and stern. It will be well for us if it be so taken to heart that the natives of India may see in our acts nothing but the evidence of a disinterested desire to promote their welfare in the highest and best sense of the word.

INDEX.

Spottiswoode & Co., Printers, New-street Square, London.